CORNMEAL COUNTRY

An American Tradition

CORNMEAL COUNTRY

An American Tradition

Compiled,
Annotated and
Illustrated

by

ELIZABETH ROSS

McClanahan
Publishing House

Cover design and book layout by James Asher Graphics
Cover illustration by James Asher from a U.S. Dept. of Agriculture photo, circa 1915
Line drawings by Elizabeth Ross
Photograph by Nancy Lee Ross

Manufactured in the United States of America

All book order correspondence should be addressed to:

McClanahan Publishing House, Inc.
P.O. Box 100
Kuttawa, KY 42055
270-388-9388
1-800-544-6959
email: kybooks@apex.net
www.kybooks.com

TABLE OF CONTENTS

DEDICATION

This cookbook is dedicated to my late father, the honorable Andrew J. Ross, a Southern gentleman and attorney. He liked nothing better than to crumble chunks of cornbread into a tall glass of cold sweet milk and to eat it with an iced tea spoon.

CORNMEAL CULTURE

The culture of corn takes us far back into the history of the Americas. Traces of the corn cuisine created by the royal houses of the Mayas, Aztecs and Incas can still be enjoyed in the quality and variety of the contemporary cooking of Mexico. For about 2,500 years before Europeans reached the American shores in the 15th Century, the Indians from Canada to Mexico were cultivating corn and making a variety of breads using ground corn. The proper generic name for corn is maize, but America's use of the term "corn" comes from British English, where the term means any kind of grain. Corn has been cultivated for at least six thousand years and yet no wild corn or fossil evidence of it exists today. Corn is dependent on man's cultivation and man is dependent on corn for his survival. The oldest known corn grew on a cob no larger than a man's little fingernail. However, its ability to hybridize very quickly produced sweet, dent, flint and flour varieties. It may have come to the United States from the West Indies or Mexico, however it was not until Columbus arrived that corn was introduced to Europe. After that, corn went everywhere because it will grow anywhere.

The ancient Pueblo Indians revered corn as the 5th element. There was earth, air, fire, water and corn. Corn was grown, ground, baked and boiled by the native Indians who introduced it to the first American settlers. They called the cornmeal "injun meal" and probably would not have survived without it. The Indians called these cornmeal breads "suppone" and "appone" and pone is still the basic form of cornbread eaten in the United States. Today its preparation is the primary feature associated with Southern cooking. Although most corn is grown in the Midwest, Southern cooks have always excelled in its preparation as food.

All good cooks in the American South find the cornmeal culture close to a religious experience. Everyone uses cornmeal and enjoys it. It is used almost daily, not only to make hot cornbread, but also to make chess pie, for dressings or stuffings, to make dumplings and to coat chicken and fish for frying. It is so connected to the Southern pioneer past that it is truly a heart and soul food.

All corn types can be grown in any color, which is no indication of its flavor, so white and yellow are interchangeable. Some cooks prefer to use yellow cornmeal while others swear by white. Some prefer fine-ground and others like coarse-ground.

Simply defined, cornmeal is ground kernels of any kind of corn which can be ground to any degree of coarseness or fineness. It is made from corn that goes unharvested until after autumn frost. By then the husks and kernels are hard and dry and the ears are stored or shucked and the kernels shelled off the cob. Also, they can be shelled at the time of grinding. Cornbread is a bread prepared using cornmeal, boiling water, maybe flour and sugar, lard or a substitute, and baking powder. The coarsely ground cornmeal is best for polenta or cornmeal mush while the fine grade is best for cornbread, muffins and for breading fish or chicken and thickening casseroles.

The first cornbread was "ashe" cake, baked in hearth ashes about 1600 at Jamestown. Later came "hoe" cake, baked in front of a fire on the metal part of a hoe. These "pones" were made according to the Indian method of mixing cornmeal and water. Another bread, "johnnycake," is probably a derivation of journey cake, a pone that traveled well in the pocket.

The hard corn dodgers are so named because if thrown, the intended target dodged to avoid being hit. They were said to have been eaten daily by George Washington. It must have been difficult considering his dental problems.

As the pioneer life style became less primitive and the frontier receded, cornbread became more refined along with the Southern lifestyle. The cooks and bakers added eggs, sweet milk or buttermilk, baking powder, baking soda, flour and sugar. Refinements included corn light bread, griddle cakes, dressings, muffins and cornsticks, hushpuppies and the elegant, ultimate cornmeal dish, spoonbread. Today blue cornmeal has become a trendy ingredient. However, Southwesterners will tell you that they have been using it for at least one thousand years. It has a nuttier taste than white or yellow cornmeal but it is interchangeable with them. From the lowly ash cake to the patrician spoonbread, cornbread is one of our most versatile foods.

The secrets to making good cornbread are using a hot cast iron skillet or mold, greasing it well and pouring the liquid into the dry ingredients. There is a period of about five minutes when it comes out of the oven that it is at its peak of flavor and texture. However, it will still be delicious, even cold.

Once you have decided on white or yellow cornmeal, take care of it to insure it will be fresh. Buy small amounts and store it in a tightly covered container in the refrigerator. This will prevent it from getting moldy or weevils from spoiling it. Just remember to store it as you would milk.

You don't have to be a Southern cook to make a superior cornmeal bread. Just enjoy all of the following recipes to enhance your eating pleasure. Remember that you are following your pioneer heritage.

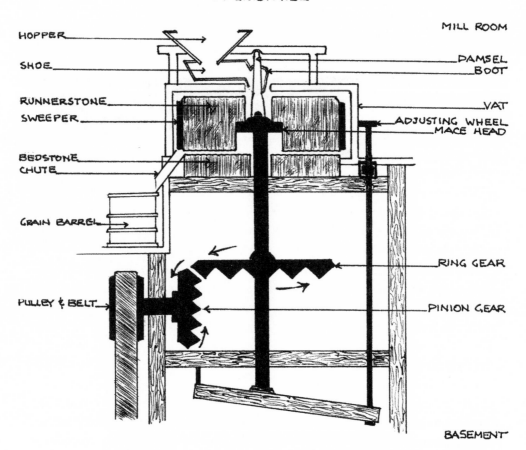

A GRISTMILL

GRISTMILLS

The most important technique of food preservation the American pioneers learned from the American Indians was how to dry corn. Consequently, it was milled, roasted, boiled, baked, dried, parched, pickled and made into whiskey. Rural streams were once lined with creekside gristmills. For bread making, people could take their homegrown corn and wheat to be ground into cornmeal and flour. Cornmeal was and still is the most prevalent grain used in the kitchen. Scattered throughout the country are some old rural gristmills where you can still buy cornmeal made by water-powered stones. It may be labeled either "stone-ground" or "water-ground" and is almost without exception, excellent and meant for immediate use. These local mills may be gasoline or diesel-powered now and most people take only one or two bushels at a time to be ground. This is to insure that the cornmeal does not get stale or that weevils will not get in and ruin it. It is best to refrigerate all stone-ground cornmeal to keep it fresh. It is only superior that way. Otherwise any store-bought brand will do.

Over a century ago, industrial milling replaced grinding stones with steel rollers. Because of its high percentage of oil, cornmeal requires great care because the kernels scorch easily and as in storage, heat is the enemy. Grinding with stones does not guarantee quality, freshness or less heat than steel rollers. But if the miller "keeps his nose to the grindstone," he can detect from the smell of the granite if the stones are too close. Steel rollers may have replaced grinding stones, but now good millers who know the qualities of the corn they grind are able to control the process from cornfield to buyer. Fortunately, there are quite a few restored and new gristmills, especially in the South, where these dedicated millers ply their trade. They know and care that cornbread made with stone-ground cornmeal has a different taste than the store-bought kind. It is more coarse in texture and faintly crunchy with a distinct tangy flavor.

A stone gristmill works very much like an old-fashioned stone mortar and pestle, only on a much larger scale. The grain is poured into the hopper. There it feeds into the shoe which is agitated by the damsel. This motion is caused by the turning of the mace head to which the damsel is attached and on which the runnerstone rides. The corn moves down through the boot through a hole in the center of the runnerstone called the eye. By means of centrifugal force, the corn is carried between the two grinding stones all the way to cornmeal. The cornmeal falls into a trough which goes around the bedstone and is forced into the chute by metal sweepers attached to the stone. The bedstone is stationary, while the runnerstone is moved by a series of belts, pulleys and gears linked together. The miller can adjust the aperture between the stones by turning the adjusting wheel, raising or lowering the runnerstone.

CAST IRON-BLACK MAGIC COOKERY

Any cook who is fortunate enough to possess pieces of family-treasured and well-used cast iron cookware knows that they are heirlooms. Cast iron is the true ancestor of nonstick cookware. It is durable and healthful to use because cooking without fat is possible. Because they are porous, well-seasoned cast iron pieces form a protective covering of oil that keeps foods from sticking and prevents rusting. Its heavy iron density conducts heat evenly, gets very hot and cooks food very quickly. It has only two disadvantages: it is heavy and it cannot be put in the dishwasher. These are small prices to pay for heaven in a bread basket.

If you haven't had the good fortune to inherit some cast iron cookware, look for old pieces at estate sales, tag sales, flea markets or yard sales. Look for such American manufacturers' names on pieces as Griswold, Erie, Wagner, Wapak, Favorite Stove and Range, Sidney, W.C. Davis, G.F. Filley and Lodge. They could be valuable collector's items. Don't be deterred if they look to be in poor condition. If they are not cracked, they can be cleaned, re-seasoned and returned to good use. Houseware departments, discount stores, hardware stores and mail-order catalogs carry new cast iron pieces in the old style. They also offer pieces such as a wok, a 2-quart casserole and a top-of-the-stove broiler. Victor Cast Iron Ware, imported from England, also has a classic line of

cookware including meat or pudding presses, round and oval casseroles and saucepans with flat-top lids that double as frying pans, baking or gratin dishes. Their snug lids make it possible to cook "waterless."

Prior to using new, old or antique cast iron, it must be seasoned. But first, however, it has to be cleaned. New pieces have a pre-seasoning coat of wax that should be scrubbed off. To do this, use steel wool pads and hot water. Hand wash with a mild soap (detergent may flavor cast iron) and dry completely to prevent rust from forming. If older pieces have a buildup of carbon on the outside or are rusted, use oven cleaner. This should be done outdoors or in a well-ventilated area. Let the pieces stand for four hours and then scrub with a scouring pad, rags or a wire brush. Repeat if necessary. Another method is to run heavily caked pieces through a regular cycle in a self-cleaning oven and then scrub, wash and dry thoroughly. A third method is to place pieces in a 300° oven for an hour to loosen old grease. Remove from oven and sprinkle with a generous amount of coarse salt. Rub salt over the hot pieces with a cotton cloth to remove any dirt and grease. Wash with soapy water and dry. Always season new cast iron and once you have cleaned down to bare iron, begin the seasoning process. This may seem like a time-consuming nuisance, but it is necessary and well worth the effort.

To season cast iron, preheat oven to 350°. Spray all surfaces liberally with shortening spray or wipe with vegetable oil, lard or suet. Do not use safflower or corn oils, butter or margarine because they will leave a sticky residue. Place piece in oven for 15 minutes then remove and wipe oil around the interior to make sure surfaces are evenly covered. Return piece to oven to "cure" for one hour where it should develop a smooth, shiny glaze. Remove from oven and allow piece to cool to the touch. Wipe out any excess oil and repeat the process two or three times over several days.

New cast iron may need more treatments because it reportedly isn't as porous as the old, since the factories now use electric furnaces instead of open-fire hearths. A drop of water will "dance" on the hot surface of a properly seasoned piece of cast iron cookware. After use, it will eventually need to be reseasoned. You will know if food begins to stick, it starts to rust or you begin to experience a metallic taste.

After the cookware has been seasoned, don't scrub or scrape it. If you really must remove a stubborn buildup of food, use table salt and a clean dishcloth or a plastic scrubber. Always remove leftover food from a cast iron piece after cooking. If possible, clean while pan is still warm by rubbing it with a handful of cornmeal. If necessary, quickly hand wash with a mild liquid soap. Don't soak in water or put in the dishwasher because the seasoning will be damaged. Always towel dry or place in a warm oven until dry or dry over low heat on top of the stove. If rust does form, pour some salt over it, scour, wipe off the salt and reseason.

Before cooking, even though a pan seems to be well seasoned, grease it well or spray it with shortening and heat it in a 450° oven for six minutes. To prevent damaging the seasoning, never marinate, steam or poach food in cast iron. Soups and stews tend to remove the seasoning while foods high in fat aid the seasoning process.

When ready to store cast iron cookware, rub the cooking surface with a light film of oil. Place a paper coffee filter or paper toweling between pieces to minimize scratching and to absorb any excess moisture. Store cookware and lids separately in a warm, dry place. Never store seasoned cookware unless it is completely dry or it will rust. Take good care of your cookware and it will truly seem like black magic cookery when the marriage of cast iron and cornbread produces a perfect taste treat from your oven.

Boston Brown Bread

Early colonists learned to mix baking soda with cornmeal and rye or whole-wheat flour to make a reasonably light bread. When the country expanded west, settlers took the recipe with them but it remains associated with Boston, where it was served with Boston baked beans on Saturday night. Today most people like to serve it with cream cheese. Tradition demands that it be cut into slices by looping a clean string around the loaf and pulling the ends of the string.

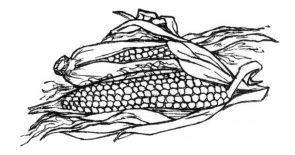

STEAMED BOSTON BROWN BREAD #1

1 c. rye flour	1 3/4 c. buttermilk
1 c. cornmeal	2 T. melted butter
1 c. whole-wheat flour	3/4 c. molasses
1/4 c. flour	Boiling water
1 t. salt	

Mix together rye flour, cornmeal, whole-wheat flour, flour and salt. In another bowl mix together buttermilk, butter and molasses. Add to cornmeal mixture; mix well. Grease two 1 pound coffee cans. Fill each can 2/3 full with batter. Cover tightly with foil and secure with twine or a heavy rubber band. Place cans on a rack in a large kettle. Add boiling water to come halfway up the cans. Cover the kettle; reduce heat to simmer. Cook for 3 hours, adding more boiling water if necessary. Remove bread from cans and cool on a wire rack. Makes 2 loaves.

STEAMED BOSTON BROWN BREAD #2

1 c. whole-wheat flour	1 t. salt
1 c. cornmeal	2 c. buttermilk
1 c. rye flour	1 c. molasses
1 t. baking powder	1 c. raisins
1 t. baking soda	Boiling water

In a mixing bowl combine whole-wheat flour, cornmeal, rye flour, baking powder, baking soda and salt. In another bowl mix the buttermilk and molasses together. Add to cornmeal mixture; stir until blended. Stir in raisins. Grease two 1 pound coffee cans and fill each 2/3 full with batter. Cover tightly with foil and secure with twine or a heavy rubber band. Place cans on a rack in a large kettle. Add enough boiling water to come halfway up the cans. Cover kettle, reduce heat to simmer; cook for 3 hours. Add more boiling water if necessary. Remove bread from cans and cool on a wire rack. Makes 2 loaves.

Corn Dodgers and Corn Pone

The simplest and oldest type of cornbread, corn dodgers, hoecakes and corn pone were and are easy to make and easy to eat. Now, they are basically the same, just called either dodgers or pones. They are as tasty served with roast beef as they are with fried chicken, fried fish, turnip greens, collards or cabbage. They should be crisp, crunchy hard, light brown and served with lots of butter.

CORN DODGERS #1

1 1/2 c. cornmeal	1/2 t. baking soda
1 T. flour	Buttermilk
1 t. salt	Vegetable oil for baking sheet
1 egg	

In a mixing bowl combine cornmeal, flour, salt and egg. Add baking soda and enough buttermilk to make a stiff batter. Shape into cakes about 3"x2" in size. Place on an oiled baking sheet and bake at 450° for 30 minutes. Makes 8 servings.

CORN DODGERS #2

1/8 t. salt	2 T. cream
1 c. boiling water	2 stiffly beaten egg whites
1 c. cornmeal	Vegetable oil for baking sheet
1 1/4 t. butter	

In a mixing bowl gradually stir salted boiling water into cornmeal. Mix until smooth and add butter. Allow to cool for 10 minutes; mix in cream. Fold in egg whites. Drop batter by teaspoonfuls onto an oiled baking sheet. Bake at 350° for 40 minutes. Makes 8 servings.

CORN PONE #1

2 c. cornmeal	1 T. baking powder
1/4 t. salt	1 1/2 c. buttermilk
1/4 t. baking soda	1 T. melted shortening
	Vegetable oil for skillet

Preheat oven to 450°. In a mixing bowl combine cornmeal, salt, baking soda and baking powder. Stir in buttermilk and shortening. Shape into cakes about 3"x2" in size. Place in a preheated oiled 10" cast iron skillet and bake for 25 minutes. Makes 6 servings.

CORN PONE #2

2 c. cornmeal	1/2 c. sugar
1/2 c. flour	1/2 c. molasses
1 qt. boiling water	1 t. salt
1/4 t. baking soda	2 T. shortening

In a mixing bowl combine cornmeal and flour. Stir in boiling water; cover and let stand overnight. When ready to cook, add baking soda, sugar, molasses and salt. Stir to mix well. Preheat oven to 350°. When hot, melt shortening in a 10" cast iron skillet. Spoon mixture into hot skillet and bake for 1 1/2 hours. Makes 10 servings.

Cornsticks

Cornsticks have endeared themselves to many cornbread lovers because of their crisp and crunchy exterior. Having a high ratio of crust to center, their shape makes them great "pushers" for beans and greens. The cast iron cornstick irons available usually have corn-shaped molds for seven sticks. There are sizes for miniature to large cornsticks. The Shaker cornstick irons make cylindrical cornsticks much like breadsticks. They come in both long and short molds.

CORNSTICKS #1

1 c. cornmeal	1 t. salt
1 t. baking powder	1 egg
1/2 t. baking soda	1 c. buttermilk

Preheat oven to 425°. Grease and heat cast iron cornstick molds in oven until hot. Combine cornmeal, baking powder, baking soda and salt in a mixing bowl. Beat egg with buttermilk; stir into cornmeal mixture. Spoon batter into hot molds and bake 15-20 minutes or until golden. Makes 12 servings.

CORNSTICKS #2

1 1/4 c. cornmeal	1 T. sugar
3/4 c. flour	2 beaten eggs
3 t. baking powder	1 c. milk
3/4 t. salt	1/4 c. vegetable oil

Preheat oven to 425°. Heat greased cast iron cornstick molds in the oven until hot. In a mixing bowl combine cornmeal, flour, baking powder, salt and sugar. In another bowl mix together eggs, milk and vegetable oil. Add to cornmeal mixture; stir just until moistened. Fill hot molds 2/3 full with batter and cook 20 minutes until brown. Makes 18 servings.

ANGEL CORNSTICKS

3/4 c. cornmeal	3/4 t. baking powder
1/2 c. flour	1/4 t. baking soda
1/2 pkg. dry yeast	1 beaten egg
1/2 T. sugar	1 c. buttermilk
1/2 t. salt	1/4 c. vegetable oil

Preheat oven to 450°. Grease cornstick molds and heat in oven until hot. Combine cornmeal, flour, yeast, sugar, salt, baking powder and baking soda. Combine eggs, buttermilk and oil. Add to cornmeal mixture; stir until smooth. Spoon batter into molds, filling 2/3 full. Bake 15 minutes until golden. Makes 18 servings.

BEREA KENTUCKY CORNSTICKS

2 c. cornmeal	1/2 t. baking soda
1/2 c. flour	2 c. buttermilk
1/2 t. salt	2 beaten eggs
1 t. baking powder	4 T. melted shortening

Preheat oven to 450°. Grease cornstick molds and heat in oven until hot. Sift cornmeal, flour, salt and baking powder into a mixing bowl. Mix baking soda and buttermilk; add to cornmeal mixture, stirring to blend well. Add eggs and mix well. Spoon batter into molds until level. Bake in middle of oven for 10-15 minutes until golden brown. Makes 12 servings.

SHAKER CORNSTICKS

1 c. plus 2 T. cornmeal	1/2 t. baking powder
1/2 c. flour	1 c. buttermilk
1 T. sugar	1 beaten egg
1/2 t. salt	2 T. vegetable oil
1/2 t. baking soda	

Preheat oven to 450°. Grease cast iron cornstick molds and heat in oven until hot. In a mixing bowl combine cornmeal, flour, sugar, salt, baking soda and baking powder. Stir until well blended. In another bowl beat together buttermilk, egg and oil. Add to cornmeal mixture; stir until smooth. Spoon batter into hot molds, filling them half full. Bake in the middle of the oven for 10 minutes until golden brown. Makes 14 servings.

TENNESSEE CORNSTICKS

3 c. plus 2 T. cornmeal	1/2 t. baking soda
1 c. boiling water	1 t. salt
2 T. butter or shortening	2 eggs
2 c. buttermilk	

Preheat oven to 450°. Grease cast iron cornstick molds and heat in oven until hot. Combine the 2 T. cornmeal with water, stirring to make a gruel. Add butter, stirring until it melts. Add remaining cornmeal, buttermilk, baking soda, salt and eggs, stirring to combine well. Pour batter into hot molds and bake for 15 minutes until golden brown. Makes 18 servings.

BRAN CORNSTICKS

2 T. shortening	3/4 c. bran
2 T. sugar	1 c. flour
1 beaten egg	3 t. baking powder
1 c. milk	1 t. salt
1/2 c. cornmeal	

Preheat oven to 400°. Heat greased cast iron cornstick molds in oven until hot. Cream shortening and add sugar. Mix well; add egg, milk, cornmeal and bran. Sift flour, measure and sift with baking powder and salt. Add to cornmeal mixture, stirring just until blended. Pour batter into hot molds. Bake for 20 minutes until golden brown. Makes 12 servings.

CHEESE CORNSTICKS #1

1 c. cornmeal	1 c. milk
1 c. flour	3/4 c. grated Parmesan cheese
1 T. baking powder	2 drops Tabasco sauce
1 t. salt	
1 1/4 c. vegetable oil	

Preheat oven to 400°. Heat greased cast iron cornstick molds in oven until hot. Combine cornmeal, flour, baking powder, and salt; mix well. Add oil, milk, cheese and Tabasco. Mix until batter is just moistened. Fill each mold 2/3 full and bake 20 minutes until golden brown. Makes 12 servings.

CHEESE CORNSTICKS #2

Vegetable cooking spray
2 c. self-rising cornmeal
1/4 t. baking soda
10 3/4-oz. can golden
   corn soup, undiluted
1 c. buttermilk

2 eggs
1/3 c. vegetable oil
1 T. chopped green chilies
1 1/2 c. shredded
   Cheddar cheese

Preheat oven to 350°. Spray iron cornstick molds and heat in oven until hot. Combine cornmeal and soda in a mixing bowl. Make a well in the center. Combine soup, buttermilk, eggs, oil, chilies and cheese. Add to cornmeal mixture, stirring just until moistened. Spoon batter into hot molds; bake for 15 minutes until golden brown. Makes 24 servings.

CILANTRO CORNSTICKS

Vegetable cooking spray
2 jalapeño peppers, seeded
   and chopped
2 cloves garlic, minced
1/3 c. vegetable oil
1/2 c. cornmeal
1/2 c. flour

2 t. baking powder
3/4 t. salt
1 T. sugar
1 t. dried cilantro
1 beaten egg
1/2 c. milk

Preheat oven to 425°. Coat cornstick molds with vegetable spray and heat in oven until hot. Sauté peppers and garlic in oil over medium heat, stirring constantly, until tender. Set aside. Combine cornmeal, flour, baking powder, salt, sugar and cilantro. Add pepper mixture, egg and milk; stir until smooth. Spoon batter into molds and bake 15-20 minutes or until golden brown. Makes 6 servings.

CORN FILLED CORNSTICKS

1/2 c. cornmeal	1/2 c. fresh corn kernels
1/2 c. flour	5 T. butter, melted
2 T. sugar	and cooled
1 1/2 t. baking powder	1 c. less 2 T. cream
1 t. salt	1 egg, separated

Preheat oven to 425°. Heat greased cast iron cornstick molds in the oven until hot. Combine cornmeal, flour, sugar, baking powder, salt and corn. In another bowl stir together butter, cream and egg yolk. Add to cornmeal mixture; stir until well combined. In a third bowl beat egg white until it just holds stiff peaks. Gently fold into the batter. Spoon batter into hot molds and bake for 15-20 minutes or until golden brown. Makes 10 servings.

CORN SYRUP CORNSTICKS

1 c. cornmeal	4 T. vegetable oil
1/4 t. salt	1 c. buttermilk
1/4 t. baking soda	2 T. light corn syrup

Preheat oven to 400°. Heat greased cast iron cornstick molds in the oven until hot. Sift cornmeal; add salt and soda; mix well. Stir in oil. Add buttermilk and syrup and stir well. Pour into molds. Bake for about 30 minutes or until golden brown. Makes 24 servings.

CRACKLING CORNSTICKS

1 c. cornmeal	1/4 t. baking soda
1/4 t. salt	3/4 c. finely chopped cracklings
1/2 c. buttermilk	or crumbled cooked bacon
1/2 c. cold water	

Preheat oven to 400°. Heat greased cast iron cornstick molds in the oven until hot. Combine cornmeal, salt, buttermilk, water, baking soda and cracklings or bacon. Pour batter into molds. Bake for 20 minutes or until golden brown. Makes 24 servings.

GREEN PEPPER CORNSTICKS

1/2 c. cornmeal	1/2 c. diced and
1/2 c. flour	sautéed green pepper
2 T. sugar	1 egg, separated
1 1/4 t. baking powder	1 c. less 2 T. heavy cream
1 t. salt	4 1/2 T. melted butter

Preheat oven to 475°. Heat greased cast iron cornstick molds in the oven until hot. Sift cornmeal, flour, sugar, baking powder and salt in a mixing bowl. Add green pepper and stir. In another bowl mix together egg yolk and cream. Stir into cornmeal mixture. Beat egg white until stiff; fold into batter. Fill each mold half full with batter and bake 20 minutes until golden brown. Makes 14 servings.

GRITS CORNSTICKS

1 c. cornmeal	1/4 c. butter
3/4 c. flour	1 c. milk
1/2 t. salt	1 egg, beaten
3 t. baking powder	1/2 c. hot cooked grits

Preheat oven to 400°. Heat greased cast iron cornstick molds in the oven until hot. Sift cornmeal, flour, salt and baking powder into a mixing bowl. Add butter, milk and egg to grits; add to cornmeal mixture. Spoon batter into molds. Bake for about 20 minutes until golden brown. Makes 24 servings.

JALAPEÑO CORNSTICKS #1

2 eggs	1/2 c. vegetable oil
1 c. cornmeal	1/2 c. buttermilk
8 3/4-oz. can cream-style corn	1 t. baking soda
1 c. shredded sharp	1/2 t. salt
Cheddar cheese	3 jalapeño peppers, chopped

Preheat oven to 400°. Heat greased cast iron cornstick molds in the oven until hot. In a large mixing bowl beat eggs and add cornmeal, corn, cheese, oil, buttermilk, baking soda and salt. Stir until well blended; add peppers. Spoon into hot molds and bake for about 7 minutes or until golden brown. Makes 20 servings.

JALAPEÑO CORNSTICKS #2

3/4 c. flour	3/4 c. milk
1/2 c. cornmeal	2 1/2 T. vegetable oil
1 1/2 t. baking powder	2 minced jalapeño peppers
1 t. sugar	2 cloves garlic, minced
1/4 t. salt	3 T. chopped cilantro
1 egg	

Preheat oven to 400°. Heat greased cast iron cornstick molds in the oven until hot. In a mixing bowl combine flour, cornmeal, baking powder, sugar and salt. In another bowl stir egg with milk and oil. Add jalapeños, garlic and cilantro. Add to flour mixture and stir just until moistened. Fill molds 3/4 full of batter and bake 12 minutes until golden brown. Makes 18 servings.

MAPLE SYRUP CORNSTICKS

1/4 c. sesame seeds	1 t. salt
1 1/4 c. cornmeal	3/4 c. sour cream
1/4 c. flour	1/3 c. milk
1/2 t. baking soda	1/3 c. maple syrup
2 t. baking powder	1 egg

In a small skillet toast sesame seeds over medium-low heat, shaking and stirring, until they are golden. Place in a small bowl; set aside to cool. Preheat oven to 425°. Heat greased cast iron cornstick molds in the oven until hot. Meanwhile, stir together cornmeal, flour, baking soda, baking powder, salt and 3 T. of the sesame seeds. In another bowl mix together sour cream, milk, maple syrup and egg until well blended. Add to cornmeal mixture; stir just until combined. Sprinkle remaining sesame seeds into hot molds and spoon the batter over the seeds. Bake for 13-15 minutes or until cornsticks are golden brown. Makes 12 servings.

PECAN CORNSTICKS

1/2 c. self-rising cornmeal
1/2 c. self-rising flour
2 T. sugar
2 eggs

1 c. milk
1/2 c. bacon drippings
1/2 c. chopped pecans

Preheat oven to 400°. Combine cornmeal, flour, sugar, eggs, milk, bacon drippings and pecans. Spoon batter into greased iron cornstick molds. Bake for 20 minutes until cornsticks are golden brown. Makes 24 servings.

SOUR CREAM CORNSTICKS

1 c. less 1 T. self-rising
   cornmeal
1 c. sour cream
2 T. milk

2 eggs
1 t. sugar
1/8 t. baking soda
4 T. melted butter

Preheat oven to 425°. In a large bowl combine cornmeal, sour cream, milk and eggs; stir to blend. Add sugar, baking soda and butter; mix thoroughly. Spoon batter into greased cast iron cornstick molds and bake 20 minutes until golden brown. Makes 12 servings.

THYME CORNSTICKS

3 eggs
10 T. melted butter, cooled
1/3 c. vegetable oil
2 c. plain yogurt
2 c. cornmeal

1 c. flour
1 1/2 T. baking powder
2 t. salt
2 t. sugar
1 t. crumbled dried thyme

Preheat oven to 400°. Grease cast iron cornstick molds and heat in oven until hot. Combine eggs, butter, oil and yogurt in a mixing bowl. In another bowl combine cornmeal, flour, baking powder, salt, sugar and thyme. Add to egg mixture; combine well. Spoon batter into hot molds and bake 15-17 minutes or until golden brown. Makes 24 servings.

THYME AND GARLIC CORNSTICKS

1 1/4 c. cornmeal	1 t. dried thyme, crumbled
3/4 c. flour	3/4 t. garlic powder
1 T. sugar	2 eggs, beaten
1 T. plus 1 t. baking powder	1 c. milk
3/4 t. salt	1/4 c. vegetable oil

Preheat oven to 425°. Grease iron cornstick molds and heat in oven until hot. Combine cornmeal, flour, sugar, baking powder, salt, thyme and garlic powder. Make a well in center of mixture. Combine eggs, milk and oil; add to cornmeal mixture. Spoon batter into hot molds, filling 2/3 full. Bake for 12 minutes or until golden brown. Makes 18 servings.

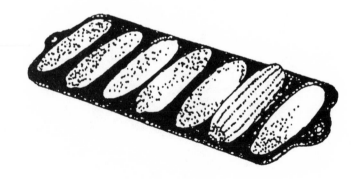

Cornbread Dressing

Is it "dressing" or "stuffing"? Either term may be used. Stuffing first appeared in print in the 1500s replacing the term "force-meat." In the late 1800s the Victorian Era made the propriety "dressing" more acceptable. To be consistent, I have used "dressing" throughout this section. Many people prefer to cook their dressing in a pan rather than stuffing it in the turkey or chicken. They say that it takes away too much of the moisture and flavor from the meat of the bird. They also claim that it is better to stuff game birds in order to absorb some of the wild taste of the meat. For stuffing a bird, just follow the directions for roasting chicken, duck, turkey or quail. When preparing the dressing, chicken or turkey broth may be used, depending on which bird you are cooking. And, oh yes, one 8" skillet of cornbread makes about 4 cups of crumbled cornbread.

CORNBREAD FOR DRESSING

1 c. flour	1 c. milk
1 1/2 c. cornmeal	1 egg
1 T. baking powder	3 T. melted butter, cooled
1 t. salt	Vegetable oil for baking pan

Preheat oven to 425°. In a mixing bowl combine flour, cornmeal, baking powder and salt. In another small bowl stir together milk, egg and butter. Add to cornmeal mixture, stirring just until combined. Pour batter into an oiled 8x8x2" baking pan; bake for 25 minutes until golden. Cool in pan on a wire rack for 5 minutes. Turn out onto rack; cool completely. If desired, crumble cornbread onto a baking sheet and toast at 325°, stirring occasionally, for 30 minutes until it is dry and golden. Makes 4 cups.

CORNBREAD DRESSING #1

3 c. crumbled cornbread	2 eggs
1 c. bread crumbs	1/2 t. pepper
2 c. chicken broth	1 t. rubbed sage or
1 c. chopped celery	poultry seasoning
1 c. chopped onion	Vegetable oil for baking pan

In a mixing bowl combine cornbread, bread crumbs, broth, celery, onion, eggs, pepper and sage. Spoon mixture into an oiled 8x8x2" baking pan; bake at 350° for 45 minutes. Makes 6 servings.

CORNBREAD DRESSING #2

4 c. crumbled cornbread	2 t. rubbed sage
8 slices stale bread,	1 t. ground thyme
cut into 1/2" cubes	1 t. celery salt
3/4 c. chopped celery	1/2 c. melted butter
3/4 c. chopped onion	3 beaten eggs
1/2 c. chopped fresh parsley	2 cans chicken broth
2 t. poultry seasoning	Vegetable oil for baking dish
2 t. pepper	

Combine cornbread and bread cubes in a mixing bowl. Stir in celery, onion, parsley, poultry seasoning, pepper, sage, thyme, celery salt, butter, eggs and broth. Mix well; spoon dressing into a lightly oiled 13x9x2" baking dish. Bake at 325° for 1 hour until golden brown. Makes 10 servings.

CORNBREAD DRESSING BALLS

3/4 c. finely chopped onion	1 t. rubbed sage or
1 c. chopped celery	poultry seasoning
1/2 c. butter	1 beaten egg
3 c. crumbled cornbread	1 t. baking powder
2 c. cubed stale white bread	1 3/4 c. warm chicken broth
1 t. salt	Vegetable oil for baking sheet
1/2 t. pepper	

In a skillet sauté onion and celery in butter until soft. In a mixing bowl combine cornbread, bread cubes, salt, pepper, sage and onion mixture. Mix gently but thoroughly. Add egg and stir in. Blend in baking powder. Add enough broth to moisten but keep mixture crumbly. With cupped hands, shape dressing into small, golf ball size balls. Arrange on an oiled baking sheet and bake at 400° for 10 minutes until crisp and browned. Makes 12 servings.

CORNBREAD APPLE DRESSING

1 c. chopped onion	1 t. vegetable broth mix
1 c. chopped celery	1 Granny Smith apple,
2 garlic cloves, minced	unpeeled, chopped
1/4 t. poultry seasoning	3 c. crumbled cornbread
1/4 t. ground sage	1/2 c. water
1/4 t. dried thyme	Vegetable oil for baking dish
2 T. parsley flakes	

Preheat oven to 350°. In a skillet sauté onion, celery and garlic over medium heat until soft. Remove from heat and sprinkle with poultry seasoning, sage, thyme, parsley flakes and broth mix. Stir to blend well. Add apple and cornbread; toss. Gradually stir in water to desired consistency. Spoon into a lightly oiled 1-quart baking dish; cover and bake 30 minutes. Makes 6 servings.

CORNBREAD CHESTNUT APPLE DRESSING

3 c. crumbled cornbread
2 c. chopped onion
1 1/2 c. chopped celery
Salt and pepper to taste
3/4 c. softened butter, divided
3/4 lb. can chestnuts,
   coarsely chopped

1 T. crumbled dried sage
2 T. crumbled dried thyme
1/2 c. minced fresh parsley
3 Granny Smith apples,
   peeled and cut into 1/4" pieces
1 c. chicken broth
Vegetable oil for baking dish

In a baking pan bake crumbled cornbread at 325°, stirring occasionally for 30 minutes until it is dry and deep golden. In a skillet sauté onion and celery, salt and pepper in 1/4 cup of the butter over medium-low heat until soft. In a mixing bowl combine cornbread, onion mixture, chestnuts, sage, thyme, parsley, remaining 1/2 cup of butter, which has been melted, and apples. Spoon dressing into a lightly oiled 2-quart baking dish and drizzle with broth. Cover loosely with foil; bake at 325° for 1 hour. Makes 8 servings.

CORNBREAD COUNTRY HAM DRESSING #1

2 onions, finely chopped
1 leek with some of the
   green part, finely chopped
1 large garlic clove, minced
1/2 c. butter
1/2 lb. baked country ham,
   sliced 1/4" thick and diced

10 c. crumbled cornbread
1 green onion, finely chopped
1/2 c. chopped fresh parsley
Pepper to taste
2 c. chicken broth
Vegetable oil for baking dish

In large skillet cook onions, leek and garlic in butter until soft. Add ham and cook, stirring, for 1 minute. Gradually stir in cornbread. Add green onion, parsley and pepper. Cook over medium heat, stirring, until cornbread is coated with butter. Spoon dressing into a bowl; add broth tossing mixture well. Transfer to a lightly oiled 3-quart casserole dish and bake at 350° for 40 minutes. Makes 12 servings.

CORNBREAD COUNTRY HAM DRESSING #2

2 med. onions, chopped
1 leek with 3" green,
    finely chopped
2 cloves garlic, minced
2 ribs celery, finely chopped
1/2 c. butter
1/2 lb. baked country ham,
    sliced 1/4" thick and diced

1 t. crumbled dried sage
1 t. dried thyme
Pepper to taste
10 c. crumbled cornbread
1/2 c. finely chopped
    fresh parsley
2 c. chicken broth

In a skillet sauté onion, leek, garlic and celery in butter over medium heat until soft. Add ham, sage, thyme and pepper. Stirring constantly, cook for 1 minute. Gradually stir in cornbread; add parsley. Cook over medium heat until cornbread is coated with butter. Transfer dressing to a mixing bowl; add broth. Toss well and spoon into a 13x9x2" baking pan. Cover with foil and bake at 375° for 35 minutes. Makes 12 servings.

CORNBREAD CRANBERRY DRESSING

1 1/2 c. chopped onion
1 1/2 c. chopped celery
1/2 c. melted butter
6 c. crumbled cornbread
3 c. dry white bread cubes
1 T. salt
1 1/2 t. poultry seasoning
1/2 t. pepper

2 beaten eggs
1 1/4 c. fresh cranberries
1/3 c. sugar
11-oz. can mandarin
    orange sections, drained
1/2 c. orange juice
Vegetable oil for baking dish

In a skillet sauté onion and celery in butter until soft. In a mixing bowl combine cornbread, bread cubes, onion mixture, salt, poultry seasoning and pepper. Add eggs; toss lightly. Mix cranberries with sugar and let stand 5 minutes. Combine cranberry mixture, orange sections and orange juice. Spoon into a lightly oiled 3-quart covered baking dish. Bake, covered, at 325° for 45 minutes. Makes 6 servings.

CORNBREAD EGG DRESSING

4 c. crumbled cornbread
1 large onion, chopped
1/2 c. chopped celery
6 hard cooked eggs, chopped

8 slices white bread,
  softened in chicken broth
1 t. rubbed sage
Salt and pepper to taste
Vegetable oil for baking dish

In a mixing bowl combine cornbread, onion, celery and eggs. Mix in softened white bread; add sage, salt and pepper. Spoon dressing into an oiled 12x8x2" baking dish. Bake at 350° for 1 hour until lightly browned. Makes 10 servings.

CORNBREAD GRAPE DRESSING

2 c. chopped onion
2 c. chopped celery
1/4 c. butter
3 c. cubed cornbread
2 c. cubed white bread
3 beaten eggs

Salt and pepper to taste
Poultry seasoning to taste
1/2 c. chicken broth
2 c. seedless red grapes, halved
Vegetable oil for baking pan

In a skillet sauté onion and celery in butter. In a large bowl combine cornbread and bread cubes. Add onion mixture to cornbread mixture. Stir in eggs, salt, pepper, poultry seasoning, broth and grapes. Spoon dressing into a lightly oiled 13x9x2" baking pan; bake at 375° for 35 minutes. Makes 12 servings.

CORNBREAD JALAPEÑO DRESSING

3 c. crumbled cornbread
1 c. chopped celery
2 med. onions, chopped

1 jalapeño pepper,
  seeded and chopped
1/4 t. pepper
3 c. chicken broth
Vegetable oil for baking pan

In a mixing bowl combine cornbread, celery, onions, jalapeño pepper and pepper. Stir in broth and spoon mixture into a lightly oiled 11x7x1 1/2" baking pan. Bake at 350° for 20 minutes until light brown. Makes 8 servings.

CORNBREAD MAYONNAISE DRESSING

1 c. cornmeal	2 beaten eggs
2 c. chicken broth	1/4 t. poultry seasoning
5 c. toasted bread cubes	1 t. salt
1/3 c. mayonnaise	1/4 t. pepper
1 c. chopped celery	Vegetable oil for baking pan
1/2 c. chopped onion	

In a saucepan combine cornmeal and broth. Cook over medium-high heat until mixture is thick. Add bread cubes, mayonnaise, celery, onion, eggs, poultry seasoning, salt and pepper. Spoon dressing into an oiled 13x9x2" baking pan. Bake at 325° for 1 hour. Makes 10 servings.

CORNBREAD MUSHROOM DRESSING #1

3 c. sliced fresh mushrooms	1 1/2 t. dried thyme
1 t. salt	1/2 t. dried marjoram
1 c. butter, divided	2 t. rubbed sage
1 1/2 c. chopped onion	1/2 c. minced fresh parsley
1 celery stalk, chopped	2 c. chicken broth
2 T. minced green onion	3 c. crumbled cornbread
1 t. pepper	Vegetable oil for baking pan
1 1/2 t. ground rosemary	

Preheat oven to 350°. In a skillet sauté mushrooms and salt in 1/2 cup of the butter until soft. Spoon into a bowl and set aside. Add remaining 1/2 cup of butter to skillet and sauté onion, celery, green onion, pepper, rosemary, thyme, marjoram and sage for 10 minutes. Add parsley, onion mixture, mushrooms and broth to cornbread in a mixing bowl. Mix well; spoon dressing into an oiled 9x9x2" pan; cover with foil and bake for 35 minutes. Uncover and bake 15 minutes longer. Makes 6 servings.

CORNBREAD MUSHROOM DRESSING #2

1/2 c. chopped onion	2 c. sliced celery
1/2 c. butter	2 1/2 c. chicken broth
3 c. crumbled cornbread	2 beaten eggs
6 c. cubed soft white bread	4 t. poultry seasoning
3 c. sliced fresh mushrooms	1/2 t. salt

In a skillet sauté onion in butter. Combine cornbread, bread cubes, mushrooms, celery, broth, eggs, poultry seasoning and salt. Add onions, toss lightly; mix well. Spoon into a 3-quart casserole dish; cover and bake at 325° for 1 hour. Makes 10 servings.

CORNBREAD OYSTER DRESSING #1

2 c. cornmeal	3 eggs, beaten
4 T. flour	Vegetable oil for cast iron skillet
2 t. baking powder	10 slices white bread,
1 t. baking soda	toasted and crushed
1 t. salt	1 c. melted butter
1 T. sugar	1 qt. hot chicken broth
1/2 c. chopped onion	2 beaten eggs
1/2 c. chopped celery	1 1/2 pt. small oysters with liquid
1 1/2 c. buttermilk	Vegetable oil for baking pan
1/2 c. vegetable oil	

Preheat oven to 400°. Combine cornmeal, flour, baking powder, baking soda, salt, sugar, onion and celery in a mixing bowl. Add buttermilk, oil and eggs. Pour into an oiled 8" cast iron skillet; bake for 40 minutes. Allow to cool. Reduce oven heat to 350°. Crumble cornbread into a large bowl. Combine with crushed toast. Add butter, broth, eggs and oysters with liquid. Stir until lightly mixed. Spoon into an oiled 13x9x2" baking pan so dressing is no more than 2" thick. Bake 1 hour. Makes 10 servings.

CORNBREAD OYSTER DRESSING #2

2 c. chopped celery
1 c. chopped onion
1/2 c. chopped fresh parsley
3/4 c. butter
4 c. crumbled cornbread
15 slices stale white bread,
  torn into pieces

1 c. oysters, drained
2 beaten eggs
1 c. chopped and floured pecans
1 1/2 t. dried sage
Salt and pepper to taste
Broth
Vegetable oil for baking pan

In a skillet sauté celery, onion and parsley in butter until soft. Combine cornbread and white bread in a large bowl. Add celery mixture, oysters, eggs, pecans, sage, salt and pepper. Toss to mix thoroughly. Gradually add some broth to moistness desired. Spoon mixture into a lightly oiled 13x9x2" baking pan and bake at 400° for 30 minutes. Makes 10 servings.

CORNBREAD PECAN DRESSING #1

4 thick slices bacon, diced
2 c. chopped onion
2 c. chopped celery
1/2 t. salt
1/2 t. pepper
1/2 t. thyme

3 c. crumbled cornbread
1 can chicken broth
3/4 c. chopped toasted pecans
1/4 c. chopped fresh parsley
Vegetable oil for baking dish

In a large skillet cook bacon until crisp. Drain on paper towels. Sauté onion, celery, salt, pepper and thyme in bacon drippings until soft. In a mixing bowl combine cornbread, onion mixture, bacon, broth, pecans and parsley until well blended. Heat oven to 325°. Spoon dressing into an oiled 13x9x2" baking dish; cover with foil. Bake 45 minutes, uncover and bake 15 minutes longer. Makes 10 servings.

CORNBREAD PECAN DRESSING #2

10 c. crumbled stale cornbread
3 c. chopped onion

Poultry seasoning to taste
Salt and pepper to taste
Chicken broth

1 c. chopped celery

1 c. chopped pecans

Vegetable oil for baking dish

In a large bowl combine cornbread, onion, celery, pecans and seasonings and mix well. Add enough broth to make a sticky mixture. Form into balls about the size of a lemon. Place balls in an oiled baking dish; bake at 350° until slightly browned. Makes 30 servings.

CORNBREAD RICE DRESSING

4 c. crumbled cornbread

3 c. dried toast croutons

1 1/2 c. cooked rice

1 large onion, diced

1 c. chopped celery

1 t. pepper

1 t. parsley flakes

1/4 t. poultry seasoning

1 t. Season-All

1 egg

1/2 c. milk

1/2 c. chicken broth

1/2 c. melted butter

1 1/2 c. orange juice

Vegetable oil for baking dish

In a mixing bowl combine cornbread, croutons, rice, onion, celery, pepper, parsley flakes, poultry seasoning and Season-All. In a small bowl beat egg with milk. Add broth, egg mixture and butter to cornbread mixture. Add orange juice; mix well. Spoon into a shallow oiled baking dish. Bake at 375° for 40 minutes. Makes 10 servings.

CORNBREAD SAUSAGE DRESSING #1

1 lb. ground pork sausage

1 c. chopped onion

1 c. chopped celery

6 c. crumbled cornbread

3 c. toasted white bread cubes

2 t. rubbed sage

1/4 t. salt

1 t. pepper

4 c. chicken broth

2 eggs, beaten

Vegetable oil for baking pan

In a large skillet combine sausage, onion and celery. Cook over medium-heat, stirring until sausage is no longer pink. Drain well and set aside. In a mixing bowl combine cornbread, bread cubes, sage, salt and pepper. Add sausage mixture and stir to combine. Add broth and eggs, mixing well. Spoon into a lightly oiled 13x9x2" baking pan. Bake at 350° for 45 minutes until browned. Makes 10 servings.

CORNBREAD SAUSAGE DRESSING #2

1 lb. ground pork sausage
1/4 c. butter
3/4 c. chopped onion
1 c. chopped celery
8 c. crumbled cornbread
2 t. salt

1/2 t. pepper
2 t. poultry seasoning
1 c. chicken broth
2 eggs
Vegetable oil for baking pan

In a skillet cook sausage until crumbly. Drain, reserving 2 tablespoons of drippings in skillet. Add butter and sauté onion and celery in mixture of drippings and butter. Crumble cornbread into a mixing bowl. Add sausage, onion mixture, salt, pepper, poultry seasoning and broth; lightly combine. Stir in eggs. Spoon mixture into a lightly oiled 13x9x2" baking pan; bake at 350° for 45 minutes until browned. Makes 8 servings.

CORNBREAD SPANISH SAUSAGE DRESSING

4 onions, chopped
5 celery ribs, chopped
2 T. butter
1 lb. Spanish sausage (chorizo)
6 cups crumbled,
   stale cornbread

3 c. cubed stale white bread
2 c. fresh corn kernels
2 t. dried cilantro
2 T. chopped fresh parsley
Salt and pepper to taste
Vegetable oil for baking dish

In a skillet sauté onion and celery in butter until soft. Remove to a large bowl. Sauté the sausage in the same skillet until lightly browned. Add to onion mixture in bowl. Add cornbread, bread cubes, corn, cilantro, parsley, salt and pepper. Toss to combine. If mixture seems too dry, add some chicken broth. Spoon mixture into a lightly oiled baking dish. Bake at 375° for 40 minutes. Makes 10 servings.

Hot Water Cornbread

These corncakes are delicious served with soups, fresh vegetables, stews or fried fish. They are quick to fix and easy to make with a little practice.

HOT WATER CORNBREAD #1

2 c. white cornmeal	Solid shortening or bacon
1 t. salt	drippings for frying (drippings
2 c. boiling water	are the most flavorful)

In a medium bowl mix together cornmeal and salt. Gradually add the boiling water, stirring constantly to make a medium thick and smooth mush. Mixture should be thick enough to hold its shape when dropped from a spoon. In an iron skillet melt shortening to 1/4" depth; heat until hot but not smoking. Drop the batter by spoonfuls into the hot skillet. Smooth the top of the cornbread with the back of a spoon. Fry on medium-high heat until golden, turning once, for 5 - 6 minutes. Cakes should be lightly browned and crispy on the outside. Drain on paper towels. Serve immediately, spread with butter. Makes 8 servings.

HOT WATER CORNBREAD #2

2 c. white cornmeal	2 c. water
1 t. salt	1/2 t. baking powder
2 T. shortening or	2 T. warmed milk
bacon drippings	

Combine cornmeal and salt in a bowl. Add shortening to water and bring to a rolling boil. Add to cornmeal mixture, stirring hard until mixture reaches the consistency of a moist croquette. Let cool 20 minutes. Combine baking powder and milk; add to cornmeal mixture, stirring to combine. Shape dough into 1" balls. Press each ball between 2 fingers to make a slight indentation on 2 sides. Heat an iron skillet containing 1/4" shortening until smoking. Carefully slide shaped dough into hot shortening. Cook only a few at a time until golden brown. Turn and cook on other side. Drain on paper towels; keep warm in oven until all cakes are cooked. Serve with lots of butter. Makes 24 servings.

HOT WATER CORNBREAD #3

1 c. white cornmeal   2 T. vegetable oil
1/4 t. salt   or bacon drippings
1 c. boiling water   2 T. milk

Combine cornmeal and salt in a mixing bowl. Add 1/4 c. water and oil. Continue adding water until mixture reaches the consistency of thick mush. Heat an iron skillet containing vegetable oil to a depth of 1/4". Drop batter by spoonfuls into the hot skillet. With the back of a spoon, smooth the tops of the corncakes and cook on medium heat until brown, turning once. Drain on paper towels and serve hot with butter. Makes 4 servings.

HOT WATER CORNBREAD #4

1 c. white cornmeal   1 c. boiling water
2 T. sugar   2 T. milk
1/8 t. salt

Mix dry ingredients in a mixing bowl. Add boiling water and mix thoroughly. Then add milk to the mixture. Heat iron skillet with 1/8" of shortening. Spoon cakes into the skillet and brown on both sides. Drain on paper towels and serve hot with butter. Makes 4 servings.

HOT WATER CORNBREAD #5

1 c. white cornmeal   1/2 t. salt
1 T. plus 1t. flour   1 T. sugar
2 t. baking powder   1 1/4 c. boiling water

Combine cornmeal, flour, baking powder, salt and sugar in a bowl. Stir in the boiling water and heat fat or oil to hot in an iron skillet. Drop the batter by tablespoons into the hot fat and cook until golden, turning once. Drain on paper towels and serve hot. Makes 4 servings.

LIGHT HOT WATER CORNBREAD

1 c. white cornmeal
1 t. salt
1 1/2 c. boiling water

1 T. vegetable oil
Nonstick vegetable spray

Combine cornmeal and salt in a bowl. Add boiling water and oil. Mix well. Fry 1/3 cup mixture on hot griddle or skillet coated with nonstick vegetable spray, pushing mixture into shape of a cake with the back of a spatula. Fry cakes on both sides until golden brown, about 3 minutes per side. Drain on paper towels. Serve hot. Makes 6 servings.

Hushpuppies

There is much speculation on how and where the "hushpuppy" got its name. It is the classic accompaniment at outdoor fish fries and at Kentucky fried catfish dinners. It is said that fishermen in Georgia or Alabama created these little deep-fried corn fritters as they cooked their catches at their campsites. They would mollify their barking dogs by throwing them bits of the fritter with the command "hush, puppy." In Florida, the workers boiling sugar cane syrup supposedly would have fish fries and the hushpuppy evolved as they watched the boiling vats. The smell of the frying fish would start their dogs barking, and so we get the "Tallahassee Hushpuppy." In Maryland, it is supposed to have been invented by women holding a combination fish fry and quilting party. In North Carolina, hushpuppies are even served at barbecue stands with fish sandwiches. Whatever its origin, this Southern institution has spread all over the country and every fish lover knows how good hushpuppies can taste!

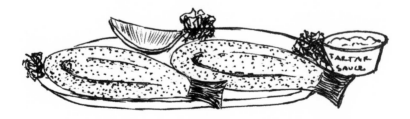

HUSHPUPPIES #1

1 c. cornmeal	1 beaten egg
1 T. flour	3/4 c. milk
1 t. baking powder	3 T. minced onion
3/4 t. salt	Vegetable oil for frying

Combine cornmeal, flour, baking powder and salt. Beat egg and milk together in a separate bowl and stir into cornmeal mixture. Add onion; blend well. Heat 3" deep oil to 375° in a Dutch oven. Drop batter by tablespoonfuls into hot oil. Deep fry 4-5 at a time for about 3 minutes, turning once, until brown and crispy. Drain on paper towels. Makes 24 servings.

HUSHPUPPIES #2

1/4 c. flour	3/4 to 1 c. buttermilk
4 t. baking powder	1 T. finely chopped onion
1/2 t. salt	1 t. finely chopped garlic
1 1/2 c. cornmeal	Vegetable oil for Dutch oven
2 eggs	

Stir flour, baking powder and salt into a mixing bowl. Stir in cornmeal and beat in eggs, one at a time. Add 3/4 cup of buttermilk and stir until well combined. If batter is too thick, add remaining 1/4 cup buttermilk. Add onion and garlic; mix well. Heat 3" deep oil to 375° in a Dutch oven. Drop batter by tablespoonfuls, 4-5 at a time, into the hot oil. Cook 3 to 5 minutes, turning once, until cakes are golden brown. Drain on paper towels. Makes 24 servings.

FLORIDA HUSHPUPPIES #1

2 c. sifted cornmeal	1 c. grapefruit juice
1/2 t. baking soda	1 beaten egg
1 t. salt	Vegetable oil for Dutch oven
3 T. minced onion	

Combine cornmeal, baking soda and salt. Add onion, grapefruit juice and egg; mix well. Use pan in which fish was fried or heat 3" deep oil in a Dutch oven to 375°. Drop batter by tablespoonfuls, 4-5 at a time, into hot oil. Cook 3-5 minutes, turning once, until golden brown. Drain on paper towels. Makes 24 servings.

FLORIDA HUSHPUPPIES #2

1 1/4 c. self-rising cornmeal	2 onions, chopped
1 1/2 c. self-rising flour	3 oz. grapefruit juice
1 T. baking powder	Vegetable oil for Dutch oven
1/4 c. plus 1 T. sugar	Salt

Combine cornmeal, flour, baking powder, sugar, onions and grapefruit juice; mix well. Batter should be fairly dry. Spray top with vegetable cooking spray and let rise 1 hour. Shape into golf ball size balls. Heat 3" deep oil in Dutch oven to 375°. Drop balls, 4-5 at a time, into hot oil and cook 5 minutes, turning once, until done on the inside and golden brown. Drain on paper towels. Sprinkle with salt. Makes 36 servings.

KENTUCKY HUSHPUPPIES

2 c. cornmeal	1 t. sugar
1/4 c. flour	1/2 c. chopped onion
1/2 t. baking soda	1 beaten egg
1 t. baking powder	1 c. buttermilk
1 t. salt	Vegetable oil for Dutch oven

Combine cornmeal, flour, baking soda, baking powder, salt and sugar in a mixing bowl. Blend in onion, egg and buttermilk. Batter should be thick; add more cornmeal if it is too thin. Heat 3" deep vegetable oil to 375° in a Dutch oven. Drop batter by rounded tablespoonfuls, 4-5 at a time, into the hot oil. Cook until brown and crispy, turning once, about 3-5 minutes. Drain on paper towels. Makes 24 servings.

LOUISIANA HUSHPUPPIES

1 c. cornmeal
1 c. flour
1 t. salt
1/2 t. sugar
1 t. baking powder
3/4 c. milk

1 egg
1/8 t. cayenne pepper
1/4 c. chopped green onion tops
1 T. finely minced onion
Vegetable oil for Dutch oven

Sift cornmeal, flour, salt, sugar and baking powder into a bowl. Make a well in cornmeal mixture. Mix together milk and egg; stir into cornmeal mixture until blended. Add cayenne pepper, green onion tops and onion. Heat 3" deep oil in a Dutch oven to 375°. Drop 5 rounded tablespoonfuls at a time into hot oil. Cook, turning once, about 5 minutes. Drain on paper towels. Makes 24 servings.

TENNESSEE HUSHPUPPIES

2 c. cornmeal
2 T. flour
1 T. baking powder
1 t. baking soda
1 t. salt

6 T. chopped onion
1 egg
2 c. buttermilk
Vegetable oil for Dutch oven

Combine cornmeal, flour, baking powder, baking soda and salt. Add onion, then egg and buttermilk beaten together. Heat 3" deep oil to 375° in a Dutch oven. Drop batter, by rounded tablespoonfuls, 4-5 at a time, into hot oil. Cook until golden brown, about 3-5 minutes, turning once. They should float when done. Drain on paper towels. Makes 24 servings.

BACON HUSHPUPPIES

6 slices bacon
1 1/2 c. cornmeal
1/2 c. flour
1 T. baking powder
1/4 t. salt

1/2 c. chopped onion
1 beaten egg
1 c. buttermilk
Vegetable oil for Dutch oven

Cook bacon in a cast iron skillet until crisp. Remove slices to paper towels to drain, then crumble. Reserve 2 tablespoons bacon drippings. Set bacon and drippings aside. Combine cornmeal, flour, baking powder and salt. Add onion and bacon. Make a well in the center of the mixture. Mix together egg, buttermilk and bacon drippings; add to cornmeal mixture. Stir just until moistened. Heat 3" deep oil in Dutch oven to 375°. Drop batter by rounded tablespoonfuls into hot oil, 4-5 at a time. Cook 3 minutes, turning once, until golden. Drain on paper towels. Makes 20 servings.

BEER HUSHPUPPIES

2 c. cornmeal	2 beaten eggs
2 t. baking powder	1/4 t. baking soda,
1 t. salt	dissolved in 1/4 c. water
1/2 c. grated onion	Vegetable oil for Dutch oven
Beer	

Combine cornmeal, baking powder and salt. Add onion and enough beer to make a stiff batter. Add eggs and baking soda; stir to combine. Heat 3" deep oil in a Dutch oven to 375°. Drop batter by tablespoonfuls, 4-5 at a time, into hot oil. Cook 3-5 minutes, turning once, until golden. Drain on paper towels. Makes 24 servings.

CHEESE AND CHILI HUSHPUPPIES

3/4 c. cornmeal	4-oz. can chopped
1/2 c. flour	green chilies, drained
1 1/2 t. baking powder	1 T. minced onion
1/2 t. salt	1 egg
1/8 t. red pepper	1/2 c. milk
1 c. shredded	Vegetable oil for Dutch oven
Monterey Jack cheese	

Combine cornmeal, flour, baking powder, salt, red pepper, cheese, chilies and onion. Mix together egg and milk; add to cornmeal mixture. Stir until just moistened. Pour 3" deep oil in a Dutch oven and heat to 375°. Drop batter, by rounded tablespoonfuls, 5 at a time, into hot oil. Cook 3-4 minutes, turning once, until golden brown. Drain on paper towels. Makes 24 servings.

JALAPEÑO HUSHPUPPIES #1

2 c. cornmeal	2 jalapeño peppers,
1/2 c. pancake mix	seeded and diced
1 t. baking powder	1 egg
2 1/2 t. sugar	1 c. buttermilk
1 t. salt	2 T. vegetable oil
1/2 c. diced onion	1/8 t. Tabasco sauce
1/2 c. diced green pepper	Vegetable oil for Dutch oven

Combine cornmeal, pancake mix, baking powder, sugar, salt, onion, green pepper and jalapeño pepper. Stir to combine well. Add egg, buttermilk, vegetable oil and Tabasco sauce. Mix well. Pour 2-3" deep oil into Dutch oven and heat to 375°. Drop batter by rounded tablespoonfuls into hot oil. Cook 4-5 at a time, turning once, for 2 minutes on each side until golden brown. Drain on paper towels. Makes 24 servings.

JALAPEÑO HUSHPUPPIES #2

1 c. self-rising cornmeal	4 T. chopped onion
3/4 c. self-rising flour	1/2 c. whole kernel corn, drained
1/3 c. sugar	2 T. jalapeño pepper,
1 egg	seeded and diced
1/2 c. milk	Vegetable oil for Dutch oven

Combine cornmeal, flour and sugar. Add egg and milk; stir to mix well. Add onion, corn and peppers; stir until well blended. Heat 3" deep oil to 375°. Drop batter, 5 at a time, into hot oil. Turning once, cook 2 minutes on each side until golden. Drain on paper towels. Makes 24 servings.

SAUSAGE HUSHPUPPIES

1/4 lb. cooked smoked sausage	1/4 c. flour
1/4 c. chopped red bell pepper	1 1/4 t. baking powder
1/2 t. vegetable oil	1/8 t. cayenne pepper
1 egg	1/4 t. salt
1/4 c. milk	1/4 c. thinly sliced green onion
1/2 c. cornmeal	Vegetable oil for Dutch oven

Quarter sausage lengthwise and cut crosswise into 1/4" pieces. Sauté with bell pepper in oil, over medium heat, for 5 minutes or until bell pepper is tender-crisp. Stir occasionally. In a large mixing bowl stir together the egg and milk; sift in cornmeal, flour, baking powder, cayenne pepper and salt. Stir until well combined. Add sausage mixture and green onion; stir until just combined. Heat 1 1/2" deep oil in a Dutch oven to 320°. Drop batter by tablespoonfuls into hot oil and cook, turning once, for 2 minutes until they are golden. Drain on paper towels. Makes 10 servings.

ACORN SQUASH HUSHPUPPIES

1 3/4 lb. acorn squash	1/2 c. milk
2 c. self-rising cornmeal	1/2 c. finely chopped onion
1/4 c. flour	Vegetable oil for Dutch oven
1 beaten egg	

Cut squash in half crosswise and remove seeds. Place halves, cut side down, in a baking dish and add 1/2" deep water. Bake at 375° for 45 minutes or until tender. Drain and scoop out pulp. Place pulp in electric blender and process until smooth. Measure out 1 1/4 cup squash puree. Combine cornmeal and flour; make a well in the center. Combine squash puree, egg, milk and onion; add to cornmeal mixture. Stir until just moistened. Pour 2" deep oil into Dutch oven and heat to 360°. Drop batter by tablespoonfuls into hot oil; cook, turning once, for 2 minutes or until golden. Drain on paper towels. Makes 24 servings.

TOMATO HUSHPUPPIES

2 c. cornmeal	1 egg
2 t. sugar	3/4 c. grated onion
1 t. baking powder	1/2 c. chopped tomatoes
2/3 t. salt	1 c. buttermilk
1/2 t. baking soda	Vegetable oil for Dutch oven
1/8 t. pepper	

Sift together cornmeal, sugar, baking powder, salt, baking soda and pepper into a mixing bowl. In another bowl, mix together egg, onion, tomatoes and buttermilk. Add to cornmeal mixture; stir until well combined. Let batter stand for 15 minutes. Heat 3" deep oil to 375° in a Dutch oven. Drop batter by rounded tablespoonfuls, 4-5 at a time, into hot oil. Cook 4-5 minutes, turning once, until golden brown. Drain on paper towels. Makes 24 servings.

BAKED HUSHPUPPIES #1

1/2 c. cornmeal	1 beaten egg
1/2 c. flour	1/3 c. skim milk
1 1/2 t. baking powder	1/4 c. thinly sliced green onion
1/2 t. salt	2 T. vegetable oil
1/2 t. sugar	Vegetable cooking spray
1/8 t. red pepper	

Combine cornmeal, flour, baking powder, salt, sugar and red pepper in a mixing bowl. Make a well in the center. Combine egg, milk, green onion and oil; add to cornmeal mixture. Stir just until moistened. Coat 1 1/2" muffin pans with cooking spray. Spoon 1 T. batter into each cup of pans and bake at 425° for 15-20 minutes until lightly brown. Remove from pans at once. Makes 18 servings.

BAKED HUSHPUPPIES #2

2/3 c. cornmeal	1 T. vegetable oil
1/3 c. flour	1 T. chopped parsley
1 t. baking powder	1/8 t. pepper
1/2 t. salt	2 beaten egg whites
1/3 c. finely chopped onion	Vegetable cooking spray
1/3 c. skim milk	

Combine cornmeal, flour, baking powder and salt in a mixing bowl and make a well in the center. Combine onion, milk, oil, parsley, pepper and egg whites. Add to cornmeal mixture, stirring just until moistened. Spoon 1 tablespoon batter each into miniature muffin pans coated with cooking spray. Cups should be 3/4 full. Bake at 450° for 10 minutes until lightly browned. Remove from pans at once. Makes 18 servings.

Indian Pudding

Early American colonists originally cooked this dish, (they called anything with cornmeal in it "Indian"), in a pot over an open hearth. Recipes for Indian pudding go back to the 1700s when cooks tried to make it taste as close as possible to English Christmas pudding. It is probably the oldest New England dessert on record.

Originally, it was very dense. Suet was used if the cook had it, molasses was used instead of expensive sugar and cornmeal replaced wheat. They also added dried fruit if it was available. Today, it tastes like a cross between custard and gingerbread. It is often served warm or cold topped with whipped cream, heavy cream, ice cream or a caramel or bourbon sauce.

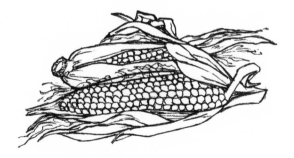

INDIAN PUDDING #1

4 c. scalded milk, divided	1/2 t. ground cinnamon
1/4 c. cornmeal	1/2 t. ground ginger
6 T. molasses	1/2 t. nutmeg
1/4 c. sugar	1 beaten egg
1 T. butter	Vegetable oil for baking dish
1/4 t. salt	

In a saucepan combine 1 cup of the milk and cornmeal; stir until thickened. Remove from heat; add molasses, sugar, butter, salt, cinnamon, ginger and nutmeg. In another bowl stir egg into remaining milk. Add to cornmeal mixture and pour into an oiled 1-quart casserole. Bake at 250° for 4 hours. Makes 6 servings.

INDIAN PUDDING #2

1/2 c. cornmeal	1/2 t. salt
1/4 c. flour	1/4 t. ground ginger
1/4 c. molasses	1/4 t. ground cinnamon
1/4 c. sugar	4 c. scalded milk
1 beaten egg	Vegetable oil for baking dish

In a mixing bowl combine cornmeal, flour, molasses, sugar, egg, salt, ginger and cinnamon. Mix well and gradually add milk, stirring constantly until mixture begins to thicken. Pour into an oiled 2-quart casserole dish and bake at 325° for 30 minutes until set. Makes 8 servings.

COLONIAL INDIAN PUDDING #1

5 c. milk	2 T. butter
2/3 c. cornmeal	1/2 t. ground ginger
1/2 t. salt	1/2 t. ground cinnamon
1 c. maple syrup	1 c. finely chopped dates
1 T. molasses	Vegetable oil for baking dish

Preheat oven to 300°. In a large heavy saucepan heat milk over medium heat.

Gradually sprinkle in cornmeal, stirring constantly for 10 minutes until mixture thickens. Reduce heat, add salt, syrup, molasses, butter, ginger, cinnamon and dates; stir for 2 minutes longer. Pour into an oiled 13x9x2" baking dish and bake for 2 1/2 hours. Makes 8 servings.

COLONIAL INDIAN PUDDING #2

1/4 c. cornmeal	2 T. packed brown sugar
1/4 t. salt	2 T. sugar
3 c. milk, divided	1 t. ground ginger
2 T. butter	1 1/2 t. ground cinnamon
2 eggs	1/3 c. raisins
1/2 c. molasses	Vegetable oil for baking dish

Preheat oven to 300°. In a heavy saucepan combine cornmeal and salt. Gradually stir in 2 1/2 cups of the milk, cooking over medium heat to a boil. Reduce heat; simmer until mixture is thick, stirring occasionally, about 10 minutes. Stir in butter; remove from heat. In a mixing bowl mix together eggs, molasses, brown sugar, sugar, ginger and cinnamon. Gradually stir in cornmeal mixture. Fold in raisins. Pour mixture into an oiled 8x8x2" baking dish. Gently pour remaining 1/2 cup of milk over pudding. Bake 1 1/2 hours until just set. Makes 10 servings.

COLONIAL INDIAN PUDDING #3

2 c. milk	1/2 t. ground nutmeg
1 c. half & half	1/2 t. ground cinnamon
1/2 c. molasses	1/2 t. ground ginger
1/4 c. brown sugar	4 eggs, beaten
6 T. butter, melted	1 c. raisins
1 c. cornmeal	Vegetable oil for baking dish
1 t. salt	

Preheat oven to 300°. In a saucepan, combine milk, half & half, molasses and brown sugar. Bring to a simmer and add butter. Pour over cornmeal in a mixing bowl. Stir in salt, nutmeg, cinnamon and ginger. Fold in eggs and the raisins. Pour mixture into an oiled 2-qt. baking dish and bake for 1 1/2 hours until pudding is set. Makes 6 servings.

COLONIAL INDIAN PUDDING #4

4 c. milk	1/2 c. raisins
1/4 c. butter	4 1/2 t. ground cinnamon
1/2 c. cornmeal	1 1/2 t. ground ginger
1/2 c. molasses	1/2 t. salt
1/4 c. sugar	1 egg, beaten
1 c. apples, pared, cored and chopped	Vegetable oil for baking dish

Preheat oven to 325°. In a saucepan, combine 2 1/2 cups of the milk and but-ter and heat until butter melts. In a small bowl, mix together remaining 1/2 cup of milk and cornmeal and add to milk and butter mixture. Bring to a boil. Reduce heat and simmer 20 minutes, stirring often, until mixture thickens. Mix in molasses, sugar, apple, raisins, cinnamon, ginger and salt. In a small bowl, stir a little of the mixture into the egg and return to saucepan, stirring to mix. Cook 5 minutes longer, stirring constantly. Pour mixture into an oiled 1 1/2-qt. baking dish and bake for 1 1/2 hours. Makes 10 servings.

SHAKER INDIAN PUDDING #1

Vegetable oil for baking dish	1/4 t. ground ginger
3/4 c. cornmeal	1/4 t. ground nutmeg
1 c. molasses	1 T. butter
1/2 t. salt	2 c. cold milk, divided
4 c. scalded milk	

Oil a casserole dish which has a cover. Put in cornmeal and combine with molasses and salt. Add scalded milk, cover and let stand for 2 hours, then refrigerate for 8 hours. Add ginger, nutmeg, butter and 1 cup of cold milk, stirring well. Bake, uncovered, at 250° until a crust forms on top. Stir well and add the remaining 1 cup of cold milk. Bake for 4 more hours, stirring occasionally. When crust has formed, cover casserole dish; remove from oven. Let cool slightly. Makes 6 servings.

SHAKER INDIAN PUDDING #2

1/3 c. cornmeal	1 t. salt
4 c. scalded milk	1/4 t. ground cinnamon
1 c. molasses	1/2 t. ground nutmeg
2 T. butter	1 c. cold milk
2 beaten eggs	Vegetable oil for baking dish

Slowly add cornmeal to milk in the top of a double boiler, stirring constantly. Cook for 15 minutes. Add molasses, butter, eggs mixed with a little hot cornmeal mix, salt, cinnamon and nutmeg. Pour into an oiled 3-quart casserole dish. Gently pour cold milk over mixture and bake at 300° for 1 hour. Reduce heat to 275° and bake for 4 hours. Makes 10 servings.

Corn Light Bread

CORN LIGHT BREAD #1

2 c. cornmeal
1 c. flour
1/2 c. sugar
1 t. salt
2 t. baking powder

1 t. baking soda
2 c. buttermilk
3 T. vegetable oil
Vegetable oil for loaf pan

In a mixing bowl combine cornmeal, flour, sugar, salt, baking powder and baking soda. Add buttermilk and vegetable oil; stir to mix well. Pour into an oiled loaf pan and bake at 300° for 1 hour. Makes 10 servings.

CORN LIGHT BREAD #2

1/3 c. vegetable oil
3 c. self-rising cornmeal
2/3 c. flour

2/3 c. sugar
1/2 t. salt
3 c. buttermilk

Preheat oven to 325°. Heat oil in a tube pan. Using a heat resistant bowl, combine cornmeal, flour, sugar and salt. Stir in buttermilk. Add hot oil from pan. Pour mixture into tube pan and bake for 1 hour. Remove from pan and cover with a towel. Makes 10 servings.

CORN LIGHT BREAD #3

1 c. flour
1 c. cornmeal
2 T. sugar
4 t. baking powder
1/2 t. salt

1 c. half & half
2 beaten eggs
1/4 c. vegetable oil
Vegetable oil for baking pan

Preheat oven to 425°. In a large mixing bowl combine flour, cornmeal, sugar, baking powder and salt. In another bowl stir half & half and eggs together. Add to cornmeal mixture; stir until just blended. Stir in oil and pour into an oiled 8x8x2" baking pan. Bake for 25 minutes. Let cool. Makes 8 servings.

CORN LIGHT BREAD #4

1 egg	1 T. flour
1 1/4 c. cold water	1 c. cornmeal
1/2 t. salt	1 c. half & half
1 t. sugar	Vegetable oil for baking pan
1 T. baking powder	

Preheat oven to 375°. In a mixing bowl, using an electric mixer, mix together egg, cold water, salt, sugar, baking powder, flour and cornmeal. Add half & half; stir well. Pour mixture into an oiled preheated 9x9x2" baking pan. Bake for 25 minutes. Let cool for 20 minutes. Makes 16 servings.

CORN LIGHT BREAD #5

6 T. melted shortening	2 T. sugar
1 2/3 c. milk	4 1/2 t. baking powder
2 eggs	1 t. salt
1 1/2 c. flour	Vegetable oil for baking pan
1 1/2 c. cornmeal	

In a mixing bowl pour shortening into milk and eggs; stir hard. In another bowl combine flour, cornmeal, sugar, baking powder and salt. Add shortening mixture to cornmeal mixture; stir until just blended. Pour into an oiled 9x9x2" baking pan; bake at 400° for 30 minutes. Makes 12 servings.

CORN LIGHT BREAD #6

1 1/2 c. cornmeal	1/2 T. salt
1/2 c. flour	2 1/2 c. boiling water
1/2 c. sugar	Vegetable oil for baking pan

Sift cornmeal, flour, sugar and salt into a mixing bowl. Add boiling water all at once and stir until batter is consistency of mush. Pour into an oiled preheated 9x9x2" baking pan; bake at 450° for 30 minutes. Makes 12 servings.

CORN LIGHT BREAD #7

1/4 c. butter
2 c. cornmeal
1 c. flour
1/2 t. salt
1/4 c. sugar

1 t. baking powder
1/2 t. baking soda
1 pkg. dry yeast
2 1/2 c. lukewarm buttermilk

Over low heat, melt butter in a cast iron skillet, tilting and rotating to grease sides. Mix together cornmeal, flour, salt, sugar, baking powder, baking soda and yeast in a large bowl. Add buttermilk; mix well. Pour mixture into the warm skillet. Cover with a towel and let rise in a warm place for 30 minutes. Uncover and bake at 350° for 30 minutes. Makes 10 servings.

CORN LIGHT BREAD # 8

2 c. cornmeal
1/2 c. flour
3/4 c. sugar
1 t. baking soda
1 t. salt

1 t. dry yeast
2 c. buttermilk
3 T. melted shortening
Vegetable oil for loaf pan

Sift cornmeal, flour, sugar, baking soda and salt into a mixing bowl. Add yeast, buttermilk and shortening; mix lightly. Pour into an oiled loaf pan and bake at 375° for 55 minutes. Makes 1 loaf.

Loaf Breads

CORNMEAL LOAF BREAD #1

1 1/2 c. flour	2 eggs
1 1/4 c. cornmeal	1/2 c. vegetable oil
3/4 c. sugar	1/2 c. milk
1/2 t. baking powder	1/2 c. buttermilk
1/2 t. baking soda	1 c. fresh corn kernels
1/2 t. salt	Vegetable oil for loaf pan

Preheat oven to 350°. In a mixing bowl combine flour, cornmeal, sugar, baking powder, baking soda and salt. In another bowl mix together eggs, oil, milk and buttermilk. Add egg mixture and corn to cornmeal mixture; stir just until combined. Pour into an oiled loaf pan dusted with cornmeal. Bake 15 minutes, reduce heat to 325° and bake 1 hour longer. Cool in pan on a wire rack for 30 minutes. Makes 1 loaf.

CORNMEAL LOAF BREAD #2

3 c. self-rising cornmeal	1 beaten egg
3/4 c. self-rising flour	1/2 c. vegetable oil
1 c. sugar	Vegetable oil for loaf pans
2 3/4 c. milk	

In a mixing bowl combine cornmeal, flour and sugar. In another bowl add enough milk to egg to measure 3 cups. Add egg mixture and oil to cornmeal mixture and mix well. Pour batter into 2 oiled loaf pans and bake at 350° for 45 minutes. Cool in pans and turn out onto a wire rack. Makes 2 loaves.

CORNMEAL LOAF BREAD #3

1/2 c. rolled oats	1/2 t. baking soda
1/2 c. cornmeal	1 1/2 t. salt
1/4 c. honey	3/4 c. plain yogurt
1 1/2 c. boiling water	3 T. butter, melted
1 1/2 c. flour	2 eggs, beaten
1/2 c. whole wheat flour	Vegetable oil for loaf pans
2 t. baking powder	

Preheat oven to 375°. In a mixing bowl combine oats, cornmeal and honey. Gradually stir in boiling water until mixture is smooth. Let stand for 15 minutes. Add flour, whole wheat flour, baking powder, baking soda and salt. Stir in yogurt, butter and eggs, mixing just until moistened. Pour batter into an oiled preheated loaf pan and bake for 50 minutes. Makes 1 loaf.

CORNMEAL LOAF BREAD #4

2 c. graham flour	3 T. butter, melted
1/2 c. cornmeal	1/2 c. maple syrup
1 t. baking soda	2 c. buttermilk
1 t. salt	Vegetable oil for loaf pan

In a mixing bowl, combine graham flour, cornmeal, baking soda and salt. In another bowl, mix together butter, maple syrup and buttermilk. Add to cornmeal mixture, stirring quickly to blend well. Pour into an oiled loaf pan and bake at 350° for 45 minutes. Makes 1 loaf.

RYE BREAD

1 c. rye flour	3/4 c. molasses
1 c. cornmeal	2 c. water
1 c. graham flour	1/2 c. raisins
1 t. baking soda	Vegetable oil for cans
1 t. salt	

In a mixing bowl combine rye flour, cornmeal, graham flour, baking soda and salt. Mix in molasses and water, stirring to mix. Fold in raisins. Spoon into 2 oiled, 1-pound coffee cans, filling 2/3 full. Cover tops with foil wrap and place in a deep pot. Add enough water to come halfway up cans and bring to a boil. Cover pot and reduce heat to a simmer. Cook for 2 hours. Remove bread from cans and cool on a wire rack. Makes 2 loaves.

Salt-Rising Bread

Salt-rising bread is an old-fashioned bread, the kind that many Americans remember from their childhoods. Since it is based on a starter made from scratch, it is very difficult to make, considering the unpredictability of the starter. It depends on yeast spores in the air to start fermentation. This starter, if it is working, has a strong cheesy odor, some refer to as the smell of dirty gym socks. The old-fashioned way to make the starter was to soak potato slices, cornmeal and sugar in warm water to ferment like a natural yeast. Why bother to go to all the trouble to make this bread — because it is so good! Toasted, there is nothing else like it.

Here are a few helpful tips for successfully making salt-rising bread:

1) Some cooks say that today's cornmeal won't make good starter, so use stone-ground, undegerminated and the most unrefined cornmeal you can find.

2) Have cornmeal and flour at room temperature before starting.

3) Warm all utensils before starting; mixing bowls, spoons and measuring cups.

4) Since the starter must be kept at a constant temperature for an active mixture to develop, things get tricky here. To get the starter to ferment, some cooks use electric yogurt makers. If you don't have one, you can use an electric heating pad covered with a terrycloth bath towel. To do this, pull the towel around the starter jar to hold in warmth, turning heat to low setting. After an hour, if starter is less than lukewarm to the touch, increase heat to medium. If fermentation (foamy consistency with a cracked surface and a cheesy aroma) does not occur, discard and start over.

SALT-RISING BREAD #1

1 med. potato, thinly sliced	1/4 t. baking soda
1 t. sugar	1 t. sugar
1/4 t. baking soda	6 c. sifted flour
1/8 t. salt	1/8 t. salt
2 c. boiling water	2 T. shortening
3/4 c. cornmeal	1 1/2 c. warm water
3/4 c. flour	Vegetable oil for tops

In a medium mixing bowl combine potatoes, sugar, baking soda and salt. Add boiling water and cornmeal. Pour mixture into a 1-quart jar and seal. Set in a warm place to rise overnight. It should double in bulk. The next morning, strain mixture into a mixing bowl. Add the 3/4 cup flour, baking soda and sugar. Beat well, cover with a plate and set in a warm place until mixture is bubbly, about 2 hours. Sift the 6 cups of flour and salt in a mixing bowl. Add shortening and mix well. Add to cornmeal mixture. Gradually add water, 1/4 cup at a time, to make a firm dough. Knead until smooth. Divide dough into 2 parts and place in 2 loaf pans. Brush tops with vegetable oil, cover with a towel and let loaves rise in a warm place until doubled in bulk, about 2 hours. Bake at 350° for 45 minutes. Makes 2 loaves.

SALT RISING BREAD #2

3 c. milk, divided	5 T. butter
1/2 c. cornmeal	5 c. sifted flour
1 3/4 t. salt	Vegetable oil for bowl
2 T. sugar	

In a saucepan scald 1 cup of the milk and pour over cornmeal in a mixing bowl. Let stand in a warm place until bubbles rise to the top, about 6 hours. In another saucepan heat remaining 2 cups of milk to lukewarm. Add salt, sugar and butter and dissolve. Add the cornmeal mixture and place in a bowl. Set the bowl in a pan of lukewarm water until bubbles rise in mixture. Work in sifted flour and knead until dough is very elastic. Place in an oiled bowl and let rise in a warm place for 2 hours. Divide dough into 3 parts and shape into loaves. Place in loaf pans, cover with a towel and let rise until doubled in bulk. Place in 375° oven for 15 minutes. Lower heat to 350° and bake for 30 minutes longer. Makes 3 loaves.

SALT-RISING BREAD #3

2/3 c. milk	1 T. salt
1/2 c. cornmeal	3 T. sugar
2 c. warm water	2 c. boiling water
1/4 t. baking soda	Melted butter
11 c. sifted flour	Vegetable oil for loaf pans
1/4 c. shortening	

In a saucepan bring milk to a boil. Add cornmeal and beat thoroughly. Cover with a towel and let stand in a warm place overnight. The next day the mixture should be light, spongy and bubbly. If the mixture has not been kept warm enough and hasn't fermented, place container in hot water and let stand until mixture is full of bubbles, about 1 hour. To the 2 cups of warm water add baking soda and 3 cups of the flour in a mixing bowl. It should make a thick batter. Add cornmeal mixture and beat well. Place in a pan of lukewarm water and set in a warm place until very light and full of bubbles, about 1 hour. Stir down dough. Add shortening, salt and sugar to the boiling water in a saucepan. Let cool to lukewarm. Add to the dough and mix thoroughly. Add enough of the remaining flour to make a stiff dough. Turn out onto a lightly floured board and knead until smooth and satiny, about 10 minutes. Divide dough into 3 parts and form into balls. Cover with a towel and let stand 10 minutes. Shape into loaves; place in oiled loaf pans and brush with melted butter. Let stand in a warm place for 2 hours until doubled in bulk. Bake at 400° for 50 minutes. Brush tops of baked loaves with melted butter. Makes 3 loaves.

CORNMEAL SOURDOUGH BREAD

Sourdough Starter

1 c. milk	1 c. flour

In a glass jar allow milk to stand at room temperature for 24 hours. Add flour and mix. Cover with cheesecloth and set outdoors for several hours. Bring indoors and let set, uncovered, for 2-5 days until bubbling. Store in refrigerator.

Cornbread

1 c. sourdough starter	1/4 c. melted butter
1 1/2 c. cornmeal	1/2 t. salt
1 1/2 c. evaporated milk	3/4 t. baking soda
2 beaten eggs	Vegetable oil for skillet
2 T. sugar	

In a mixing bowl stir together sourdough starter, cornmeal, milk, eggs and sugar. Add butter, salt and baking soda; stir to combine. Pour mixture into an oiled 10" cast iron skillet and bake at 425° for 30 minutes. Makes 10 servings.

Meats and Seafood

BEEF

CORNMEAL TAMALE PIE #1

1 T. vegetable oil	Salt and pepper to taste
2 finely chopped onions	1 1/2 c. grated sharp
2 finely minced garlic cloves	Cheddar cheese
1 chopped green pepper	Vegetable oil for baking dish
3/4 lb. ground chuck	3/4 c. cornmeal
1 T. chili powder	1/2 t. salt
1/2 t. ground cumin	2 c. water
2 c. canned tomato sauce	2 T. butter
12-oz. can whole kernel corn, drained	

To prepare filling, heat oil in a large skillet and sauté onions, garlic and green peppers until soft. Add meat, stirring to break up lumps; cook until meat is no longer red. Sprinkle with chili powder and cumin. Stir in tomato sauce, corn, salt and pepper. Simmer 30 minutes; remove from heat. Let mixture cool slightly. Preheat oven to 375°. Alternate layers of filling and cheese in an oiled 1 1/2-quart baking dish. To prepare crust, stir cornmeal and salt into water in a saucepan. Cook, stirring constantly, until mixture is thick. Mix in butter; spoon over the meat filling, smoothing with a rubber spatula. Bake for 40 minutes. Makes 6 servings.

CORNMEAL TAMALE PIE #2

1 c. cornmeal	1/2 c. chopped green pepper
3 1/2 c. cold water, divided	1 c. diced celery
1 t. salt	3/4 lb. ground chuck
1 c. grated sharp Cheddar cheese	2 1/2 c. canned whole tomatoes, cut up
1/2 t. Worcestershire sauce	1 t. salt
2 T. vegetable oil	1 bay leaf
1 sm. garlic clove, minced	Vegetable oil for baking pan
1/2 c. chopped onion	

In a small bowl mix cornmeal and 1 cup of cold water. In a saucepan bring 2 1/2 cups water to a boil and add salt. Add cornmeal mixture and cook over low heat for 10 minutes, stirring constantly. Add cheese and Worcestershire sauce, stirring until cheese melts. Spoon into an oiled 8x8x2" baking pan. Set aside in a warm place. In a large skillet heat oil and sauté garlic, onion, green pepper and celery until soft. Add meat and brown. Drain off fat. Add tomatoes, salt and bay leaf; simmer for 20 minutes. Discard bay leaf; pour mixture over cornmeal crust. Makes 6 servings.

CHICKEN

CHICKEN CORNBREAD SHORTCAKE

Topping #1

1 large chicken	2 T. melted butter
2 c. chicken stock	Salt and pepper to taste
2 T. flour	1 recipe baked cornbread,
1 lb. cleaned chopped	seasoned with dried
mushrooms	poultry seasoning

In a stock pot boil chicken in water to cover. When done, remove and allow to cool. Reserve stock in pot. When cool enough to handle, remove skin and bones from chicken. Cut meat into small pieces. In a saucepan make a sauce with 2 cups of the chicken stock and flour. In a skillet sauté mushrooms in butter. Add chicken and mushrooms to sauce; season with salt and pepper. Cut cornbread into 4" squares. Split and butter. Cover bottom halves with chicken topping. Replace top halves and top with more chicken mixture. Makes 6 servings.

Topping #2

3 T. butter	3/4 c. heavy cream
2 T. finely chopped celery	Salt and pepper to taste
2 T. finely chopped onion	3 c. coarsely chopped cooked
3 T. flour	chicken
2 c. chicken broth	1 recipe baked cornbread

In a large skillet melt butter over medium-high heat. Add celery and onion; cook until soft, stirring occasionally. Add flour; cook, stirring constantly for 1 minute. Slowly add broth and cream; salt and pepper to taste. Reduce heat; stir constantly until slightly thickened, about 3 minutes. Fold in chicken pieces. Cut cornbread into 4" squares; split and butter. Cover bottom halves with chicken sauce. Replace top halves and top with more of the chicken mixture. Makes 6 servings.

Topping #3

6 oz. process cheese spread
1/3 c. chicken broth
1 1/2 c. chopped
    cooked chicken

4 1/2-oz. can chopped chilies,
    undrained
1 recipe cooked cornbread

In a saucepan combine cheese and chicken broth. Stirring constantly, cook over medium heat until cheese melts. Add chicken and chilies. Cook until heated through. Cut cornbread into 4" squares; split and butter. Cover bottom halves with chicken sauce. Replace top halves and top with more of the chicken sauce. Makes 6 servings.

Topping #4

1/2 c. butter
1/4 c. flour
2 c. milk
1/2 t. salt
1/8 t. pepper
1 T. Worcestershire sauce

1/2 t. A-1 steak sauce
2 T. grated onion
2 c. chopped cooked chicken
Shortcake Cornbread

In a skillet melt butter. Add flour and cook for 1 minute. Add milk, stirring until thickened. Fold in salt, pepper, Worcestershire sauce, A-1 sauce, onion and chicken. Heat through. Cut cornbread into 4" squares. Split and butter. Cover bottom halves with chicken sauce. Replace top halves and top with more of the chicken mixture. Makes 6 servings.

SHORTCAKE CORNBREAD

1 c. cornmeal	1/3 t. baking soda
3 T. flour	1 c. buttermilk
1 T. baking powder	1 egg
1 t. salt	3 T. bacon drippings
	or melted shortening

Preheat oven to 400°. In a mixing bowl combine cornmeal, flour, baking powder, salt and baking soda. Add buttermilk; stir to mix. Beat in egg and 1 tablespoon bacon drippings. Put 2 tablespoons bacon drippings in an 8x8x2" baking pan and heat. Spoon cornmeal batter into pan; bake for 25 minutes.

CORNBREAD CHICKEN CASSEROLE

1 med. onion, chopped	1 can condensed mushroom soup
2 T. butter	1 c. water, divided
1 chicken boiled,	1 can cream of onion soup
broth reserved	Salt and pepper to taste
8" skillet of baked cornbread	

In a medium skillet cook onion in butter until soft. Remove skin and bones from chicken; cut meat into cubes. Crumble cornbread into a mixing bowl, add 1 cup chicken broth to soften. Add mushroom soup and 1/2 cup water, stirring to combine. Add onion soup and remaining 1/2 cup water, stirring to combine. Fold in chicken cubes, onion, salt and pepper. Spoon mixture into a baking dish and bake at 350° for 30 minutes until golden brown. Makes 8 servings.

CORNMEAL CHICKEN AND AVOCADO CASSEROLE

4 boneless, skinless	3 T. vegetable oil
chicken breast halves	1 ripe avocado, peeled and sliced
2 T. cornstarch	1 1/2 c. shredded
1 t. ground cumin	Monterey Jack cheese
1 t. garlic salt	1/2 c. sour cream, divided
1 beaten egg	1/4 c. sliced green onion tops
1 T. water	1/2 c. chopped sweet red pepper
1/3 c. cornmeal	

Preheat oven to 350°. Flatten chicken pieces to 1/4" thickness. In a shallow bowl combine cornstarch, cumin and garlic salt. Coat each breast in this mixture. In another bowl stir together egg and water. In a shallow dish spread out cornmeal. Dip chicken in egg mixture and then in cornmeal, coating both sides. Heat oil in a large skillet over medium heat. Add chicken pieces and cook 2 minutes on each side. Place chicken in a shallow baking dish. Top with avocado slices and sprinkle with cheese. Bake for 15 minutes. Top each breast with sour cream and sprinkle with green onion tops and red pepper pieces. Makes 4 servings.

CORNMEAL FRIED CHICKEN #1

Vegetable oil for frying	1/2 t. salt
1 c. flour	2 eggs
1 c. cornmeal	2 Three-lb. fryers, cut up
1/2 t. baking powder	

Heat 1" deep oil to 400° in a deep cast iron skillet. Combine flour, cornmeal, baking powder and salt in a brown paper bag. Beat eggs in a shallow dish. Dip chicken, a piece at a time, in egg. Place in paper bag; shake well to coat chicken pieces. When oil is hot, place half of chicken pieces in hot oil, not crowding them. When undersides are done, turn pieces and brown the other side. Reduce heat to 350° and cook 15 minutes longer. Drain on paper towels. Repeat with remaining chicken. Makes 8 servings.

CORNMEAL FRIED CHICKEN #2

1 c. flour	2 T. butter
1 c. cornmeal	2 T. flour
1 t. salt	1 1/4 c. milk
1/2 t. pepper	1/4 t. salt
1 fryer, cut up	1/8 t. pepper
1/2 c. vegetable oil	

Combine flour, cornmeal, salt and pepper in a brown paper bag. Add chicken pieces; shake well to coat with cornmeal mixture. Heat oil and butter in a large cast iron skillet to 375°. Add chicken and brown on both sides. Cover, reduce heat to medium; cook for 20 minutes. Uncover and cook 10 minutes longer until golden. Drain on paper towels. For gravy reserve 2 tablespoons of drippings in skillet. Add flour and stir until smooth; cook about 1 minute over medium heat. Gradually add milk, stirring constantly, until mixture thickens. Add salt and pepper. Serve this gravy with the chicken. Makes 4 servings.

CORNMEAL OVEN-FRIED CHICKEN #1

3/4 c. buttermilk	3/4 c. cornmeal
1 t. lemon zest	1/2 c. fine dry bread crumbs
1/3 c. plus 1 T. fresh	1/4 c. grated Parmesan cheese
lemon juice, divided	2 T. minced fresh parsley
1/4 c. olive oil	1/2 t. paprika
2 green onions, minced	2 eggs
1 T. fresh thyme leaves	2 T. cold water
2 t. salt, divided	2 T. melted butter
1 1/2 t. cayenne pepper, divided	Vegetable oil for baking pan
1 fryer, cut up	

In a mixing bowl combine buttermilk, lemon zest, 1/3 cup lemon juice, olive oil, green onions, thyme, 1 teaspoon salt and 1 teaspoon cayenne pepper. Add chicken pieces, cover and refrigerate overnight. Preheat oven to 425°. In another bowl combine cornmeal, bread crumbs, Parmesan cheese, parsley, remaining 1 teaspoon salt, paprika and remaining 1/2 teaspoon cayenne pepper. In a small bowl mix together eggs, water and lemon juice to make a wash. Dip chicken pieces in egg wash and coat with cornmeal mixture. Place pieces on a wire rack and let dry for 30 minutes. Arrange chicken, skin side up, on a lightly oiled baking sheet. Drizzle with butter and place in prepared baking pan; bake for 35 minutes until crisp and golden. Drain on paper towels. Makes 6 servings.

CORNMEAL OVEN-FRIED CHICKEN #2

1/3 c. fresh lime juice
1/3 c. vegetable oil
1 1/2 t. Tabasco sauce
3/4 t. cayenne pepper
3/4 t. dried oregano
3/4 t. ground cumin
3 garlic cloves, minced
1/2 med. onion, minced
1 fryer, cut up
1 c. cornmeal

1/2 c. grated Parmesan cheese
1/2 t. paprika
1/2 t. salt
1/4 t. pepper
1 T. minced fresh parsley
2 eggs
2 T. cold water
2 T. fresh lemon juice
2 T. melted butter

Combine lime juice, oil, Tabasco sauce, cayenne pepper, oregano, cumin, garlic and onion in a mixing bowl. Add chicken pieces; cover and chill in refrigerator overnight. In a second bowl combine cornmeal, Parmesan cheese, paprika, salt, pepper and parsley. In a small bowl mix together eggs, water and lemon juice to make a wash. Dip chicken in egg wash and coat with cornmeal mixture. Arrange pieces on a wire rack and let them dry for 30 minutes. Preheat oven to 425°. Arrange pieces on a lightly oiled baking sheet. Drizzle butter over pieces and bake for 35 minutes until golden and crisp. Makes 6 servings.

FISH

All small fish are best fried and they are called "pan fish" for this reason. Although all regions of the country fry fish coated with cornmeal, the South most often claims credit for this technique. Wherever the credit goes, bass, bream, crappie, perch, sunfish and trout are sweetly delicious cooked this way. There is no better meal than a traditional summer fish fry, accompanied by coleslaw, hushpuppies, iced tea or beer.

FRIED FISH #1

6 pan fish	1 T. milk
1 t. salt	1 c. cornmeal
1/8 t. pepper	Vegetable oil for frying
1 egg	

Clean and wash fish. Sprinkle both sides with salt and pepper. Combine egg and milk. Dip fish in egg mixture and coat with cornmeal. Heat 1/8" oil in a cast iron skillet to hot but not smoking. Add the fish being sure not to crowd them. Fry on one side until golden brown. Turn carefully; brown on the other side. The fish will take about 5 minutes on each side. Drain on paper towels. Makes 6 servings.

FRIED FISH #2

8 small pan fish	1/2 t. pepper
1 c. cornmeal	Vegetable oil, butter
1 t. salt	or bacon drippings for frying

Wash and clean fish. Combine cornmeal with salt and pepper. Coat fish with cornmeal mixture. Heat 1/2" deep oil in a cast iron skillet to hot but not smoking. Add fish, being careful not to crowd them. Fry 5 minutes on each side, turning once, until golden brown. Drain on paper towels and serve with lemon wedges. Makes 4 servings.

OVEN-FRIED FISH

1/4 c. cornmeal	1 lb. fish fillets, cut into 1" strips
1/4 c. dry breadcrumbs	1/3 c. milk
1/2 t. salt	3 T. butter, melted
1/8 t. pepper	

Preheat oven to 450°. Combine cornmeal, breadcrumbs, salt and pepper. Dip fish in milk; coat with cornmeal mixture. Place on a lightly greased baking sheet. Coat fillet strips with butter and bake for 10 minutes or until fish flakes easily when tested with a fork. Serve with lemon wedges, if desired. Makes 6 servings.

BAKED CATFISH

1/4 c. cornmeal	1/8 t. ground red pepper
1/4 c. flour	1 egg
1/4 c. grated Parmesan cheese	2 T. milk
1 t. paprika	4 catfish fillets
1/2 t. salt	Vegetable cooking spray
1/2 t. pepper	1/2 t. sesame seeds

Preheat oven to 350°. Combine cornmeal, flour, cheese, paprika, salt, pepper and red pepper in a shallow bowl. Mix together egg and milk. Dip fillets in the milk mixture and then coat them with the cornmeal mixture. Place the fillets on a baking sheet coated with vegetable spray. Sprinkle sesame seeds over fillets; spray with cooking spray. Bake for 30 minutes until fish flakes easily when tested with a fork. If desired, serve with lemon slices. Makes 4 servings.

FRIED CATFISH #1

1 c. flour	1/2 t. salt
Salt and pepper	1/4 t. cayenne pepper
for seasoning	1 c. cornmeal
Flour	4 1/2 lbs. catfish fillets,
2 eggs	halved crosswise
	Vegetable oil for deep frying

Using 3 separate shallow bowls have ready the flour seasoned lightly with salt and pepper in one, the egg beaten with the salt and cayenne pepper in the second and the cornmeal in the third. Dredge each fillet half in the flour, shaking off excess. Dip it in the egg mixture, letting excess drip off; dredge in the cornmeal. In a Dutch oven, heat 1" oil to 375° and fry fillets in batches for 4 minutes on each side until done and crisp. Drain on paper towels. Makes 8 servings.

FRIED CATFISH #2

6 catfish fillets	1 1/2 c. self-rising cornmeal
1 c. buttermilk	1/2 c. self-rising flour
1 1/2 T. salt	Vegetable oil for frying
1 T. pepper	

Rinse fillets. Place in a large shallow dish. Combine buttermilk, salt and pepper; pour over fish. Cover with plastic wrap; chill in refrigerator overnight. Turn fillets occasionally. When ready to fry, remove fillets from buttermilk mixture, discarding mixture. Combine cornmeal and flour. Coat chilled fillets completely. Heat 1 1/2" deep oil in a Dutch oven to 375°. Fry fillets, two at a time, for 5 minutes or until golden brown. Drain on paper towels. Makes 6 servings.

PARMESAN CATFISH

1/2 c. grated Parmesan cheese	1/8 t. ground red pepper
2 T. cornmeal	8 catfish fillets
1 t. paprika	Vegetable cooking spray

Combine cheese, cornmeal, paprika and red pepper in a paper bag. Add fillets and shake to coat with cheese mixture. Remove fillets from bag and place on broiler pan coated with cooking spray. Broil 3" from heat with oven door partially open for 10 minutes until fish flakes easily when tested with a fork. Makes 8 servings.

SALMON CASSEROLE

1/2 c. cornmeal
3 c. boiling water
1 t. salt
1 small onion, chopped

2 T. chopped green pepper
1 c. canned tomatoes, drained
8-oz. can salmon, drained
1/2 c. grated American cheese

Preheat oven to 350°. Cook the cornmeal in boiling salt water for 45 minutes. Add onion and green pepper. In a buttered casserole, place alternate layers of the cooked cornmeal, tomatoes, flaked salmon and cheese. Bake for 30 minutes. Makes 8 servings.

SMOKED SALMON CORNCAKES

1/4 c. plus 2 T. cornmeal
3 T. flour
1/4 t. baking soda
1/4 t. salt
1 egg, beaten
2 T. softened cream cheese
1/4 c. plus 2 T. buttermilk
1/2 c. fresh corn kernels,
   divided

3 T. chopped fresh chives
1/4 c. chopped green pepper
1/3 c. chopped smoked salmon
2 T. vegetable oil
Sour cream, chopped red onion
   and lemon slices
   as accompaniments

In a bowl combine cornmeal, flour, baking soda and salt. In another bowl mix together egg, cream cheese and buttermilk. Coarsely chop half of the corn and stir into buttermilk mixture. Add remaining corn, chives, green pepper, salmon and cornmeal mixture. Mix until just combined. In a large cast iron skillet, heat oil over medium-high heat. Drop batter by 1/4 cupfuls into skillet. Spread batter slightly to form 4" cakes. Cook 3 minutes on each side, turning once, until golden brown. If desired, serve with sour cream, chopped red onion and lemon slices. Makes 6 servings.

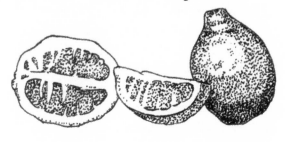

SALMON CROQUETTES #1

8-oz. can salmon	1 c. cornmeal
1 egg	Vegetable oil for frying
1 c. mashed potatoes	Tomato catsup
1/8 t. salt	

Remove skin and bones from salmon and flake with a fork. Add egg, mashed potatoes and salt. Roll into balls and coat well with cornmeal. Heat oil in a Dutch oven and fry croquettes until golden. Serve with tomato catsup. Makes 4 servings.

SALMON CROQUETTES #2

2 eggs	1/4 c. cornmeal
1/4 t. baking powder	8-oz. can salmon
1/4 c. flour	Vegetable oil for frying

Mix eggs, baking powder, flour and cornmeal. Add undrained salmon and mix thoroughly. Heat oil in a Dutch oven and drop batter from teaspoonfuls into hot oil; fry 3 minutes on each side, until golden. Turn once. Makes 8 servings.

BAKED STUFFED FISH

3-lb. whole fish	1 T. butter
6 saltine crackers, crushed	Fish broth
1 t. salt	Cornmeal
1 T. minced fresh parsley	4 strips bacon
1 T. minced fresh thyme	

Preheat oven to 300°. Scrape fish to remove scales. Wash thoroughly and remove head and tail to make broth. Cover head and tail with water and cook over medium-high and simmer while preparing fish. Combine crackers, salt, parsley, thyme and butter. Moisten with broth. Stuff fish and fasten with toothpicks; lace up with string. Cut 4 diagonal slashes at 1-2" intervals across fish. Dredge in cornmeal and lay strips of bacon over slashes. Place fish in a lightly greased baking dish. Bake for 1 hour. Remove to serving platter and, if desired, serve with lemon slices. Makes 6 servings.

FRIED CLAMS

2 c. cornmeal	4 dozen soft-shelled clams
12-oz can evaporated milk	Vegetable oil for frying

Put cornmeal and milk in 2 separate bowls. Shuck clams and dip each one in milk then coat with cornmeal. Place on a dish. In a Dutch oven, heat oil to 350°. Fry clams, a dozen at a time, for 5 minutes or until brown and crisp. Drain on paper towels and, if desired, sprinkle with salt. Makes 4 servings.

CRAB CAKES

1/4 c. melted butter, cooled	1/2 t. salt
4 beaten eggs	1/4 t. cayenne pepper
6 T. sour cream	2 lbs. lump crab meat,
1/2 c. minced fresh parsley	picked over
2 T. lemon juice	2 c. fine bread crumbs
1 t. Worcestershire sauce	1/3 c. cornmeal, divided
1 t. paprika	1/2 c. vegetable oil for frying

In a bowl combine butter, eggs, sour cream, parsley, lemon juice, Worcestershire sauce, paprika, salt and cayenne pepper. Fold in crab meat and bread crumbs. Divide mixture into 12 half cup cakes 1/4" thick. Sprinkle the cakes with half the cornmeal and place sprinkled side down on a baking sheet. Sprinkle tops of cakes with remaining cornmeal. Cover with plastic wrap; chill in refrigerator for 1 hour. Heat oil in a large cast iron skillet over medium-high heat. Fry the cakes in batches, 4 minutes on each side, turning once until golden. Drain on paper towels. If desired, serve with tartar sauce and lemon slices. Makes 12 servings.

FRIED OYSTERS #1

1 c. self-rising cornmeal	3 T. milk
1 c. self-rising flour	1 qt. oysters, drained
1/4 t. ground red pepper	Vegetable oil for frying
2 eggs	

Combine cornmeal, flour and red pepper. Beat together eggs and milk. Dip oysters in egg mixture and coat with cornmeal mixture. Heat 3 deep oil to 375° in a Dutch oven. Fry oysters until golden brown, turning once. Drain on paper towels. Makes 6 servings.

FRIED OYSTERS #2

4 beaten eggs	1/2 t. salt
1 t. salt	1/2 t. pepper
1/2 t. pepper	1 qt. oysters, drained
2 T. vegetable oil	2 T. bacon drippings
2 c. cornmeal mixed with	1/3 c. vegetable oil

In a bowl combine eggs, salt, pepper and oil. Place seasoned cornmeal in a shallow dish. Dip each oyster in the egg mixture and then lightly in the cornmeal. Set aside for 5 minutes before frying. In a large cast iron skillet, heat the bacon drippings and oil over high heat. Fry the oysters 4 minutes per side, turning once, until golden brown. Drain on paper towels. Makes 6 servings.

OYSTER PANCAKES

1/2 c. cornmeal	1/2 t. lemon juice
1/2 c. flour	2 beaten eggs
1 t. baking powder	2 c. fresh corn kernels
1/4 t. baking soda	2 T. diced sweet red pepper
1 t. salt	1 T. minced fresh chives
1/2 t. pepper	1 T. chopped fresh cilantro
2 T. melted butter	2 c. oysters, drained and chopped
1 c. buttermilk	

Preheat a lightly greased cast iron skillet. Combine cornmeal, flour, baking powder, baking soda, salt and pepper in a large bowl. Beat together butter, buttermilk, lemon juice and eggs; add to cornmeal mixture, stirring well to combine. Fold in corn kernels, red pepper, chives, cilantro and oysters. Spoon the batter into the hot skillet to make 2-3" wide cakes. Brown on both sides, turning once. Makes 18 servings.

ROLLED OYSTERS

1/2 c. flour	1/4 c. milk
1 t. baking powder	18 oysters, drained
1/4 t. salt	1 c. cornmeal
1 beaten egg	Vegetable oil for frying

Combine flour, baking powder and salt. Mix the egg and milk; add to flour mixture to make a stiff dough. Stir until batter is smooth. Place oysters in batter and coat well. Remove 3 oysters at a time; form them into a roll. Quickly roll them in the cornmeal, covering them well. Repeat process and set the 6 rolls aside. Heat 4" oil to 375° in a Dutch oven. Put oyster rolls, 3 at a time, in a basket and lower into oil. Lower heat; cook on one side and turn with a slotted spoon and cook on the other, about 4 minutes altogether. Drain on paper towels and serve hot. Makes 6 servings.

LOUISIANA FRIED OYSTER SANDWICHES

2 c. cornmeal	2 loaves soft-crusted French bread
mixed with 1/2 t. pepper	Tartar sauce
and 1/8 t. cayenne	Tomato slices
24 oysters, drained	Iceberg lettuce, shredded
Vegetable oil for frying	

Put cornmeal mixture in a paper bag. Working in batches of 6, shake oysters in bag to coat with cornmeal. Heat 1 1/2" oil in a Dutch oven to 375°. Fry oysters for 1 1/2 minutes, turning as they cook, until golden. Drain each batch on paper towels. Cut bread loaves in half crosswise and lengthwise, cutting all the way through. Spread each piece with 2 tablespoons tartar sauce. Layer tomato slices, lettuce and oysters on bottom pieces of bread. Top with remaining pieces of bread and press together. Makes 4 servings.

PORK

The corn dog is as much a part of country fairs and festivals as rides and games of chance. The condiments of choice are catsup, mustard, chili sauce and/or pickle relish.

CORN DOGS #1

1 c. self-rising cornmeal	2 T. vegetable oil
1/2 t. pepper	Wooden skewers
1/2 c. milk	8-10 hot dogs
1 beaten egg	Vegetable oil for frying

In a mixing bowl mix cornmeal and pepper. Stir in milk, egg and oil. Insert a wooden skewer into the end of each hot dog. Dip into cornmeal mixture. Heat 2" oil to 375° in a heavy skillet. Fry hot dogs, a few at a time, for 2-3 minutes until golden brown. Drain on paper towels. Makes 10 servings.

CORN DOGS #2

1/2 c. flour	1 egg
1/4 c. cornmeal	Wooden skewers
1/4 t. salt	8-10 hot dogs
1/4 t. baking soda	Vegetable oil for frying
1/2 c. buttermilk	

In a mixing bowl combine flour, cornmeal, salt and baking soda. Mix together buttermilk and egg; add to cornmeal mixture. Insert a wooden skewer into the end of each hot dog. Dip into cornmeal mixture. Heat 2" oil to 375° in a heavy skillet. Fry hot dogs, a few at a time, for 2-3 minutes until golden brown. Drain on paper towels. Makes 10 servings.

CORNMEAL AND HAM FRITTERS

1/2 c. sour cream
1/4 t. ground cumin
1/4 t. ground coriander
Salt and pepper to taste
1 egg yolk
5 T. milk
2 egg whites
1/2 c. cornmeal

1/4 c. flour
1 1/4 t. baking powder
1/2 c. coarsely grated carrot
1/2 c. diced cooked ham
1/4 c. chopped green onion
Salt and pepper to taste
Vegetable oil for frying

Mix together sour cream, cumin, coriander, salt and pepper in a small bowl. Cover and chill in refrigerator. In another bowl stir together egg yolk and milk. In a separate bowl beat egg whites until they form soft peaks. Sift cornmeal, flour and baking powder into the milk mixture and stir to combine. Stir in egg whites. Add carrot, ham, green onion and salt and pepper to taste. Heat 1 1/2" deep oil to 340° in a deep skillet. Fry 1/4 cupfuls of the batter in batches for 5 minutes, turning once, until golden. Drain on paper towels. Serve with sour cream sauce. Makes 6 servings.

HAM AND CORNBREAD PIE #1

1 lge. onion, chopped
1/4 c. chopped green pepper
1 clove garlic, minced
2 T. butter
1 T. flour
2 t. chili powder

2 c. diced cooked ham
12-oz. can whole kernel corn
2 1/4 c. tomato juice
1/4 c. seedless raisins

For Cornbread Topping

2 T. butter
1 T. sugar
1 egg
1/2 c. flour

1/2 c. cornmeal
1/2 c. milk
1 t. paprika
1 t. baking powder

In a large skillet cook onion, green pepper and garlic in butter for 5 minutes. Stir in flour and chili powder. Add ham, corn, tomato juice and raisins; heat through. Pour mixture into a large baking dish. For topping, cream butter with sugar.   Beat in egg; add flour, cornmeal, milk, paprika and baking powder. Mix well and spoon this mixture around the edge of pie to form a border. Bake at 375° for 30 minutes. Makes 6 servings.

HAM AND CORNBREAD PIE #2

1 c. cubed ham	1 1/2 t. salt
2 T. shortening	1/4 t. pepper
1/2 c. finely diced onion	2 T. flour
1 c. finely diced celery	2 c. canned tomatoes
1/4 c. finely diced	1/2 c. drained whole kernel corn
green pepper,	
cooked until partially tender	

For Cornbread Biscuit Topping

3/4 c. flour	3/4 c. cornmeal
2 1/2 t. baking powder	1/4 c. shortening
1/2 t. salt	3/4 c. milk

In a 10" skillet brown ham in shortening. Add onion, celery and green pepper. Stir in salt, pepper and flour. Blend in tomatoes and corn. Cook until mixture has thickened. Pour mixture into a shallow baking dish. To make cornmeal biscuit topping, sift together flour, baking powder and salt. Stir in cornmeal. Cut in shortening until mixture resembles coarse meal. Add milk all at once; stir just until mixture is moistened. Drop by tablespoonfuls onto meat and vegetable mixture. Bake at 400° for 35-40 minutes. Makes 6 servings.

PORK AND CORNBREAD TAMALE PIE

1 c. chopped onion	1 T. ground cumin
1 c. chopped green pepper	1/2 t. ground allspice
2 T. vegetable oil	2 t. chili powder
1 1/2 lbs. lean ground pork	1 T. Worcestershire sauce
12-oz. can tomato sauce	1 t. Tabasco sauce
2 T. tomato paste	1 T. cornmeal
10-oz. pkg. frozen corn, thawed	Salt and pepper to taste

For Cornbread Topping

1 c. flour	1 egg
1 c. cornmeal	1/2 c. grated
3 T. sugar	Monterey Jack cheese
2 t. baking powder	4-oz. can green chili peppers,
3 T. melted butter, cooled	drained and chopped
3/4 c. milk	

Preheat oven to 400°. Using a large skillet, cook the onion and green pepper in the oil over medium-low heat, stirring constantly, until onion is soft. Add pork over medium-heat, stirring constantly, until it is no longer pink. Add tomato sauce, tomato paste, corn, cumin, allspice, chili powder, Worcestershire sauce, Tabasco, cornmeal, salt and pepper. Simmer, stirring occasionally, for 30 minutes. Pour mixture into a 2 1/2-quart shallow baking dish. To make topping, sift flour, cornmeal, sugar and baking powder into a mixing bowl. Add butter, milk and egg. Stir batter until it is just blended and mix in cheese and chili peppers. Drop batter by rounded tablespoonfuls around edge of dish. Bake for 10 minutes, reduce heat to 350° and bake for 30 minutes longer. Makes 6 servings.

SAUSAGE CORNBREAD PIE #1

1 lb. pork sausage	1 can whole kernel corn, drained
1 c. cornmeal	1 bell pepper, diced
1/2 c. self-rising flour	1 small onion, chopped
1 c. buttermilk	

Preheat oven to 400°. Heat a lightly greased large cast iron skillet in oven until hot. Cook sausage in skillet until it is no longer pink, but not brown. Remove from heat; do not drain. In bowl mix cornmeal, flour, buttermilk, corn, green pepper and onion. Stir in cooked sausage and combine well; pour into hot skillet. Bake for 30 minutes until done. Makes 8 servings.

SAUSAGE AND CORNBREAD PIE #2

> 1 lb. pork sausage links

For Topping

> 1 c. flour   3/4 t. salt
> 1 c. cornmeal   3 T. sausage drippings
> 2 T. sugar   1 c. buttermilk
> 2 T. baking powder

For
Sausage Gravy

> 1/4 c. sausage drippings   2 c. milk
> 1/4 c. flour

In a 10" iron skillet brown sausage links. Drain off drippings into a measuring cup. Leave 8-9 links in skillet arranged in a sunburst pattern. Reserve remaining links for gravy. To make topping, combine flour, cornmeal, sugar, baking powder, salt, sausage drippings and buttermilk. Pour this batter over sausage links in skillet. Bake at 400° for 25 minutes. Meanwhile, make sausage gravy. In a skillet pour in sausage drippings; add flour and brown over medium-heat. Add milk all at once and bring to a boil for 1 minute. Cut remaining links into quarters and stir into gravy. Serve with pie. Makes 8 servings.

SCRAPPLE

Originally scrapple was a Pennsylvania Dutch dish called "panhaus," which was a simple mixture of cornmeal and pork trimmings. When marjoram, sage and black pepper were added to the mixture, it became known as scrapple. The name "scrapple" may have come from the word "schrapel," a German word meaning a scraping or scrap, such as the scraps from the hog. Scrapple has traditionally been made when hogs were butchered in the fall. A few years ago, canned scrapple was introduced, making it available anytime and anywhere. Here are some recipes using fairly simple ingredients and easy techniques.

SCRAPPLE #1

6 c. water	1 1/2 t. salt
1 lb. pork sausage	1/2 t. sage
2 c. cornmeal	

Bring 5 cups water to boil and crumble sausage into the water. Reduce heat and simmer for 15-20 minutes. Chill in refrigerator and skim fat. Bring mixture back to a boil. Meanwhile, combine cornmeal, salt, sage and 1 cup water; add to the sausage and water mixture. Reduce heat and stir until mixture thickens. Cover and cook for 10 minutes longer. Pour into an ungreased loaf pan and refrigerate overnight. When ready to cook, turn scrapple out of loaf pan and slice 1/2" thick. Fry in a medium-high lightly oiled skillet. Serve with syrup or sorghum, if desired. Makes 8 servings.

SCRAPPLE #2

3 c. water	1 T. finely chopped onion
1 t. salt	Flour
1 1/2 c. cornmeal	Vegetable oil or
1/2 lb. sausage	bacon drippings for frying

Make cornmeal mush, using water, salt and cornmeal. Fry sausage with onion until cooked through. Drain and add to the cornmeal mush. Pour into a lightly oiled loaf pan and chill in refrigerator overnight. When ready to use, unmold scrapple from loaf pan and cut into 3/4" slices. Dip slices in flour and fry in oil or bacon drippings until golden brown. Makes 12 servings.

Mexican Style Cornbread

A Tex-Mex specialty, these cornbreads are hot and spicy. They are excellent served with such dishes as chili, barbecue or stews. Just remember when preparing them: WEAR RUBBER GLOVES WHEN HANDLING ANY OF THE HOT PEPPERS!

CONFETTI CORNBREAD

1 c. cornmeal	1/4 t. ground cumin
3/4 c. flour	2 T. chopped green onions
1 T. sugar	1 c. plain yogurt
2 t. baking powder	1 egg
1/2 t. baking soda	2-oz. jar diced pimiento, drained
1/2 t. salt	3 T. vegetable oil
1/2 t. chili powder	

Preheat oven to 400°. In a mixing bowl combine cornmeal, flour, sugar, baking powder, baking soda, salt, chili powder, cumin and onions. In another bowl combine yogurt, egg and pimiento. Add to cornmeal mixture; stir until just moistened. In oven heat oil in an 8" cast iron skillet for about 5 minutes. Remove from oven and pour oil into batter. Stir until blended; pour into hot skillet. Bake for 25 minutes until golden. Makes 6 servings.

GREEN CHILI CORNBREAD #1

1 c. cornmeal	2 eggs
1/2 t. salt	Vegetable oil for skillet
1/2 t. baking soda	1 c. shredded Cheddar cheese
1/3 c. melted shortening	4-oz. can chopped green chilies,
1 c. sour cream	drained
8-oz. can cream style corn	

Preheat oven to 375°. In a mixing bowl combine cornmeal, salt and baking soda. Add shortening, sour cream, corn and eggs; mix well. Spoon 1/2 batter into an oiled preheated 8" cast iron skillet. Sprinkle with cheese and chilies. Top with remaining batter. Bake for 40 minutes until golden. Makes 8 servings.

GREEN CHILI CORNBREAD #2

1 c. cornmeal	1 1/2 c. fresh corn kernels
1 t. baking powder	1 clove garlic, minced
1 t. salt	4-oz. can chopped green chilies,
1 1/2 c. shredded sharp	drained
Cheddar cheese	1/3 c. melted butter
2 beaten eggs	Vegetable oil for baking dish
2 c. milk	

In a mixing bowl combine cornmeal, baking powder, salt and cheese; add eggs and milk. Stir in corn, garlic, green chilies and butter. Pour into an oiled 1 1/2-quart casserole dish and bake at 350° for 1 hour. Makes 8 servings.

GREEN PEPPER CORNBREAD #1

1 egg	3 T. chopped onion
8-oz. can cream style corn	1 1/2 c. self-rising cornmeal
1/2 c. vegetable oil	1 c. shredded sharp
1/4 c. buttermilk	Cheddar cheese
3 T. chopped green pepper	Vegetable oil for skillet
2 T. hot pepper,	
seeded and chopped	

Preheat oven to 350°. In a mixing bowl combine egg, corn, oil, buttermilk, green pepper, hot pepper, onion and cornmeal. Pour half the mixture into an oiled preheated 10" cast iron skillet. Sprinkle with half the cheese. Pour remaining cornmeal mixture on top. Top with remaining cheese. Bake for 45 minutes. Makes 10 servings.

GREEN PEPPER CORNBREAD #2

3 beaten eggs	1 sm. onion, grated
2/3 c. vegetable oil	1 c. chopped green pepper
1 c. milk	1 c. cream-style corn
1 1/2 c. cornmeal	1 c. grated sharp Cheddar cheese
2 T. flour	Vegetable oil for baking pan

In a mixing bowl combine eggs, oil, milk, cornmeal, flour, onion, green pepper and corn; mix well. Pour half the mixture into an oiled 13x9x2" baking pan. Sprinkle cheese over cornmeal mixture. Top with remaining cornmeal mixture and bake at 400° for 30 minutes. Makes 10 servings.

JALAPEÑO CORNBREAD #1

1 c. cornmeal	1 c. grated sharp Cheddar cheese
1/2 t. baking soda	17-oz. can cream-style corn
1/2 t. salt	2 jalapeño peppers,
2 eggs	seeded and chopped
1/2 c. vegetable oil	1 clove garlic, minced
1 c. sour cream	Vegetable oil for baking pan

In a mixing bowl combine cornmeal, baking soda, salt, eggs, oil, sour cream, cheese, corn, peppers and garlic. Mix well and pour into an oiled 13x9x2" baking pan. Bake at 400° for 30 minutes. Makes 12 servings.

JALAPEÑO CORNBREAD #2

1 c. cornmeal	1 jalapeño pepper,
1/2 c. flour	seeded and minced
1 1/2 t. baking powder	2 eggs
1/4 t. baking soda	1 c. buttermilk
1/4 t. salt	1/4 c. melted butter
1 c. grated sharp	Vegetable oil for baking pan
Cheddar cheese	

Preheat oven to 350°. In a mixing bowl combine cornmeal, flour, baking powder, baking soda and salt. Add cheese and pepper; mix well. In another bowl stir together eggs, buttermilk and butter; add to the cornmeal mixture and stir until just combined. Pour batter into an oiled 8x8x2" baking pan. Bake for 30 minutes. Let it cool in the pan on a rack for 5 minutes. Makes 6 servings.

HOT PEPPER CORNBREAD #1

1 c. cornmeal	1 1/2 hot peppers,
1/2 c. vegetable oil	seeded and finely minced
1 sm. can cream-style corn	2 eggs
1/2 t. salt	1 med. onion, finely chopped
1 c. buttermilk	Vegetable oil for skillet
3/4 t. baking soda	1/2 lb. sharp Cheddar cheese,
	grated

Preheat oven to 375°. In a mixing bowl combine cornmeal, oil, corn, salt, buttermilk, baking soda, hot peppers, eggs and onion. Pour half the mixture into an oiled preheated 8" cast iron skillet. Sprinkle with cheese and top with remaining batter. Bake for 30 minutes until golden. Makes 8 servings.

HOT PEPPER CORNBREAD #2

1 lge. onion, chopped	8-oz. carton sour cream
2 eggs	1 1/2 c. self-rising cornmeal
1/2 c. vegetable oil	Vegetable oil for skillet
1 hot pepper,	4 oz. grated sharp
seeded and chopped	Cheddar cheese
1 c. cream-style corn	

Preheat oven to 400°. In an electric blender process onion, eggs, oil and hot pepper until well blended. In a mixing bowl combine corn, sour cream and cornmeal. Add onion mixture and mix well. Pour half the mixture into an oiled preheated 8" cast iron skillet. Sprinkle with 3/4 of cheese; pour on remaining cornmeal mixture. Top with remaining cheese. Bake for 40 minutes until golden. Makes 8 servings.

RED PEPPER CORNBREAD

2 c. self-rising cornmeal	1/2 c. melted butter
2 t. sugar	1 c. milk
1 1/2 t. crushed dried	1/4 c. buttermilk
red pepper	Vegetable oil for skillet
1 beaten egg	

Preheat oven to 450°. In a mixing bowl combine cornmeal, sugar and red pepper. Add egg, butter, milk and buttermilk; stir until smooth. Pour mixture into an oiled preheated 10" cast iron skillet. Bake for 15 minutes until golden. Makes 10 servings.

PICANTE CORNBREAD

1 c. flour	1 c. buttermilk
3/4 c. cornmeal	2 eggs
1 1/2 t. baking powder	1/3 c. picante sauce
1/2 t. baking soda	1/4 c. butter
1/2 t. salt	

Preheat oven to 425°. In a mixing bowl combine flour, cornmeal, baking powder, baking soda and salt. In another bowl combine buttermilk, eggs and picante sauce. Add to cornmeal mixture and stir just until moistened. Heat an 8" cast iron skillet in oven for 5 minutes. Add butter and heat in oven about 1 minute. Pour melted butter into batter, stirring to blend. Pour batter into hot skillet and bake for 20 minutes until golden. Makes 8 servings.

SOUTHWEST BLUE CORNBREAD #1

1 c. blue cornmeal	1 egg
1 c. flour	1 c. milk
1 T. sugar	1/4 c. melted butter
1 t. salt	Vegetable oil for baking pan
2 t. baking powder	1 c. shredded
1/2 t. dried oregano, rubbed fine	Monterey Jack cheese
1/4 t. garlic salt	Paprika

Preheat oven to 425°. In a mixing bowl combine cornmeal, flour, sugar, salt, baking powder, oregano and garlic salt. In another bowl mix together egg and milk. Add cornmeal mixture and stir in butter. Pour half the batter into an oiled preheated 8x8x2" baking pan. Spread with half the cheese. Add remaining cornmeal batter and sprinkle with remaining cheese and paprika. Bake for 20 minutes. Makes 9 servings.

SOUTHWEST BLUE CORNBREAD #2

1 1/4 c. blue cornmeal
1 c. flour
2 T. sugar
1 T. baking powder
1 t. salt
1/8 t. baking soda
2 T. butter
3 serrano chilies, unseeded
  and finely chopped
3 cloves garlic, minced

1 sweet red pepper, finely chopped
1 green pepper, finely chopped
2 beaten eggs
1 c. buttermilk
1/3 c. melted butter
1/3 c. melted shortening
2 T. plain yogurt
11-oz. can white corn, drained
3 T. chopped fresh cilantro
Vegetable oil for skillet

Preheat oven to 450°. In a bowl combine cornmeal, flour, sugar, baking powder, salt and baking soda. Melt butter in a 10" cast iron skillet. Add chilies, garlic, red and green peppers; sauté until soft. In another bowl combine eggs, buttermilk, melted butter, shortening, yogurt and corn; add to cornmeal mixture, stirring just until moistened. Add vegetable mixture and cilantro. Spoon batter into oiled preheated skillet and bake for 25 minutes until browned. Makes 10 servings.

Muffins

Muffins and gems are the same delicious hot bread. Gems got their name from old-time recipes using a heavy muffin pan known as a "gem pan." Muffins got their name from the days when muffs were worn. These "little muffs" were served hot to warm the fingers and satisfy the appetite.

When making cornmeal muffins, use either white or yellow cornmeal; it is your choice. Blue cornmeal is very popular in the Southwest. The use of sugar is also a matter of preference. Northerners like it, Southerners don't!

The secret of making light muffins is the quick mixing of the dry and liquid ingredients. The batter may look lumpy, but it is ready to be put in the muffin pan. If possible, leave one of the cups empty and fill with water. The muffins will not scorch.

Cornmeal muffins are good served with chili, soups, stews, fried apples, sausage, bacon and eggs or split and topped with creamed beef or chicken. And, of course, they are best served hot with lots of butter!

CORNMEAL MUFFINS #1

1 c. sifted flour	2 beaten eggs
1 c. cornmeal	1 c. milk
1 T. sugar	1/4 c. melted butter
4 t. baking powder	Vegetable oil for muffin pan
1 1/2 t. salt	

Sift flour, cornmeal, sugar, baking powder and salt into a mixing bowl. Add eggs, milk and butter, stirring until smooth. Spoon batter into oiled muffin cups, filling 2/3 full. Bake at 425° for 20 minutes until golden. Makes 12.

CORNMEAL MUFFINS #2

1 egg, at room temperature	2/3 c. cornmeal
1/2 c. melted butter, cooled	1 T. baking powder
1/4 c. vegetable oil	1/2 t. salt
1 c. lukewarm milk	1 T. sugar
1 c. cake flour	Vegetable oil for muffin pan

Preheat oven to 400°. In a mixing bowl combine egg, butter and oil. Add milk in a stream; mix until well combined. In another bowl mix together flour, cornmeal, baking powder, salt and sugar. Add to egg mixture; stir just until combined. Spoon batter into oiled muffin cups, filling 2/3 full. Bake for 20 minutes until golden. Makes 12.

CORNMEAL APPLE MUFFINS

1/2 c. flour	1 beaten egg
1 c. cornmeal	1/2 c. milk
1/2 t. salt	2 T. melted butter
1 T. sugar	1/2 c. finely chopped apples
2 1/2 t. baking powder	Vegetable oil for muffin pan

Preheat oven to 400°. Sift flour, cornmeal, salt, sugar and baking powder into a mixing bowl. Add egg and milk to make a medium batter. Mix well; add butter and apples. Mix well; spoon into oiled muffin cups, filling 2/3 full. Bake for 20 minutes until golden. Makes 12.

CORNMEAL BACON MUFFINS #1

1 3/4 c. cornmeal
1 t. salt
1 t. sugar
1 t. baking powder
1/2 t. baking soda

1 beaten egg
1 1/2 c. buttermilk
4 strips bacon,
    crisply cooked and crumbled
Vegetable oil for muffin pan

Preheat oven to 450°. In a mixing bowl combine cornmeal, salt, sugar, baking powder and baking soda. Add egg and buttermilk; stir to combine. Mix in bacon. Spoon batter into oiled muffin cups, filling 2/3 full. Bake for 15 minutes. Makes 12.

CORNMEAL BACON MUFFINS #2

8 slices bacon,
    crisply cooked and crumbled
1/2 c. finely chopped onion
1 c. cornmeal
2/3 c. flour
1 t. baking powder
1 t. baking soda

1/2 t. salt
2 eggs
1/4 c. melted butter, cooled
1 1/2 c. sour cream
1/4 c. milk
Vegetable oil for muffin pan

Preheat oven to 425°. After frying bacon, pour off all but 1 tablespoon drippings; sauté onion in bacon drippings in skillet until soft. Into a mixing bowl sift together cornmeal, flour, baking powder, baking soda and salt. In another bowl stir together eggs, butter, sour cream and milk. Add bacon, onion and cornmeal mixture; beat well. Spoon batter into oiled muffin cups, filling 2/3 full. Bake 20 minutes until golden. Makes 12.

CORNMEAL BLUEBERRY MUFFINS #1

1 c. flour
1 c. cornmeal
1 T. baking powder
1 t. salt
1/4 c. melted butter, cooled
1 egg

1/3 c. honey
1/3 c. sugar
3/4 c. milk
2 c. fresh blueberries
Vegetable oil for muffin pan

Preheat oven to 425°. In a mixing bowl combine flour, cornmeal, baking powder and salt. In another bowl mix together butter, egg, honey, sugar and milk. Add to cornmeal mixture; stir just until combined. Fold in blueberries; spoon batter into oiled muffin cups, filling 2/3 full. Bake 20 minutes until golden. Makes 12.

CORNMEAL BLUEBERRY MUFFINS #2

1 c. cornmeal	2 c. fresh blueberries
1 c. flour	4 T. melted butter
1 T. baking powder	2 beaten eggs
1/2 t. salt	1 c. sour cream
1/4 t. baking soda	Vegetable oil for muffin pan
1 T. sugar	

Preheat oven to 400°. Sift cornmeal, flour, baking powder, salt, baking soda and sugar into a mixing bowl. Add blueberries; stir to mix. In another bowl combine butter, eggs and sour cream. Add to cornmeal; stir just until combined. Spoon into oiled muffin cups, filling 2/3 full. Bake for 20 minutes until golden. Makes 12.

CORNMEAL BROWN BREAD MUFFINS

1/2 c. rye flour	1/3 c. molasses
1/2 c. cornmeal	1/3 c. brown sugar, packed
1/2 c. whole-wheat flour	1/3 c. vegetable oil
3/4 t. salt	1 c. buttermilk
1 1/2 t. baking soda	1 c. raisins, cut into pieces
1 egg, at room temperature	Vegetable oil for muffin pan

Preheat oven to 400°. In a large mixing bowl combine rye flour, cornmeal, whole-wheat flour, salt and baking soda. In another bowl mix together egg, molasses, brown sugar, oil and buttermilk. Add to the cornmeal mixture, stirring just until combined. Fold in raisins. Fill oiled muffin cups 2/3 full. Bake for 20 minutes and turn out on a rack to cool. Makes 12.

CORNMEAL BROWN SUGAR MUFFINS

1 c. sifted flour	1/4 c. melted shortening
3/4 t. baking soda	2 T. brown sugar
1 t. salt	2 beaten eggs
1 t. baking powder	1 1/2 c. buttermilk
1 c. cornmeal	Vegetable oil for muffin pan

Sift flour, baking soda, salt and baking powder into a mixing bowl; stir in cornmeal. In another bowl combine shortening, brown sugar and eggs. Add buttermilk; combine with cornmeal mixture, stirring just until smooth. Spoon batter into oiled muffin cups, filling 2/3 full. Bake at 425° for 20 minutes until golden. Makes 12.

CORNMEAL BUTTERMILK MUFFINS #1

1 c. flour	1/4 c. melted butter
3/4 t. baking soda	2 T. brown sugar
1 t. salt	2 beaten eggs
1 t. baking powder	1 1/2 c. buttermilk
1 c. cornmeal	Vegetable oil for muffin pan

Sift flour and measure. Sift with baking soda, salt and baking powder into a mixing bowl. Add cornmeal; stir to combine. In another bowl combine butter, brown sugar and eggs. Add buttermilk; combine with cornmeal mixture. Stir only just until smooth. Spoon batter into oiled muffin cups, filling 2/3 full. Bake at 435° for 20 minutes. Makes 10.

CORNMEAL BUTTERMILK MUFFINS #2

2 c. cornmeal	1 egg, beaten
2 t. baking powder	2 c. buttermilk
1/2 t. baking soda	3 T. melted butter
1 t. salt	Vegetable oil for muffin pan

Preheat oven to 450°. Sift cornmeal, baking powder, baking soda and salt into a bowl. In another bowl mix egg, buttermilk and butter. Add to cornmeal mixture; stir just until moistened. Spoon into preheated muffin cups, filling 2/3 full; bake 20 minutes until golden. Makes 12.

CORNMEAL CHEDDAR CHEESE MUFFINS #1

1 1/2 c. flour	1 c. milk
1/2 c. cornmeal	1/4 c. melted butter
1 T. baking powder	1 1/4 c. coarsely grated sharp
1/2 t. salt	Cheddar cheese, divided
Pinch of cayenne pepper	Vegetable oil for muffin pan
1 egg	

Preheat oven to 425°. In a mixing bowl combine flour, cornmeal, baking powder, salt and cayenne pepper. In another bowl beat together egg, milk and butter; add to cornmeal mixture. Stir until well combined. Mix in 1 cup of cheese and fill oiled muffin cups 3/4 full. Sprinkle 1 teaspoonful of remaining cheese over each muffin. Bake 20 minutes until golden. Makes 12.

CORNMEAL CHEDDAR CHEESE MUFFINS #2

1 c. cornmeal	2 beaten eggs
1 c. flour	1 1/4 c. buttermilk
1 T. baking powder	1/4 c. melted butter
1 t. salt	1 c. fresh corn kernels
1/2 t. baking soda	1/3 c. grated sharp
1/2 t. sugar	Cheddar cheese
Pinch of cayenne pepper	Vegetable oil for muffin pan

Preheat oven to 425°. In a mixing bowl sift together cornmeal, flour, baking powder, salt, baking soda, sugar and cayenne pepper. In another bowl mix together eggs and buttermilk until well combined. Blend in butter and corn. Add cornmeal mixture to the buttermilk mixture; stir just until combined. Fill oiled muffin cups 3/4 full with batter. Sprinkle each muffin with cheese and bake for 25 minutes until golden. Makes 12.

CORNMEAL FETA CHEESE MUFFINS

1 c. cornmeal	1 c. crumbled Feta cheese
2/3 c. flour	1 c. milk
1 t. baking powder	1 egg
1/2 t. baking soda	1/4 c. melted butter
1/2 t. salt	Vegetable oil for muffin pan
1 T. finely chopped	
fresh sage leaves	

Preheat oven to 425°. In a mixing bowl combine cornmeal, flour, baking powder, baking soda and salt. Add sage and Feta cheese; mix well. In another bowl stir together milk, egg and butter. Add to cornmeal mixture; stir just until combined. Spoon batter into oiled muffin cups. Bake 20 minutes until golden. Makes 12 muffins.

CORNMEAL PARMESAN CHEESE MUFFINS

1 c. cornmeal	2 eggs
1 c. flour	1/4 c. vegetable oil
1/4 c. grated Parmesan cheese	1 1/3 c. buttermilk
1 t. baking soda	Vegetable oil for muffin pan
1/2 t. salt	

Preheat oven to 425°. In a mixing bowl combine cornmeal, flour, cheese, baking soda and salt. In another bowl mix together eggs, oil and buttermilk. Stir into cornmeal mixture just until moistened. Spoon batter into oiled muffin cups; bake for 20 minutes until golden. Makes 12.

CORNMEAL CORN MUFFINS #1

1 c. flour	1 beaten egg
2 T. sugar	8 3/4-oz. can cream-style corn
2 t. baking powder	3/4 c. milk
3/4 t. salt	2 T. vegetable oil
1 c. cornmeal	Vegetable oil for muffin pan

Sift flour, sugar, baking powder and salt into a mixing bowl. Mix in cornmeal. In another bowl combine egg, corn, milk and oil. Add to cornmeal mixture; stir just until moistened. Spoon batter into oiled muffin cups, filling 2/3 full. Bake at 425° for 30 minutes until golden. Makes 12.

CORNMEAL CORN MUFFINS #2

1 c. flour	1 egg
1 c. cornmeal	1/4 c. vegetable oil
1/4 c. sugar	1 c. milk
1 T. baking powder	8 3/4-oz. can corn, drained
1/2 t. salt	Vegetable oil for muffin pan
1/8 t. ground red pepper	

Preheat oven to 425°. In a mixing bowl combine flour, cornmeal, sugar, baking powder, salt and red pepper. In another bowl mix together egg, oil and milk. Add to cornmeal mixture; stir just until combined. Fold in corn. Spoon batter into oiled muffin cups, filling 2/3 full. Bake 20 minutes until golden. Makes 12.

CORNMEAL COUNTRY HAM MUFFINS

1 2/3 c. flour	1 1/4 c. finely chopped
1/3 c. cornmeal	baked country ham
1/4 c. sugar	2 beaten eggs,
2 t. dry mustard	at room temperature
1 1/2 t. baking powder	1 c. buttermilk
3/4 t. salt	1/3 c. vegetable oil
1/2 t. baking soda	3 T. Dijon mustard
1/8 t. pepper	Vegetable oil for muffin pan
1/8 t. ground cloves	

Preheat oven to 400°. Combine flour, cornmeal, sugar, dry mustard, baking powder, salt, baking soda, pepper and cloves in a mixing bowl; stir in ham. In another bowl mix together eggs, buttermilk, oil and Dijon mustard. Stir into cornmeal mixture just until blended. Spoon batter into oiled muffin cups, filling 3/4 full. Bake 25 minutes until golden. Cool 5 minutes. Makes 14.

CORNMEAL CURRY MUFFINS

1/4 c. chopped green onion	2 T. sugar
3 T. vegetable oil	1 T. curry powder
1 1/4 c. cornmeal	1 beaten egg
3/4 c. sifted flour	1 c. milk
3/4 t. salt	Vegetable oil for muffin pan
1 T. baking powder	

Preheat oven to 425°. In a small skillet sauté onion in oil until tender and set aside. Sift cornmeal, flour, salt, baking powder, sugar and curry powder into a mixing bowl. Add the egg, milk and onion; stir just until combined. Spoon batter into oiled muffin cups, filling 2/3 full. Bake 18 minutes. Makes 12.

CORNMEAL GRITS MUFFINS

1 c. milk	1/2 t. salt
1 egg	2 t. baking powder
1 c. cold cooked grits	1 1/4 c. cornmeal
1 T. melted shortening	Vegetable oil for muffin pan

In a mixing bowl combine milk, egg and grits. Add shortening, salt, baking powder and cornmeal; mix well. Spoon batter into oiled muffin cups, filling 2/3 full. Bake at 425° for 25 minutes until golden. Makes 12.

CORNMEAL HERB MUFFINS #1

2 c. self-rising cornmeal	2 t. grated onion
1/2 t. salt	1/2 c. sour cream
1/4 t. thyme	2 T. melted butter
1/2 t. celery seed	Vegetable oil for muffin pan
1 beaten egg	

Sift cornmeal, salt and thyme into a mixing bowl. Add celery seed, egg, onion and sour cream; mix well. Add butter, stirring well. Spoon batter into oiled muffin cups, filling 2/3 full. Bake at 450° for 20 minutes. Makes 12.

CORNMEAL HERB MUFFINS #2

1 1/3 c. flour	1 1/4 c. buttermilk
2/3 c. cake flour	2 beaten eggs
1 c. cornmeal	1/2 c. chopped packed
2 T. sugar	mixed herbs
1 T. baking powder	(basil, chives, parsley, tarragon)
1 1/2 t. salt	Vegetable oil for muffin pan
1 c. cold butter, cut into pieces	

Preheat oven to 350°. Combine flour, cake flour, cornmeal, sugar, baking powder and salt in a mixing bowl. Using an electric mixer gradually mix in butter until mixture resembles coarse meal. In another bowl mix together buttermilk, eggs and herbs. Add to cornmeal mixture; mix just until combined. Spoon batter into oiled muffin cups, filling 2/3 full. Bake 25 minutes until golden. Makes 12.

CORNMEAL JALAPEÑO MUFFINS

1 c. cornmeal	1/4 c. melted butter
3/4 c. flour	1 beaten egg
2 t. baking powder	1 T. pureed jalapeño peppers
3/4 t. salt	Vegetable oil for muffin pan
1 c. milk	

Preheat oven to 400°. In a mixing bowl combine cornmeal, flour, baking powder and salt. In another bowl mix together milk, butter, egg and peppers. Add to cornmeal mixture; stir well. Spoon batter into oiled muffin cups, filling 2/3 full. Bake 15 minutes until golden. Makes 12.

CORNMEAL MAPLE MUFFINS

1 beaten egg	1 1/2 t. baking powder
1/3 c. milk	1/4 t. salt
2 T. maple syrup	3 T. melted butter
1/2 c. cornmeal	Vegetable oil for muffin pan
3/4 c. flour	

Preheat oven to 425°. In a mixing bowl combine egg, milk and syrup. In another bowl mix together cornmeal, flour, baking powder and salt. Gradually stir in syrup mixture. Add butter; stir in. Spoon batter into oiled preheated muffin cups, filling 2/3 full. Bake 15 minutes until golden. Makes 12.

CORNMEAL MAYONNAISE MUFFINS

2 c. cornmeal	1 T. mayonnaise
1 t. baking powder	1 1/2 c. milk
1 t. salt	Vegetable oil for muffin pan
1 egg	

Sift cornmeal, baking powder and salt into a mixing bowl. Add egg, mayonnaise and milk; mix well. Spoon batter into oiled muffin cups, filling 2/3 full. Bake at 400° for 25 minutes. Makes 12.

CORNMEAL MOLASSES MUFFINS

1 c. flour	1 egg yolk
1/2 c. cornmeal	1/4 c. molasses
2 1/2 t. baking powder	3/4 c. cold milk
1/3 t. salt	1 slightly beaten egg white
1/4 c. sugar	Vegetable oil for muffin pan
1/4 c. butter	

Sift flour, cornmeal, baking powder, salt and sugar into a mixing bowl. Using a pastry blender cut in butter. Mix in egg yolk and molasses. Blend well. Add milk; stir until blended. Fold in egg white. Spoon batter into oiled muffin cups, 2/3 full. Bake at 400° for 20 minutes. Makes 12.

CORNMEAL OAT MUFFINS #1

1 1/4 c. buttermilk	1 c. whole-wheat flour
1/2 c. cornmeal	1 t. baking powder
1/2 c. uncooked regular oats	1/2 t. baking soda
1 beaten egg	1/4 t. salt
3 T. brown sugar	Vegetable oil for muffin pan
2 T. vegetable oil	

In a mixing bowl combine buttermilk, cornmeal and oats. Let stand 1 hour. Add egg, brown sugar and oil, mixing well. In another bowl combine whole-wheat flour, baking powder, baking soda and salt. Add buttermilk mixture, stirring just until moistened. Spoon batter into oiled muffin cups, filling 2/3 full. Bake at 400° for 20 minutes. Makes 12.

CORNMEAL OAT MUFFINS #2

1/2 c. cornmeal	1/2 t. salt
1/4 c. uncooked regular oats	1/2 c. buttermilk
1/4 c. flour	1/4 c. vegetable oil
1 1/2 t. wheat germ	1 beaten egg
2 T. sugar	Vegetable oil for muffin pan
1 1/2 t. baking powder	

In a mixing bowl combine cornmeal, oats, flour and wheat germ. Mix in sugar, baking powder and salt. Add buttermilk, oil and egg, stirring just until moistened. Spoon batter into oiled muffin cups, filling 2/3 full. Bake at 375° for 25 minutes until golden. Makes 10.

CORNMEAL ORANGE MUFFINS

1 c. cornmeal	1/2 c. vegetable oil
2 c. flour	2 beaten eggs
1 c. sugar	2 T. grated orange rind
1/2 t. salt	2/3 c. buttermilk
1 t. baking soda	Vegetable oil for muffin pan

Preheat oven to 375°. Combine cornmeal, flour, sugar, salt and baking soda in a mixing bowl. Add vegetable oil, eggs, orange rind and buttermilk; mix well. Spoon batter into oiled muffin cups, filling 2/3 full. Bake for 12 minutes until golden. Makes 12.

CORNMEAL PECAN MUFFINS #1

1 1/2 c. cornmeal	1 1/2 c. milk
1 1/4 c. flour	1/2 c. melted butter
2 T. sugar	2 beaten eggs
1 T. baking powder	1 c. finely chopped pecans
1/4 t. salt	Vegetable oil for muffin pan

Preheat oven to 400°. In a mixing bowl stir together cornmeal, flour, sugar, baking powder and salt. Add milk, butter and eggs; mix well. Fold in pecans. Spoon batter into oiled muffin cups, filling 2/3 full. Bake for 20 minutes until golden. Makes 18.

CORNMEAL PECAN MUFFINS #2

1 1/3 c. flour	1/2 c. chopped pecans,
2/3 c. cornmeal	lightly toasted
1 1/2 t. baking powder	1 c. sour cream
3/4 t. baking soda	2 eggs
1 t. salt	1/4 c. melted butter, cooled
	1/4 c. molasses
	Vegetable oil for muffin pan

Preheat oven to 400°. In a mixing bowl combine flour, cornmeal, baking powder, baking soda, salt and pecans. In another bowl mix together sour cream, eggs, butter and molasses. Add to cornmeal mixture; stir just until combined. Spoon into oiled muffin cups, filling 2/3 full. Bake 20 minutes until golden. Makes 12.

CORNMEAL PICANTE MUFFINS

1 1/2 c. cornmeal	1/4 c. picante sauce
1 t. baking soda	1/4 c. vegetable oil
1 t. sugar	8-oz. carton sour cream
1/2 t. salt	Vegetable oil for muffin pan
2 egg whites	

In a large mixing bowl combine cornmeal, baking soda, sugar and salt. In another bowl combine egg whites, picante sauce, oil and sour cream. Add to cornmeal mixture, stirring just until moistened. Spoon batter into oiled muffin cups, filling 2/3 full. Bake at 425° for 20 minutes. Makes 12.

CORNMEAL RASPBERRY MUFFINS

1 c. cornmeal	2 eggs
1 c. flour	1 1/4 c. sour cream
1/2 c. sugar	1/4 c. melted butter, cooled
1 t. baking powder	1 c. fresh raspberries
1 t. baking soda	Vegetable oil for muffin pan
1/4 t. salt	

Preheat oven to 375°. Combine cornmeal, flour, sugar, baking powder, baking soda and salt in a mixing bowl. In another bowl mix together eggs, sour cream and butter. Add cornmeal mixture; stir just until combined. Gently fold in raspberries. Spoon batter into oiled muffin cups, filling 2/3 full. Bake for 20 minutes. Let cool in muffin pan on a rack for 5 minutes. Turn muffins out onto rack and allow to cool completely. Makes 12.

CORNMEAL SOUR CREAM MUFFINS #1

1 1/2 c. self-rising cornmeal	1/2 c. melted butter
1 med. onion, grated	1 c. cream-style corn
2 T. sugar	1 c. sour cream
2 beaten eggs	Vegetable oil for muffin pan

Preheat oven to 350°. In a mixing bowl combine cornmeal, onion and sugar.

Add eggs, butter, corn and sour cream; stir to combine. Spoon batter into preheated oiled muffin cups, filling 3/4 full. Bake for 45 minutes until golden. Makes 12.

CORNMEAL SOUR CREAM MUFFINS #2

1 c. cornmeal	1/2 t. salt
1 c. flour	2 egg whites
2 t. baking powder	1 1/4 c. sour cream
1 t. baking soda	1/4 c. vegetable oil
1 t. sugar	Vegetable oil for muffin pan

In a mixing bowl combine cornmeal, flour, baking powder, baking soda, sugar and salt. In another bowl mix together egg whites, sour cream and oil. Add cornmeal mixture, stirring just until moistened. Spoon batter into oiled muffin cups, filling 3/4 full. Bake at 425° for 15 minutes until golden. Turn out of pan immediately. Makes 18.

CORNMEAL SWEET POTATO MUFFINS

1 c. cornmeal	1/4 c. molasses
1 c. flour	1/2 c. sour cream
1 T. baking powder	1 c. orange juice
1/2 t. salt	1 c. cooked sweet potatoes,
1 c. raisins	pureed
2 beaten eggs	Vegetable oil for muffin pan
1/4 c. vegetable oil	

Preheat oven to 400°. Sift cornmeal, flour, baking powder and salt into a mixing bowl; stir in raisins. In another bowl mix together eggs, oil, molasses, sour cream, orange juice and sweet potato puree. Add to cornmeal mixture; stir just until blended. Spoon batter into oiled muffin cups, filling 2/3 full. Bake for 20 minutes until golden. Makes 12.

CORNMEAL YEAST MUFFINS #1

1 pkg. dry yeast	1/2 c. butter
1/4 c. warm water	2 c. scalded milk
1 c. cornmeal	2 c. sifted flour
1/2 c. sugar	2 beaten eggs
1 T. salt	Vegetable oil for muffin pan

Dissolve yeast in water. In a mixing bowl combine cornmeal, sugar, salt and butter. Add milk and stir until butter melts. Cool to lukewarm. Stir in 1 cup of the flour and eggs. Beat in yeast, then remaining flour. Dough will be very stiff. Cover with a towel; let rise in a warm place until doubled in bulk, about 1 hour. Punch down. Fill oiled muffin cups 3/4 full. Cover again; let rise in a warm place until nearly doubled in bulk, about 45 minutes. Bake at 400° for 15 minutes until golden. Makes 24.

CORNMEAL YEAST MUFFINS #2

3/4 c. warm water	1 egg
1 pkg. dry yeast	1/2 t. salt
1 1/2 c. sifted flour	1/2 c. cornmeal
2 T. sugar	Vegetable oil for muffin pan
1/4 c. shortening	

In a mixing bowl combine water and yeast. Stir until dissolved. Add 1 cup flour, sugar, shortening, egg, salt and cornmeal. Using an electric mixer combine on low speed. Stir in additional flour. Spoon batter into oiled muffin cups and let rise 40 minutes. Bake at 375° for 20 minutes until golden. Makes 12.

BLUE CORNMEAL MUFFINS #1

1 1/2 c. flour	1 1/2 c. milk
1 c. blue cornmeal	2 beaten eggs
1 T. baking powder	1/4 c. vegetable oil
1/2 t. salt	Vegetable oil for muffin pan
1 1/2 t. sugar	

Preheat oven to 400°. In a mixing bowl combine flour, cornmeal, baking powder, salt and sugar. Add milk, eggs and oil; stir just until combined. Spoon batter into muffin cups, filling 2/3 full. Bake for 20 minutes until golden. Makes 12.

BLUE CORNMEAL MUFFINS #2

1 1/2 c. blue cornmeal
1 c. flour
1 T. salt
1 T. baking powder
2 T. sugar
3/4 c. plus 2 T. melted butter

1/4 c. minced onion
1 clove garlic, minced
1/2 c. chopped roasted
  bell pepper
2 T. chopped fresh coriander
Vegetable oil for muffin pan

Preheat oven to 450°. In a mixing bowl combine cornmeal, flour, salt, baking powder and sugar. In another bowl mix together butter, onion, garlic, peppers and coriander. Add cornmeal mixture; stir just until combined. Fill oiled muffin cups, filling 2/3 full. Bake for 20 minutes until golden. Makes 12.

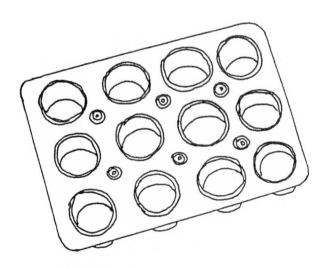

Cornmeal Mush and Polenta

Cornmeal mush, a basic native American dish, is like a cross between cornbread and spoonbread. It is found throughout the South, recipes for it being published in the early 1800s. It is especially good served combined with cheese or fried and served with pork, chicken or chili. You can use leftover mush as thickening for soups, gravies or stews or combined with cheese or vegetables in scalloped dishes.

Polenta is really just gourmet mush. They are basically the same thing. Have you ever tried to lure a guest to your table by saying you are serving mush? Try saying polenta instead. Then they will think you are preparing a gourmet dish. Before Columbus discovered America and corn, polenta in Italy was made from the flours of wheat, barley or chestnuts. After Columbus' discovery, corn thrived along the Po River and polenta soon became daily fare for Northern Italian peasants. Polenta is now the name for the corn and the dish. Traditionally, it was cooked in a copper kettle, called a "paiolo," hung from a chain over a fire in a country kitchen. It was stirred with a special wooden spoon or stick. Either as cornmeal mush or polenta, it is a dish that should not be ignored by the modern cook.

CORNMEAL MUSH #1

1 1/4 c. cornmeal	2 1/2 c. boiling water
1 t. salt	

Gradually sprinkle cornmeal into boiling salted water in a saucepan. Stirring constantly, cook until mixture comes to a boil. Boil for 4-5 minutes. Lower heat and cook, stirring occasionally, until mixture is thick. Makes 4 servings.

CORNMEAL MUSH #2

1 c. cornmeal	4 c. milk
1/2 c. cold water	1 t. salt

In a small bowl stir cornmeal into cold water. In a saucepan heat milk to boiling. Add salt; stir in cornmeal paste and mix well. When thickened, lower heat; cook 45 minutes, stirring occasionally to keep from sticking. Makes 6 servings.

FRIED CORNMEAL MUSH #1

Pour prepared cornmeal mush into a lightly oiled loaf pan and chill until firm. Turn out onto a plate and slice into 1/2" thick pieces. Dip each slice in flour and fry in a hot skillet coated with butter, bacon drippings or vegetable oil.

FRIED CORNMEAL MUSH #2

Prepare cornmeal mush and while hot, add 1 1/2 c. grated sharp Cheddar cheese and Tabasco sauce to taste. Pour into an oiled loaf pan and chill completely. Remove from pan and cut into 1/2" slices. Fry in a hot skillet coated with butter, bacon drippings or vegetable oil.

CORNMEAL MUSH AND CHEESE BAKE

1 recipe cornmeal mush	Salt and pepper to taste
3/4 c. butter	1/2 c. grated Parmesan
1 c. shredded Monterey Jack	cheese
cheese	Vegetable oil for baking dish
4-oz. can peeled green chilies,	
drained and finely diced	

Pour mush into a loaf pan and chill overnight in refrigerator. Remove from pan and cut into 1/2" thick slices. Place half the slices in an oiled 9x9x3" baking dish. Spread with butter and top with half the shredded cheese. Add chilies and remaining shredded cheese. Place remaining slices of mush on top of cheese. Dot with butter, sprinkle with salt and pepper; cover with Parmesan cheese. Bake at 350° for 20 minutes until cheese is melted and light brown. Makes 6 servings.

CORNMEAL MUSH AND SMOKED SAUSAGE

1 recipe hot cooked	Tomato sauce
cornmeal mush	Grated Parmesan cheese
Cooked smoked sausage	

Pour cornmeal mush into a 1 1/2-quart baking dish. Place sausages on top of mush. Top with a tomato sauce of your choice. Sprinkle liberally with cheese and heat thoroughly in an oven heated to 350°.

POLENTA #1

2 qts. chicken broth	3 c. cornmeal
1/2 t. salt	2 T. butter

In a heavy 4-quart saucepan bring broth and salt to a boil. Gradually add cornmeal, stirring constantly. Reduce heat and simmer, stirring frequently, for 30 minutes until consistency is that of thick oatmeal. Mix in butter and serve while hot. Makes 8 servings.

POLENTA #2

4 c. water   1 c. cornmeal
1 t. salt

Using a heavy saucepan bring water and salt to a boil. Gradually stir in cornmeal. Cook over medium-low heat, stirring constantly for 2 minutes. Cover pan and cook 45 minutes, stirring for 1 minute every 10 minutes. Remove from heat; cover. Stir just before serving, Makes 6 servings.

POLENTA, GOAT CHEESE AND MUSHROOM PIE

9"frozen pie shell, defrosted   1/2 c. sour cream
1/2 lb. mushrooms, sliced   1/4 lb. soft mild goat cheese
Salt to taste   2 beaten eggs
1/2 c. softened butter, divided   1/2 t. salt
1 c. prepared polenta, cooled   1 T. coarsely chopped fresh
        thyme sprigs

Preheat oven to 375°. Chill pie shell until ready to use. In a skillet sauté mushrooms with salt in 2 tablespoons of the butter until golden. Spread mushrooms in pie shell and bake for 20 minutes. Force polenta through a coarse sieve with the back of a spoon. In a bowl combine polenta, sour cream and remaining butter. Grate goat cheese; add to polenta mix. Add eggs and salt; stir to combine. Spread polenta mixture over mushrooms. Sprinkle with thyme and bake 35 minutes. Cool slightly on a wire rack. Makes 6 servings.

POLENTA WITH FONTINA CHEESE

2 med. onions, finely chopped   1/8 t. pepper
1/2 c. butter   1 c. heavy cream
1 1/2 c. cornmeal   1/2 c. grated Fontina cheese
4 c. hot chicken broth   Vegetable oil for baking dish
1 1/2 t. salt

Preheat oven to 350°. In a large saucepan sauté onions in butter until soft. Add cornmeal and stir to coat with butter. Gradually add broth, stirring constantly; bring to a boil. Reduce heat to low; cook about 10 minutes, stirring occasionally. Stir in salt and pepper; allow to cool slightly. Spoon half of the polenta into an oiled 13x9x2" baking dish. Pour half the cream over polenta; top with remaining polenta. Pour remaining cream over polenta; sprinkle with cheese. Bake 30 minutes until cream is bubbling up and cheese is golden. Cool 10 minutes on a wire rack before serving. Makes 8 servings.

POLENTA WITH GORGONZOLA
AND MASCARPONE CHEESE #1

4 c. plus 1 T. chicken broth
1 c. cornmeal
1 c. half & half
Salt and pepper to taste
10 oz. mild Gorgonzola cheese,
    at room temperature,
    thinly sliced

10 oz. Mascarpone cheese,
    at room temperature
5 large garlic cloves, thinly sliced
5 T. butter

In a large saucepan bring 4 cups broth to a boil and gradually add cornmeal, stirring constantly. Reduce heat and simmer, stirring constantly, until mixture is thick, about 30 minutes. Mix in half & half; stir over medium heat until heated through.   Season with salt and pepper. Arrange Gorgonzola on plates and mound Mascarpone next to Gorgonzola. Cover with polenta. To make garlic sauce, combine garlic, butter and 1 tablespoon broth in a small saucepan. Cover and cook over low heat 15 minutes; uncover and cook 5 minutes longer until garlic is golden. Spoon sauce over polenta. Makes 6 servings.

POLENTA WITH GORGONZOLA
AND MASCARPONE CHEESE #2

5 c. milk
1 c. cornmeal
1/3 c. Mascarpone cheese

1 t. salt
1/8 t. white pepper
3 T. crumbled Gorgonzola cheese

In a heavy saucepan bring milk to a boil over medium heat, stirring to prevent scorching. Gradually add cornmeal in a slow stream, stirring constantly until milk is absorbed. Reduce heat to very low and cook polenta 1 hour, stirring every 10 minutes until thick and smooth. Mix in Mascarpone, salt and white pepper. Preheat broiler. Spoon polenta into a 2-quart shallow baking dish and top with Gorgonzola cheese. Broil 2 minutes about 6" from heat until cheese melts. Makes 6 servings.

POLENTA WITH GORGONZOLA CHEESE AND MUSHROOMS

1/2 lb. fresh mushrooms, cut into 1/2" slices	1 T. chopped fresh parsley
3 T. butter	1 t. fresh lemon juice
Salt to taste	3/4 c. Gorgonzola cheese, cut into 1/2" pieces
1 chopped garlic clove	1 recipe polenta, kept warm
1/2 c. water	

In a skillet sauté mushrooms in butter until brown, stirring occasionally. Season with salt and add garlic; cook 1 minute, stirring. Add water, cover and simmer 5 minutes until mushrooms are tender. Uncover and simmer 3 minutes longer, until liquid is slightly reduced. Mix in parsley and lemon juice; keep warm. Add half cup Gorgonzola cheese to warm polenta. Stir until smooth. Spoon mushroom mixture over and top with remaining Gorgonzola. Makes 4 servings.

POLENTA WITH MASCARPONE CHEESE AND SAGE

2 c. water	1/2 c. Mascarpone cheese
1 1/2 c. chicken broth	1/4 c. grated Parmesan cheese
1 c. cornmeal	2 T. minced fresh parsley
3/4 t. crumbled dried sage	Dash of Tabasco sauce
2 garlic cloves	Salt to taste

In a 3-quart microwave-safe casserole with a cover combine water and broth. Gradually stir in cornmeal; add sage and garlic. Cover and microwave at high power (100%) for 12 minutes, stirring every 3 minutes, until mixture is thick and liquid is absorbed. Let stand 2 minutes, covered. Discard the garlic; stir in Mascarpone, Parmesan, parsley, Tabasco sauce and salt. Makes 6 servings.

POLENTA WITH PARMESAN CHEESE #1

1 1/2 c. cornmeal	1 t. salt
1 c. water	2 T. butter
3 1/2 c. boiling water	Grated Parmesan cheese

In top of a double-boiler combine cornmeal and 1 cup water. When well mixed, add boiling water. Stirring constantly, cook over low heat until mixture boils. Add salt. Place over hot water; cook for 1 hour. Add butter and sprinkle heavily with Parmesan cheese. Makes 8 servings.

POLENTA WITH PARMESAN CHEESE #2

2 c. water	Pepper to taste
1/2 t. salt	Vegetable oil for pie plate
1/2 c. cornmeal	3 T. grated Parmesan cheese
2 T. butter	

Preheat oven to 400°. In a large saucepan bring water to a boil; add salt. Gradually add cornmeal, stirring constantly, for 15 minutes until mixture is very thick. Stir in butter and pepper. Spoon mixture into an oiled 9" pie plate; smooth with a rubber spatula. Sprinkle with Parmesan cheese; chill in refrigerator for 30 minutes. Bake for 25 minutes. Brown lightly under broiler 4" from heat. Makes 2 servings.

POLENTA WITH PARMESAN
AND MOZZARELLA CHEESE

2/3 c. chopped onion	2/3 c. plus 1/4 c. grated
3 T. olive oil	Parmesan cheese
5 c. water	Salt to taste
2 c. cornmeal	Vegetable oil for baking dish
1 1/3 c. half & half	2 1/3 c. grated Mozzarella cheese

Preheat oven to 350°. In a large saucepan sauté onion in oil until soft. Add water; bring to a boil. Gradually add 1 cup of cornmeal, stirring constantly.

Lower heat and gradually add remaining cornmeal, stirring constantly. Mix half & half, 2/3 cup of Parmesan cheese and salt. Spoon mixture into an oiled 13x9x2" baking dish. Spread evenly with a rubber spatula and sprinkle with half the Mozzarella cheese. Top with remaining cornmeal mixture and sprinkle with remaining Parmesan and Mozzarella. Bake for 40 minutes until cheese is melted and golden. Allow to cool slightly before serving. Makes 8 servings.

POLENTA WITH SAUSAGE

2 qts. water	15-oz. can tomato paste
1 T. salt	Two 14 1/2-oz. cans beef broth
2 c. cornmeal	1/2 t. rubbed sage
1 lb. Italian sausage, sweet or hot, sliced	1/2 c. grated Parmesan cheese

In a heavy 4-quart saucepan combine water and salt; bring to a boil. Gradually add cornmeal, stirring constantly. Reduce heat to medium and cook for 30 minutes, stirring occasionally, until fairly thick. Remove from heat; keep warm. Cook sausage in a 10" cast iron skillet. Drain well. Add tomato paste, broth and sage. Cook over low heat for 30 minutes. Spoon polenta onto a platter; top with sausage mixture. Sprinkle with Parmesan cheese. Makes 4 servings.

BROILED POLENTA WITH TOMATO SAUCE

1 recipe polenta, kept warm	1 garlic clove, chopped
1 c. grated Fontina cheese	28-oz. can whole tomatoes, including juice
Vegetable oil for pans	
2 T. olive oil	1 T. chopped fresh parsley
1 lge. onion, chopped	Olive oil for brushing
Salt to taste	Grated Parmesan cheese

In a mixing bowl combine warm polenta and Fontina cheese. Mix until smooth and pour into a lightly oiled 1 1/2-quart loaf pan. Chill in refrigerator. In a large skillet heat olive oil over medium-high heat until hot but not smoking. Sauté onion with salt about 10 minutes, stirring, until tender. Add garlic; sauté one minute, stirring. Add tomatoes with juice. Stir to break up tomatoes, cover and simmer 30 minutes. Stir in parsley; keep warm. Preheat broiler. Unmold polenta and cut into 3/4" thick slices. Arrange slices, side-by-side, in a lightly oiled shallow baking pan; brush with olive oil. Broil about 3" from heat for about 5 minutes until edges are golden. Turn slices; broil 3 minutes longer. Place on a platter; spoon sauce over slices. Sprinkle with Parmesan cheese. Makes 4 servings.

POLENTA WITH VEGETABLES

1 c. water	1/3 c. thinly sliced red onion
3/4 c. chicken broth	2 mushrooms, stems discarded
1/2 c. cornmeal	and thinly sliced
1/4 c. heavy cream	1 minced garlic clove
1/4 t. salt	1 T. olive oil
1 sm. carrot,	1/3 c. grated Parmesan cheese
halved lengthwise and	Pinch dried red pepper flakes
thinly sliced crosswise	

In a 2-quart microwave-safe glass bowl with a lid mix together water, broth, cornmeal, cream and salt. Microwave, covered, at high power (100%) 6 minutes, stirring every 2 minutes until cornmeal is cooked but still soft. In a small cast iron skillet sauté carrot, onion, mushrooms and garlic in oil over medium heat, stirring often, for 3 minutes until vegetables are crisp-tender. Stir in Parmesan cheese and red pepper flakes; pour over polenta. Makes 2 servings.

POLENTA WITH SAUTÉED VEGETABLES

4 c. chicken broth	12 baby carrots, blanched for
2 c. water	2 minutes, drained and
3/4 t. salt	patted dry
1 c. cornmeal	12 baby eggplants,
3 T. butter, cut into pieces	halved lengthwise
1/3 c. grated Parmesan cheese	18 green onions, trimmed
Salt & pepper to taste	Olive oil for vegetables and skillet

In a large saucepan, bring broth and water to a boil. Gradually add the salt and cornmeal; cook over medium heat for 15 minutes, stirring constantly. Mix in butter, Parmesan cheese, salt and pepper. If necessary, stir in enough water so polenta will just fall from a spoon in a continuous stream. Cover and keep warm. Brush carrots, eggplants and green onions with oil and season with salt and pepper. Heat a cast iron skillet over medium-high heat, brush it with oil. Sauté vegetables, covered, in batches for 5-7 minutes until they are crisp-tender. Spoon polenta onto a platter and arrange vegetables on top. Makes 6 servings.

Cornmeal Pancakes and Waffles

It is generally acknowledged that the American Indians taught our ancestors how to make corn cakes. The Colonial settlers from Europe used the Indian staple cornmeal to supplement their often meager supply of wheat flour. Cornmeal pancakes, crepes, johnny-cakes, griddle cakes, batty cakes, hot cakes, hoe cakes, whatever your region of the country calls them, are still a mainstay of the American diet. In the South, the *Louisville Courier-Journal* newspaper used to sponsor a "Batty Cake Brekfus" on the opening day of the spring racing meet at Churchill Downs. The guests ate sausages, batty cakes with lacy edges, molasses, coffee and fried eggs. This meal has become a model for Derby breakfasts. Now, lacy-edged batty cakes always accompany turkey hash at a traditional Kentucky Derby breakfast. "Johnnycake" is said to come from "Journey Cake" because in the days of the pioneers, no man left home without his sack of cornmeal to make griddle cakes on his travels. It was mixed with water or even snow and cooked before the trail fire. In the East, cooks claim that only white stone-ground cornmeal from Rhode Island makes proper johnnycakes. This meal has grains that are flat, not rounded like regular cornmeal. Some Rhode Islanders prefer their cakes thick and some like them crisp and thin. Cornmeal pancakes are served with everything from fried chicken and cream gravy to beef stew. They are good with a bowl of bean soup or a plate of vegetables. It is traditional in the South to serve them with molasses or cane sugar syrup. Others prefer maple syrup or jams and preserves with their cakes. Just remember, they should be served hot enough to melt the butter and, as one cook declares, greasy batter cakes are "neither appetizing nor healthful."

CORNMEAL CREPES #1

1/2 c. plus 2 T. flour	1 egg
2 T. cornmeal	1 T. melted butter, cooled
1/4 c. plus 1 T. milk	1/4 t. salt
1/2 c. water	Butter for skillet

In a blender mix flour and cornmeal for 1 minute. Add milk, water, egg, butter and salt; blend for 5 seconds. Turn off motor; scrape down the sides with a rubber spatula. Blend mixture for 20 seconds longer. Pour batter into a bowl and let stand, covered, for 1 hour. Heat a 6" non-stick skillet over medium heat until hot. Brush with butter and heat skillet to hot but not smoking. Stir batter; fill a quarter measuring cup about one third full; pour batter into skillet. Tilt and rotate skillet quickly to cover bottom with a thin layer of batter. Pour excess back into bowl. Return skillet to heat. Loosen edges of crepe with a spatula; cook for 1 minute until bottom is lightly browned and top appears almost dry. Turn and cook the other side until lightly brown. Transfer crepe to a plate. Makes 12 servings.

CORNMEAL CREPES #2

1/2 c. cornmeal	1/2 c. buttermilk
1 T. flour	1 T. melted butter
1/2 t. salt	1 T. water
Pinch of sugar	Butter for skillet
1 egg	

Sift together cornmeal, flour, salt and sugar. In another bowl stir together egg, buttermilk, butter and water. Add to cornmeal mixture; stir until smooth. Let stand for 20 minutes. Heat a 6" non-stick skillet over medium heat. When it is hot, brush pan lightly with butter and remove from heat. Stir batter; pour 1 1/2 tablespoons of batter into skillet. Tilt and rotate skillet quickly to cover bottom with a thin layer of batter. Return excess batter to bowl. Return skillet to heat, loosen edges of crepe with a spatula; cook until bottom is lightly browned. Turn crepe and cook until bottom is lightly browned. Place crepe on a plate. Makes 8-12 servings.

THIN JOHNNYCAKES #1

1 c. cornmeal   1/3 c. milk
1/2 t. salt   Vegetable oil for griddle
1 c. boiling water

Combine cornmeal and salt. Slowly stir in water until batter is smooth. Let stand, uncovered, for 20 minutes. Stir in milk. Heat a lightly oiled griddle to hot but not smoking. Drop batter by quarter cupfuls onto hot griddle. Cook until tops are covered with bubbles and bottoms are set, about 5 minutes. Turn and cook bottoms until crisp, about 5 minutes. Makes 16 servings.

THIN JOHNNYCAKES #2

1 c. cornmeal   1 egg, at room temperature
1 t. sugar   1/2 c. milk, at room temperature
3/4 t. salt   Vegetable oil for griddle
1 c. boiling water

Combine cornmeal, sugar and salt. Add water; stir until smooth. Let stand 2 minutes. Beat egg and milk together; stir into cornmeal mixture and blend well. Heat a lightly oiled griddle to hot but not smoking. Drop batter by heaping tablespoonfuls onto hot griddle. Cook 2-3 minutes until bubbles appear on tops of each cake. Turn and cook 2 minutes more until bottoms are browned. Makes 20 servings.

THICK JOHNNYCAKES #1

1 c. boiling water   4 T. melted butter
1 c. cornmeal   Vegetable oil for griddle
1/4 t. salt

Slowly stir water into cornmeal. Add salt and butter; combine well. Let batter stand for 5 minutes. Shape batter into cakes about the size of sausage patties. Heat a lightly oiled griddle to hot but not smoking. Cook cakes 5-8 minutes until browned on both sides, turning once. Makes 12 servings.

THICK JOHNNYCAKES #2

1 c. cornmeal	1 1/2 c. boiling water
1/2 t. salt	1 T. butter
1 T. sugar	Vegetable oil for griddle

Combine cornmeal, salt and sugar in saucepan. Add water and butter; mix well. Cook over low heat, stirring constantly, for 15 minutes. Form into cakes about 2 1/2" round. Heat a lightly oiled griddle to hot but now smoking. Cook cakes until brown, turning once. Makes 12 servings.

CORNMEAL PANCAKES #1 (Lacy Edged Batty Cakes)

1 c. cornmeal	1 beaten egg
1/2 t. baking soda	1 1/4 c. buttermilk
1/2 t. salt	Vegetable oil for griddle

Combine cornmeal, baking soda and salt. Add egg and buttermilk; beat until smooth. The batter must be thin for the cakes to be lacy edged. Drop by tablespoonfuls on a preheated lightly oiled griddle or cast iron skillet. Allow 1 teaspoon oil for every 4 pancakes. Stir batter each time before dipping or pouring. Brown on one side; turn when tops are covered with bubbles and edges are brown. Brown on the other side. If batter gets too thick, add more buttermilk, a tablespoonful at a time. Makes 6 servings.

CORNMEAL PANCAKES #2 (Buttermilk Corn Cakes)

1 c. cornmeal	1/2 t. baking soda
1 T. flour	3/4 c. buttermilk
2 t. baking powder	2 beaten eggs
1/2 t. salt	Vegetable oil for skillet

Combine cornmeal, flour, baking powder and salt. Add baking soda to buttermilk; stir until it foams. Stir buttermilk and eggs into cornmeal mixture. Allow to stand for a few minutes. Heat 1/4" deep oil in a cast iron skillet or on a griddle. Drop batter by tablespoonfuls into the hot oil, leaving room to turn them. When brown on one side, turn and brown on the other. Drain on paper towels. The secret to lacy edges is having the batter thin and the griddle hot. Makes 8 servings.

CORNMEAL PANCAKES #3 (Batter Cakes)

2 c. cornmeal	1 T. melted butter
1/4 c. flour	2 beaten eggs
1 t. salt	1 3/4 c. buttermilk
2 t. baking powder	Vegetable oil for skillet

Combine cornmeal, flour, salt and baking powder. Stir in butter and eggs. Add enough buttermilk to make a thin batter. Heat 3 tablespoons oil in a cast iron skillet. Spoon batter into skillet, spreading them into 3" rounds. Cook in batches, adding more oil as needed. Cook for 3 minutes on each side, turning once, until golden brown. Drain on paper towels. Makes 24 servings.

CORNMEAL PANCAKES #4 (Griddle Cakes)

Shortening for griddle	1 T. sugar
1 t. baking powder	1 1/2 c. milk
1 t. salt	2 c. cornmeal
1/2 t. baking soda	1 beaten egg

Preheat a griddle coated with melted shortening until a few drops of water will dance on it. Add baking powder, salt, baking soda and sugar to milk. Mix with cornmeal and stir in the egg. Pour batter on griddle in separate cakes 5-6" across. Do not spread. Turn cakes once, when bubbles begin to break. Makes 10 servings.

CORNMEAL PANCAKES #5 (Sweet Milk Corn Cakes)

Vegetable oil for griddle	1 T. vegetable oil
1 beaten egg	1 c. self-rising cornmeal
3/4 c. milk	1/2 t. sugar

Preheat a lightly oiled griddle to medium heat. In a bowl combine egg, milk, oil, cornmeal and sugar until well blended. For thinner batter, add a little more milk. Pour batter by quarter cupfuls onto hot griddle. After cakes are brown on one side, turn and brown on the other. Makes 6 servings.

CORNMEAL PANCAKES #6 (Indian Griddle Cakes)

1 c. cornmeal	1/2 t. baking soda
1 c. flour	2 beaten eggs
1/2 t. salt	2 c. buttermilk
1/2 t. sugar	2 T. melted butter
1 t. baking powder	Vegetable oil for griddle

Sift together cornmeal, flour, salt, sugar, baking powder and baking soda. In another bowl combine eggs, buttermilk and butter. Add egg mixture to cornmeal mixture; stir until smooth. Let batter rest for 10 minutes. Heat a lightly oiled griddle to hot but not smoking. Spoon batter by tablespoonfuls onto hot griddle. Cook cakes for 1 minute until bottoms are golden. Turn and cook 1 minutes longer until undersides are golden. Makes 18 servings.

CORNMEAL PANCAKE #7 (Raised Griddle Cakes)

1 pkg. yeast	4 t. sugar
1/2 c. lukewarm water	1 t. salt
2 1/2 c. scalded milk	2 beaten eggs
2 2/3 c. sifted flour	Vegetable oil for griddle
1 1/3 c. cornmeal	

Dissolve yeast in water. Cool milk to lukewarm. Add yeast; mix well. Combine flour, cornmeal, sugar and salt; add to yeast mixture. Cover and set aside to rise overnight. Add eggs and let stand for 15 minutes. Heat a lightly oiled griddle to hot but not smoking. Drop batter by tablespoonfuls onto hot griddle; cook until brown. Turn and cook until brown on the other side. Makes 36 servings.

CORNMEAL PANCAKES #8 (Spoon Cakes)

1 1/2 c. cornmeal	2 c. buttermilk
1 t. baking powder	2 beaten eggs
1 t. baking soda	2 T. melted butter
1 t. salt	Vegetable oil for griddle

Combine cornmeal, baking powder, baking soda and salt in a mixing bowl. Add buttermilk; mix thoroughly. Add eggs and beat until batter is smooth. Cover bowl and chill in refrigerator overnight. Allow batter to warm to room temperature when ready to use. Heat a lightly oiled griddle to hot but not smoking. Drop batter by tablespoonfuls onto hot griddle; cook 2-3 minutes to a side, turning once. Makes 24 servings.

CORNMEAL PANCAKES #9 (Cornmeal Hot Cakes)

1 c. cornmeal	1 beaten egg
1 c. flour	1 1/2 c. milk
2 1/2 t. baking powder	2 T. vegetable oil
1/2 t. salt	Vegetable oil for griddle

Sift cornmeal, flour, baking powder and salt. Stir together egg and milk. Add to cornmeal mixture; stir until just smooth. Add oil and stir to blend. Heat a lightly oiled griddle to hot but not smoking. Pour quarter cupfuls of batter onto hot griddle. Turn cakes when tops are covered with bubbles and edges look cooked. Makes 24 servings.

CORNMEAL PANCAKES #10 (Cornmeal Hoe Cakes)

1/2 c. cornmeal	1/4 c. water
1/4 t. baking soda	4 beaten eggs
1/2 t. baking powder	4 T. melted butter
1/2 t. salt	Vegetable oil for griddle
1 c. buttermilk	

Sift together cornmeal, baking soda, baking powder and salt. Add buttermilk and water; stir to combine. Add eggs and mix well; stir in butter. Heat a lightly oiled griddle to hot but not smoking. Drop batter by tablespoonfuls onto hot griddle. Cook about 3 minutes on each side until golden. Makes 8 servings.

CORNMEAL APPLE PANCAKES

2/3 c. whole-wheat flour	1 T. baking powder
2/3 c. flour	1 t. ground ginger
1/3 c. cornmeal	1/4 c. vegetable oil
1/2 t. baking soda	3 eggs
1/4 c. honey	1 large apple
2 c. buttermilk	Vegetable oil for griddle

Combine whole-wheat flour, flour, cornmeal, baking soda, honey, buttermilk, baking powder, ginger, oil and eggs in blender. Blend until smooth. Peel, core and shred apple; stir into batter. Heat griddle to hot but not smoking. Add 1 tablespoon oil to griddle. Drop batter by tablespoonfuls onto hot griddle. When bubbles appear on tops, turn cakes and brown on the other side, about 2 minutes longer. Makes 16 servings.

CORNMEAL BACON AND CHEESE PANCAKES

1 c. flour	1/2 c. sour cream
1 c. cornmeal	1/4 c. melted butter
1/3 c. sugar	Vegetable oil for griddle
1 t. salt	2 c. grated Cheddar cheese
1 t. baking powder	20 slices bacon,
3 eggs	crisp-fried and crumbled
2 c. buttermilk	

Combine flour, cornmeal, sugar, salt and baking powder. Mix together eggs, buttermilk, sour cream and butter. Add buttermilk mixture to flour mixture; blend until just combined. Heat a lightly oiled griddle to hot but not smoking. Pour quarter cupfuls of batter onto griddle. Sprinkle each cake with 1 tablespoon each of cheese and bacon. Cook until golden, about 2 minutes. Turn and cook 2 minutes more. Makes 25 servings.

CORNMEAL BLUEBERRY PANCAKES

2 c. cornmeal
2 c. flour
1 1/2 t. baking soda
1/2 t. salt
3 beaten eggs
2 1/2 c. buttermilk

1/3 c. honey
3 T. vegetable oil
1 1/2 c. fresh or frozen
   blueberries, thawed
Sugar
Vegetable oil for griddle

Combine cornmeal, flour, baking soda and salt in a mixing bowl. Make a well in center of this mixture. Mix together eggs, buttermilk, honey and vegetable oil; add to cornmeal mixture. Stir just until moistened. Allow to stand 10 minutes. Sprinkle blueberries with sugar and stir into batter. Heat a lightly oiled griddle to hot but not smoking. Pour batter by quarter cupfuls onto hot griddle and cook until bubbles appear on tops and edges look cooked. Turn and cook on other side until cakes are golden. Makes 24 servings.

CORNMEAL BUCKWHEAT PANCAKES

1/2 c. cornmeal
1/2 t. salt
2 1/2 c. scalded milk
1/2 cake yeast
2 c. buckwheat flour

2 T. molasses
2 T. melted butter
1/4 t. baking soda
1/4 c. lukewarm water
Vegetable oil for skillet

In a large mixing bowl add cornmeal and salt to scalded milk; allow to cool. When mixture is lukewarm, add yeast cake; stir until it has dissolved. Add buckwheat flour; stir until batter is smooth. Set aside in a warm place overnight. The next morning, add molasses, butter and soda mixed with water; stir until smooth. Heat a lightly oiled cast iron skillet until hot but not smoking. Drop batter by quarter cupfuls into skillet, spreading to make 4" wide cakes. Cook until cake tops seem dry. Turn and cook 3 minutes more. Makes 16 servings.

CORNMEAL CORN PANCAKES

1/2 c. cornmeal	1/2 c. flour
1 c. buttermilk	1 t. baking powder
2 c. fresh corn kernels	1/4 t. baking soda
2 eggs	1/2 t. salt
2 T. melted butter	Vegetable oil for griddle

Mix cornmeal with buttermilk; set aside. Chop corn kernels and combine with eggs and butter. Add cornmeal mixture. Sift flour, baking powder, baking soda and salt together. Add to corn mixture; add quarter cup more buttermilk if batter is too thick. Heat a lightly oiled griddle to hot but not smoking. Drop batter by tablespoonfuls onto hot griddle. Cook 3 minutes to brown on one side. Turn and brown for 3 minutes more. Makes 24 servings.

CORNMEAL CORN AND BACON PANCAKES

1 c. cornmeal	2 eggs
1/2 c. flour	3/4 c. milk
1 T. sugar	2 T. melted butter, cooled
2 t. baking powder	5 slices bacon, crisp-cooked
1/4 t. salt	Vegetable oil for griddle
1 c. fresh corn kernels including pulp scraped from cobs	

Combine cornmeal, flour, sugar, baking powder and salt. Coarsely chop corn and combine with eggs, milk and butter. Add to cornmeal mixture; stir just until combined. Allow batter to rest for 10 minutes; add crumbled bacon. Heat a lightly oiled griddle over moderate heat. Drop batter by quarter cupfuls onto griddle and cook cakes 1 minute on each side until golden. Makes 12 servings.

CORNMEAL FLANNEL PANCAKES

2 c. milk	1/2 t. salt
3 T. butter	1 c. cornmeal
1 cake yeast	1 1/2 c. flour, divided
1/4 c. warmed water	2 beaten egg whites
2 beaten egg yolks	Vegetable oil for griddle

In a saucepan heat milk and butter. Set aside to cool. Dissolve yeast in water. Add egg yolks to milk mixture. Add yeast, salt, cornmeal and one cup of flour. Mix well; set aside to rise. When ready to beat down, add remaining 1/2 cup of flour; fold in egg whites. Heat a lightly oiled griddle to hot but not smoking. Drop batter by tablespoonfuls onto hot griddle and cook until golden brown, turning once. Makes 24 servings.

CORNMEAL NUTMEG PANCAKES

1 c. milk	2 beaten eggs
1/4 c. cornmeal	1 1/2 t. sugar
1 t. salt	1 t. baking powder
1/8 t. nutmeg	Vegetable oil for griddle
Pinch of cayenne pepper	

Bring milk to a boil. Remove from heat and sprinkle in cornmeal, stirring until smooth. Add salt, nutmeg and cayenne pepper. Stir in eggs, sugar and baking powder. Mix until smooth. Return to heat; stir until batter begins to thicken. Heat a lightly oiled griddle until hot but not smoking. Drop batter by tablespoonfuls onto hot griddle; cook until golden, turning once. Makes 6 servings.

CORNMEAL ONION PANCAKES

2 c. cornmeal	3 T. finely chopped onion
1/2 t. baking soda	1 c. buttermilk
1 t. salt	1 beaten egg
1 t. baking powder	Vegetable oil or bacon drippings
1 T. flour	for skillet

In a large bowl combine cornmeal, baking soda, salt, baking powder and flour. Stir in onion, buttermilk and egg. Heat 1/8" oil in a large cast iron skillet until hot but not smoking. Drop batter by tablespoonfuls into hot oil. Cook in batches and add more oil as needed. Cook until golden, turning once. Drain on paper towels. Makes 24 servings.

CORNMEAL PECAN PANCAKES

1 c. milk	1/2 t. salt
1 c. water	1 t. sugar
4 t. cornmeal	1 t. baking powder
1 t. butter	1 beaten egg
1 c. flour	Vegetable oil for griddle
1/2 c. finely ground pecans	

Combine milk and water in a saucepan; bring to a boil. Add cornmeal in a fine stream, stirring constantly. Stir in butter; remove from heat. Combine flour, pecans, salt, sugar and baking powder; stir until well mixed. Stir egg into the cornmeal mixture. Stir cornmeal mixture into pecan mixture. The batter should have the consistency of heavy cream. If necessary, thin with water. Preheat a griddle over medium-high heat until hot but not smoking. Brush griddle lightly with oil. Drop batter by quarter cupfuls onto the griddle and cook cakes until bottoms are golden, about 2 minutes. Turn cakes and cook 1 minute more. Makes 12 servings.

CORNMEAL PUMPKIN PANCAKES

1 1/2 c. flour	1/4 t. ground ginger
1/2 c. cornmeal	1/4 t. ground nutmeg
2 T. brown sugar, firmly packed	1 1/2 c. milk
	1/2 c. canned pumpkin
1 T. baking powder	1 egg
1 t. salt	2 T. vegetable oil
1 t. ground cinnamon	Vegetable oil for skillet

In a mixing bowl combine flour, cornmeal, brown sugar, baking powder, salt, cinnamon, ginger and nutmeg. In another bowl mix together milk, pumpkin, egg and oil. Add to flour mixture; stir just until moistened. The batter will be thick. Lightly oil a large cast iron skillet and heat over medium heat until a drop of water dances on the surface. Drop by quarter cupfuls into skillet, spreading to make 4" wide cakes. Cook until surface seems dry. Turn and cook 3 minutes more. Makes 16 servings.

CORNMEAL SOUR CREAM PANCAKES

1 c. cornmeal	2 c. buttermilk
1 c. flour	1/2 c. sour cream
1 t. salt	1 beaten egg
1/2 t. baking powder	Vegetable oil for griddle
1 1/4 t. baking soda	

Sift cornmeal and flour. Measure and sift with salt, baking powder and baking soda. Add buttermilk, sour cream and egg. Stir until smooth. Heat a lightly oiled griddle until hot but not smoking. Drop batter by tablespoonfuls onto hot griddle and cook until golden brown, turning once. Makes 16 servings.

CORNMEAL SUN-DRIED TOMATO PANCAKES

1/4 c. chopped sun-dried tomatoes (not oil packed)	1/4 t. salt
	1/4 t. minced fresh rosemary
1/4 c. frozen corn kernels, thawed and drained	1 c. buttermilk
	1 T. vegetable oil
3 T. flour, divided	1 egg white
3/4 c. cornmeal	Vegetable oil for griddle
1/2 t. baking soda	

In a bowl pour enough boiling water over tomatoes to cover. Let stand 15 minutes until tomatoes soften. Drain well; mix with corn and 1 tablespoon flour. Combine cornmeal, baking soda, salt, rosemary and remaining flour in a medium bowl. Add buttermilk, oil and tomato mixture; blend well. Beat egg white until firm peaks form. Fold into batter. Heat a lightly oiled griddle over medium-low heat. Drop batter by heaping tablespoonfuls onto griddle. Cook until bottoms of cakes are golden, about 1 1/2 minutes. Turn cakes and cook until bottoms are golden, about 1 1/2 minutes more. Makes 8 servings.

CORNMEAL WHOLE-WHEAT PANCAKES #1

1/2 c. cornmeal	1/4 c. vegetable oil
1 c. cold water	1 1/4 c. whole-wheat flour
1/4 c. molasses	1 1/2 t. baking powder
2/3 c. buttermilk	1/2 t. baking soda
2/3 c. milk	1/2 t. salt
2 beaten eggs	Vegetable oil for skillet

Stir together cornmeal and water in a heavy saucepan and bring to a boil. Reduce heat to medium and cook, stirring constantly, for 3 minutes until very thick. Spoon into a large bowl and stir in, one at a time, molasses, buttermilk, milk, eggs and oil. In a separate bowl, combine whole-wheat flour, baking powder, baking soda and salt. Make a well in the dry ingredients; add cornmeal mixture; stir just until blended. Allow batter to rest for several minutes. Thin with 2 tablespoons milk if necessary. Heat 1/8" deep oil in a cast iron skillet. Spoon batter by tablespoonfuls into hot oil. Cook on one side until golden and bubbles appear on top. Turn cakes and repeat process. Makes 18 servings.

CORNMEAL WHOLE-WHEAT PANCAKES #2

1 c. cornmeal	1 3/4 c. milk
1 1/2 c. whole-wheat flour	2 T. molasses
1/2 t. salt	1/4 c. vegetable oil
1 t. baking powder	Vegetable oil for griddle
3 eggs	

Stir together cornmeal, whole-wheat flour, salt and baking powder. Beat eggs and blend in milk and molasses. Make a well in the cornmeal mixture; add egg mixture and oil. Stir until batter is smooth. Let stand a few minutes before cooking. Heat a lightly oiled griddle until hot but not smoking. Drop batter by tablespoonfuls onto hot griddle. Cook 2 minutes on each side, turning once, until golden. Makes 14 servings.

Cornmeal waffles are a tasty dish for breakfast, lunch or supper. They are good served with butter, maple syrup, honey, sausage links, fruit, apple-sauce, fried apples, yogurt, salsa, chili topping or chicken or beef hash.

CORNMEAL WAFFLES #1

3/4 c. cornmeal
2 T. flour
1/3 t. salt
1/4 t. baking soda
1/2 t. baking powder

1 beaten egg
1 c. buttermilk
1/4 c. melted butter
Vegetable oil for waffle iron

Pour cornmeal into a large mixing bowl. Sift flour, salt, baking soda and baking powder into cornmeal. Add egg; beat to combine. Gradually add buttermilk and stir until smooth; stir in butter. Preheat waffle iron until hot; brush with oil. Pour batter, about 4 tablespoons at a time, onto waffle iron. Cook until brown, about 4-5 minutes. Makes 4 servings.

CORNMEAL WAFFLES #2

1 1/4 c. flour
1/2 c. cornmeal
2 t. baking powder
1/2 t. salt
2 T. sugar

3 eggs, separated
1 3/4 c. milk
6 T. melted butter
Vegetable oil for waffle iron

Sift flour, cornmeal, baking powder, salt and sugar into a mixing bowl. In another bowl beat egg yolks; add milk and butter. Stir into cornmeal mixture, just until moistened. In a small bowl beat egg whites until they form stiff peaks. Fold into batter. Preheat waffle iron until hot and brush with oil. Pour batter, about 4 tablespoons at a time, onto waffle iron. Cook until brown, about 4-5 minutes. Makes 6 servings.

CORNMEAL WAFFLES WITH BOURBON SYRUP

1 egg	1 t. salt
2 T. melted butter	2 c. buttermilk
2 c. cornmeal	Vegetable oil for waffle iron
1 t. baking soda	

For syrup

1 c. maple syrup	3 T. bourbon whiskey
2 T. butter	

In a mixing bowl beat egg and add butter. Stir in cornmeal, baking soda and salt. Add buttermilk; stir until smooth. Preheat waffle iron until hot and brush with oil. Pour batter, about 4 tablespoons at a time, onto waffle iron. Cook until brown, about 4-5 minutes. To make syrup, combine syrup, butter and bourbon. Heat over medium-low heat until bubbling. Makes 6 servings.

CORNMEAL AND BACON WAFFLES

1 c. cornmeal	2 beaten eggs
3/4 c. flour	1/4 c. melted butter
3 t. baking powder	3 strips bacon, crisply fried
1/4 t. salt	and crumbled
1 c. milk	Vegetable oil for waffle iron

Sift cornmeal, flour, baking powder and salt into a mixing bowl. Add milk, eggs and butter; stir to combine. Add bacon and mix. Preheat waffle iron until hot and brush with oil. Pour batter, about 4 tablespoons at a time, onto waffle iron. Cook until brown, about 4-5 minutes. Makes 4 servings.

CORNMEAL AND CORN WAFFLES

1/2 c. cornmeal	1 egg
1/2 c. flour	2 T. melted butter, cooled
1 T. sugar	1/2 c. water
2 t. baking powder	2/3 c. fresh corn kernels, cooked
1/4 t. salt	Vegetable oil for waffle iron

In a mixing bowl combine cornmeal, flour, sugar, baking powder and salt. In another bowl mix together egg, butter, water and corn. Add to cornmeal mixture. Stir just until combined. Preheat waffle iron until hot and brush with oil. Pour batter, about 4 tablespoons at a time, onto waffle iron. Cook until brown, about 4-5 minutes. Makes 2 servings.

CORNMEAL, CORN AND CHILI WAFFLES

1 1/2 c. cornmeal	8 1/2-oz. can cream-style corn
1 1/2 c. flour	2 1/2 c. buttermilk
1 1/2 t. baking powder	1/3 c. melted butter
1/4 t. salt	1/3 c. canned chopped green
1/2 t. chili powder	chilies, drained
3 eggs, separated	Vegetable oil for waffle iron

Combine cornmeal, flour, baking soda, salt and chili powder in a mixing bowl. Make a well in the center and set aside. In another bowl combine egg yolks, corn, buttermilk, butter and chilies. Add to cornmeal mixture; stir just until moistened. Set aside. Beat egg whites until stiff peaks form. Fold into batter. Preheat waffle iron until hot and brush with oil. Pour batter, about 4 tablespoons at a time, onto waffle iron. Cook until brown, about 4-5 minutes. Makes 10 servings.

CORNMEAL AND COUNTRY HAM WAFFLES

1 c. flour	2 beaten eggs
1 1/2 t. baking powder	2 c. buttermilk
1 t. baking soda	1/4 c. melted butter
1 T. sugar	1/4 lb. baked country ham,
1/4 t. salt	thinly slivered
1 c. cornmeal	Vegetable oil for waffle iron

Sift together flour, baking powder, baking soda, sugar and salt into a mixing bowl. Add cornmeal. In another bowl combine eggs and buttermilk; stir in butter and ham. Add to cornmeal mixture; stir just until combined. Preheat waffle iron until hot and brush with oil. Pour batter, about 4 tabl spoons at a time, onto waffle iron. Cook until brown, about 4-5 minutes. Makes 4 servings.

CORNMEAL, OAT BRAN AND FLOUR WAFFLES

1 c. oat bran	2 beaten eggs
3/4 c. cornmeal	2 c. milk
3/4 c. flour	3 T. vegetable oil
2 T. sugar	1 t. vanilla extract
1 1/2 t. baking powder	Vegetable oil for waffle iron
1/2 t. salt	

Pulverize oat bran in electric blender. Combine with cornmeal, flour, sugar, baking powder and salt in a mixing bowl. In another bowl combine eggs, milk, oil and vanilla. Mix well; add to cornmeal mixture. Preheat waffle iron until hot and brush with oil. Pour batter, about 4 tablespoons at a time, onto waffle iron. Cook until brown, about 4-5 minutes. Makes 6 servings.

CORNMEAL AND OATS WAFFLES

1 1/4 c. regular rolled oats	3/4 t. salt
1/2 c. cornmeal	2 eggs, at room temperature
1/2 c. flour	2 c. plus 2 T. milk
4 t. baking powder	6 T. melted butter
3 T. sugar	Vegetable oil for waffle iron

Process oats in an electric blender until powdered. Combine with cornmeal, flour, baking powder, sugar and salt in a mixing bowl. In another bowl beat eggs until frothy. Add milk and butter. Make a well in cornmeal mixture and add milk mixture; stir just until smooth. Let batter rest for several minutes. Preheat waffle iron until hot and brush with oil. Pour batter, about 4 tablespoons at a time, onto waffle iron. Cook until brown, about 4-5 minutes. Makes 4-5 servings.

CORNMEAL AND WHOLE-WHEAT WAFFLES

1 1/2 c. whole-wheat flour	2 eggs
1/2 c. cornmeal	2 1/3 c. milk
2 T. sugar	1/2 c. melted butter
4 t. baking powder	Vegetable oil for waffle iron
3/4 t. salt	

In a large mixing bowl combine flour, cornmeal, sugar, baking powder and salt. In another bowl beat eggs; stir in milk and butter. Make a well in cornmeal mixture; pour in egg mixture. Stir just until blended; let batter rest for several minutes. Preheat waffle iron until hot and brush with oil. Pour batter, about 4 tablespoons at a time, onto waffle iron. Cook until brown, about 4-5 minutes. Makes 4-5 servings.

Pies, Cakes and Cookies

PIES

Americans love almost any type of pie. A particular Southern favorite is the traditional chess pie, described as a pecan pie without the nuts. It is very rich and remarkably easy to make. Some people prefer it with meringue on top, but most eat it unadorned. The purpose of the addition of cornmeal is to make the attractive thin granular surface that is a characteristic of the traditional chess pie.

There are several theories on how chess pie got its name. The first, and most likely, is that before refrigeration, pies were stored in pie chests. Because of its good keeping qualities, it became known as a "chest" pie. Later the "t" in the chest was dropped. Another explanation is that someone asked a cook what she was cooking and she replied "jes pie." The "just" she had available was sugar, butter, eggs, vinegar and some cornmeal. And lastly, "chess" may be a variation of "cheese" pie. But, since it has no cheese, this may refer to the fact that it is as rich as a cheese pie. However it got its name, many Southerners consider it a must dessert for fine dining.

CHESS PIE #1

1 c. sugar	1/2 T. cornmeal
1/2 c. melted butter	1 1/2 t. vinegar
or margarine	1 t. vanilla
4 eggs	9" unbaked pie shell

Preheat oven to 350°. Cream sugar and butter just until blended. Beat in eggs, one at a time, until mixture is very light in color. Add cornmeal, vinegar and vanilla; mix thoroughly. Pour into pie shell; bake for 40 minutes or until set and top is slightly brown. If a straw inserted in center of pie comes out clean, it is done. Cool pie to room temperature on wire rack. Serve or refrigerate until ready to serve. Makes 8 servings.

CHESS PIE #2

1 1/2 c. sugar	3/4 c. water
1/4 lb. butter	1 t. vanilla
2 eggs	Nutmeg
2 T. flour	9" unbaked pie shell
1 1/2 T. cornmeal	

Cream sugar and butter. Add eggs one at a time and mix well after each addition. Combine flour and cornmeal; beat into mixture. Gradually add the water and vanilla. Sprinkle in a generous amount of nutmeg; pour into pie shell. Bake at 350° for 5 minutes then lower heat to 275° and bake for 45 minutes longer. Shake the pie gently to test for firmness. Makes 8 servings.

CHOCOLATE CHESS PIE

1 c. light brown sugar,	Pinch of salt
firmly packed	2 eggs
1/2 c. sugar	1/2 c. milk
2 T. flour	1 t. vanilla
2 T. cornmeal	1/4 c. melted butter
2 T. cocoa	9" unbaked pie shell

Combine brown sugar, sugar, flour, cornmeal, cocoa and salt. In a separate bowl beat eggs; add milk, vanilla and butter. Add to sugar mixture; mix well. Pour into pie shell; bake at 350° for 45 minutes. Makes 8 servings.

LEMON CHESS PIE #1

2 c. sugar
4 eggs
1 T. flour
1 T. cornmeal

Pinch of salt
1/2 c. melted butter
1/2 c. lemon juice
9" unbaked pie shell

Preheat oven to 350°. Cream sugar and eggs. Add remaining ingredients; mix well. Pour into pie shell; bake for 45 minutes until puffed and set in the middle. Do not over bake. Cool on a wire rack. Makes 8 servings.

LEMON CHESS PIE #2

1 1/2 c. sugar
1/2 c. melted butter
4 eggs
1/4 c. lemon juice
Grated rind of 1 lemon
1 T. flour

1 T. cornmeal
1/4 c. milk or buttermilk
1 t. vanilla
Eight 1/8"-thick lemon slices
Additional sugar
9" unbaked pie shell

Preheat oven to 350°. Cream together sugar and butter. Beat in eggs, lemon juice and lemon rind. Add flour, cornmeal, milk and vanilla; mix well. Pour into pie shell. Dip lemon slices into the additional sugar; arrange on top of filling around edge of pie. Bake for 40 minutes or until center is set. Cool on wire rack. Makes 8 servings.

Cornmeal pie is a countrified, somewhat less sweet, version of chess pie. The cornmeal flavor should be more pronounced in this pie.

CORNMEAL PIE #1

1/2 c. softened butter	1/4 t. salt
1 1/2 c. sugar	1/3 c. buttermilk
2 T. cornmeal	3 beaten eggs
1 T. flour	9" unbaked pie shell

Preheat oven to 375°. Cream butter and sugar. Stir in cornmeal, flour and salt. Add buttermilk and eggs. Mix well; pour into pie shell. Bake for 15 minutes. Reduce heat to 325°; bake for an additional 35 minutes. Cool on a wire rack. Makes 8 servings.

CORNMEAL PIE #2

1 T. flour	1/2 c. brown sugar
1/4 c. melted butter	2 beaten eggs
1/2 c. milk	1 t. vanilla
2 T. cornmeal	9" unbaked pie shell
2/3 c. sugar	

Preheat oven to 400°. Combine flour and butter. Add remaining ingredients; mix well. Pour into pie shell; bake for 30 minutes until center is set. Cool on a wire rack. Makes 8 servings.

ORANGE PUDDING PIE

1/4 c. butter	1/2 c. orange juice
1/2 c. sugar	Grated rind of 1 orange
3 egg yolks	Pinch of salt
1 1/2 T. white cornmeal	9" baked pie shell,
1/2 t. cornstarch	lightly browned

Cream butter and sugar. Add egg yolks and cornmeal. Dissolve cornstarch in the orange juice; add to cornmeal mixture. Add grated orange rind and salt. Put in top of double-boiler; set over medium-high heat on top of stove. Stir until the custard is thick. Set aside to cool; pour into prepared shell. Top with orange-flavored meringue if desired. Serve warm or at room temperature. Makes 8 servings.

Because it does not shrink, a cornmeal pie crust is a good choice for a pre-baked pie shell or tart shells. It is especially tasty used for apple or pear pies.

CORNMEAL PIE CRUST #1

1 c. unbleached flour
1/4 c. cornmeal
1 T. sugar
Pinch of salt

7 T. cold butter,
   cut into 1/4" pieces
3 1/2 T. ice-cold water

In a large bowl combine flour, cornmeal, sugar and salt. With a pastry blender cut the butter into the dry mixture until it is crumbly. Everything should be the size of split peas or smaller. Add the water, a tablespoon at a time, stirring with a fork. Stir and toss until the dough starts to cohere. When it can be collected in a cohesive mass, pack it into a ball. Flatten dough into a 3/4" disk and wrap it in plastic. Refrigerate for one hour. When ready to use, roll out dough between 2 sheets of waxed paper into a 12" circle. Remove top sheet of paper and invert the dough into a pie pan. Trim overhang to 1/2", tuck under, sculpting the edge into a ridge. Can be frozen until ready to use. Makes one 9" pie shell.

CORNMEAL PIE CRUST #2

1 c. flour	1/2 c. shortening
1/2 c. cornmeal	1/4 c. water
1/2 t. salt	

In a mixing bowl combine flour, cornmeal and salt. Using a pastry blender cut shortening into cornmeal mixture until it resembles coarse meal. Sprinkle water over mixture; stir with a fork. Form into a ball, flatten and wrap in plastic wrap. Refrigerate for 1 hour. When ready to use, roll out dough between 2 sheets of waxed paper making a 12" circle. Remove top sheet of paper; invert dough into a 9" pie pan. Trim overhang to 1/2" and tuck under, forming edge into a ridge. Crust may be frozen until ready to use. Makes 1 pie shell.

CAKES

CORNMEAL CAKE #1

1 c. buttermilk	1/4 c. plus 2 T. sugar
1/4 c. water	1 T. baking powder
1 c. cornmeal	1/2 t. baking soda
2 T. melted butter	Salt
1 egg white	Vegetable oil spray for pan
1 c. flour	

Preheat oven to 375°. In a small bowl mix together buttermilk, water, cornmeal, butter and egg white. In another bowl combine flour, 1/4 cup sugar, baking powder, baking soda and salt. Stir buttermilk mixture into flour mixture just until combined. Coat an 8" springform pan with vegetable oil spray; dust with flour. Spread batter in pan and sprinkle with remaining two tablespoons of sugar. Bake for 25 minutes. Place on a wire rack, remove side of pan and allow to cool. Makes 8 servings.

CORNMEAL CAKE #2

12 T. softened butter	1/2 c. flour
3/4 c. superfine sugar	1/2 c. cornmeal
3 eggs, at room temperature	1 1/2 t. baking powder
3 egg yolks,	1/4 t. salt
at room temperature	Powdered sugar
1/2 t. vanilla extract	Vegetable oil for baking pan
1/2 t. almond extract	

Preheat oven to 350°. In a mixing bowl cream butter and sugar with an electric mixer until light and fluffy. Add eggs, one at a time, beating after each addition. Add egg yolks, vanilla extract and almond extract. Beat until mixture is very fluffy. Sift flour, cornmeal, baking powder and salt into a bowl. Fold into batter. Spoon batter into an oiled 8" cake pan sprinkled with cornmeal. Bake for 40 minutes; cool in pan. Invert onto a wire rack and sprinkle with powdered sugar. Makes 1 cake.

COOKIES

CORNMEAL COOKIES #1

1 c. softened butter	1 1/4 c. flour
1/2 c. sugar	3/4 c. cornmeal
1 T. vanilla	Vegetable oil for cookie sheet

Preheat oven to 350°. In a mixing bowl using an electric mixer, beat butter, sugar and vanilla until fluffy. Gradually beat in flour and cornmeal. Roll out dough to 1/4" thickness between 2 sheets of waxed paper. Remove top sheet and cut out cookies with a 5" cookie cutter. Place rounds 1" apart on an oiled cookie sheet. Bake for 12 minutes until golden. Cool on a wire rack. Makes 8 cookies.

CORNMEAL COOKIES #2

1/2 lb. butter	1 1/2 c. flour
2/3 c. sugar	1 c. cornmeal
3 egg yolks	Vegetable oil for cookie sheet
1 t. vanilla	

Preheat oven to 325°. Using an electric mixer beat butter and sugar in a mixing bowl until fluffy. Add egg yolks, one at a time, beating after each addition. Mix in vanilla. In another bowl combine flour and cornmeal. Add to butter mixture; mix just until combined. Roll dough into a log 2" in diameter, wrap in waxed paper and chill 4 hours. Remove paper; slice log into 1/4" thick rounds. Place on an oiled cookie sheet 1" apart and bake 15 minutes until edges brown. Makes 24 cookies.

CORNMEAL CHOCOLATE COOKIES #1

3/4 c. butter	1/4 t. salt
3/4 c. sugar	1/4 c. cocoa
1 egg	1 t. vanilla
1 1/2 c. flour	1/2 c. milk
1/2 c. cornmeal	Vegetable oil for cookie sheet
1 t. baking powder	

In a mixing bowl combine butter and sugar. Add egg; mix well. Stir in flour, cornmeal, baking powder, salt, cocoa, vanilla and milk. Mix well and drop dough from a teaspoon onto an oiled cookie sheet. Bake at 350° for about 15 minutes until lightly browned. Makes 36 cookies.

CORNMEAL CHOCOLATE COOKIES #2

3/4 c. sifted flour	2 1/2 squares baking chocolate,
1 t. baking powder	melted
3/4 t. salt	1 t. vanilla
3 beaten eggs	3/4 c. cornmeal
1 1/2 c. sugar	3/4 c. chopped pecans
1/2 c. melted butter	Vegetable oil for baking pans

Sift flour, baking powder and salt into a mixing bowl. In another bowl combine eggs, sugar, butter, chocolate and vanilla. Mix well; add cornmeal and-flour mixture. Blend well; fold in nuts. Pour batter into 2 oiled 9x9x2" baking pans which have been dusted lightly with cornmeal. Bake at 375° for 30 minutes. Let cool slightly and cut into 1 1/2" squares. Makes 24 cookies.

CORNMEAL CRANBERRY COOKIES

3 c. flour	1 1/2 c. sugar
1 c. cornmeal	2 eggs
2 t. baking powder	2 t. vanilla
1/2 t. salt	2 c. dried cranberries
1 1/2 c. softened butter	Vegetable oil for baking sheet

Preheat oven to 350°. In a mixing bowl combine flour, cornmeal, baking powder and salt. Using an electric mixer cream butter and sugar in a large bowl. Beat in eggs, one at a time. Add flour mixture and vanilla; combine well. Fold in cranberries. Drop dough by teaspoonfuls 2" apart on an oiled baking sheet. Bake 18 minutes until golden. Cool on wire racks. Makes 45 cookies.

CORNMEAL LEMON COOKIES #1

1 1/2 c. flour	1 egg
1/2 c. cornmeal	2 t. finely shredded lemon rind
1 t. baking powder	2 T. lemon juice
1/2 t. baking soda	1/2 c. buttermilk
1/8 t. salt	1/2 c. finely chopped pecans
1/2 c. butter	Additional pecans, chopped
3/4 c. brown sugar, packed	

In a mixing bowl combine flour, cornmeal, baking powder, baking soda and salt. Using an electric mixer, beat butter in a mixing bowl for 30 seconds. Add brown sugar; beat until fluffy. Add egg, lemon rind and lemon juice; mix well. Add cornmeal mixture and buttermilk alternately to the butter mixture. Beat until well mixed. Fold in pecans. Drop dough from a teaspoon 2" apart onto an ungreased cookie sheet. Sprinkle with additional pecans. Bake at 350° for 12 minutes. Cool on wire rack. Makes 48 cookies.

CORNMEAL LEMON COOKIES #2

1 1/4 c. flour	1 c. softened butter
1 c. cornmeal	1 c. sugar
1 t. finely grated lemon zest	2 egg yolks
1/2 t. ground ginger	1/2 t. vanilla
1/8 t. salt	Vegetable oil for cookie sheet

In a mixing bowl stir together flour, cornmeal, lemon zest, ginger and salt. In another bowl using an electric mixer, beat butter and sugar until fluffy. Add egg yolks and vanilla; mix well. Add cornmeal mixture and combine well. Roll dough into 2 logs 9 1/2x1 1/2". Wrap in waxed paper and chill for 3 hours. Preheat oven to 400°. Unwrap logs and cut into 1/4" rounds. Place 2" apart on an oiled cookie sheet; bake for 10 minutes until edges turn brown. Cool on wire racks. Makes 72 cookies.

CORNMEAL ORANGE COOKIES

1 c. softened butter	1/2 c. cornmeal
1/2 c. sugar	1 c. powdered sugar
1 egg	2 T. softened butter
1 t. orange extract	1 1/2 T. orange juice
2 c. flour	

In a mixing bowl beat butter until fluffy.   Beat in sugar, egg and orange extract. In another bowl combine flour and cornmeal; mix into butter mixture. Shape dough into a ball and place on waxed paper. Roll into a 12" log. Seal and refrigerate 4 hours. Preheat oven to 350°. Remove dough from waxed paper and slice into 1/4" thick rounds; place on cookie sheets. Bake 10 minutes until edges begin to brown. Cool on wire racks. Mix powdered sugar, butter and enough orange juice to make spreadable. Frost cookies. Makes 24 cookies.

CORNMEAL PECAN COOKIES

3/4 c. butter
1 c. brown sugar
1 egg
1 c. self-rising flour

1 c. self-rising cornmeal
1 t. vanilla
1 c. chopped pecans

In a mixing bowl cream butter and brown sugar. Add egg; mix well. In another bowl combine flour and cornmeal. Add to the butter mixture a third at a time. Add vanilla; fold in pecans. On sheets of waxed paper, shape into 3 rolls 1" in diameter. Wrap and refrigerate until well chilled and firm. Unwrap and slice rolls into 1/4" thick rounds; bake at 400° for 12 minutes. Makes 48 cookies.

CORNMEAL RAISIN COOKIES #1

3/4 c. butter
3/4 c. sugar
1 egg
1 1/2 c. flour
1/2 c. cornmeal

1 t. baking powder
1/4 t. salt
1 t. vanilla
1/2 c. raisins
Vegetable oil for cookie sheet

In a large mixing bowl combine butter and sugar. Add egg; mix well. Stir in flour, cornmeal, baking powder, salt, vanilla and raisins. Drop dough from a teaspoon onto an oiled cookie sheet; bake at 350° for about 15 minutes until lightly browned. Makes 36 cookies.

CORNMEAL RAISIN COOKIES #2

1 c. shortening
1 1/2 c. sugar
2 eggs
1 t. lemon juice
2 3/4 c. cake flour
1 c. cornmeal

1 t. baking powder
1 t. ground nutmeg
1/2 t. salt
1 c. raisins
Vegetable oil for cookie sheet

Using an electric mixer beat shortening, sugar, eggs and lemon juice in a large mixing bowl until blended. In another bowl combine flour, cornmeal, baking powder, nutmeg and salt. Add to shortening mixture; mix well. Fold in raisins. Drop dough from a teaspoons 2" apart onto an oiled cookie sheet. Bake at 375° for 12 minutes. Cool on a wire rack. Makes 24 cookies.

Regional Cornbreads

For the past century, most Southern cooks have used white corn-meal, bacon grease, instead of vegetable shortening, and have not put sugar or much flour in their batter. Yankee cornbread has always been defined by the use of yellow cornmeal, sugar and flour—much like cake. Southern cornbread is crisp and crunchy on the out-side and moist on the inside. Northern cornbread is dry, fluffy and sweet. As Mark Twain is reported to have said "Perhaps no bread in the world is as good as Southern cornbread, and perhaps no bread in the world is as bad as the Northern imitation of it."

A "spider" was a cast iron frying pan with three legs, used by our Pilgrim ancestors to cook over an open fire or hot coals in a fire-place. The batter for cornbread was placed in the heavily greased pan and then coals were placed on the lid. Their legs and black color led the pans to be known as spiders. Even though the legs have been lost in the progress of modern cookware, the black cast iron pan is still called a spider by many traditional cooks.

The key to good cornbread is the crust. To get a crisp and crunchy crust the skillet and oil must be heated until very hot before putting in the batter. Many cooks add variety to their cornbread by stirring leftover vegetables and meats into their batter before baking.

SOUTHERN BUTTERMILK SPIDER CORNBREAD #1

2 c. cornmeal	2 c. buttermilk
1/4 c. flour	2 beaten eggs
1/2 t. salt	4 T. shortening, melted
1 t. baking powder	Vegetable oil for skillet
1/2 t. baking soda	

Preheat oven to 450°. Sift cornmeal, flour, salt and baking powder into a mixing bowl. In a small bowl mix baking soda and buttermilk together. Add to cornmeal mixture; mix well. Add eggs and beat to combine. Add shortening; mix well. Pour mixture into an oiled preheated 9" cast iron skillet and bake for 20 minutes until golden. Makes 8 servings.

SOUTHERN BUTTERMILK SPIDER CORNBREAD #2

2 c. self-rising cornmeal	1 egg
2 T. vegetable oil	Vegetable oil for skillet
1 1/2 c. buttermilk	

Preheat oven to 450°. In a mixing bowl combine cornmeal, oil, buttermilk and egg. Pour batter into an oiled preheated 8" cast iron skillet sprinkled with a small amount of cornmeal. Bake at 475° for 20 minutes until golden. Makes 8 servings.

SOUTHERN BUTTERMILK SPIDER CORNBREAD #3

1 c. cornmeal	2 T. vegetable oil
1/2 t. baking soda	1 c. buttermilk
1/2 t. salt	Vegetable oil for skillet
1 egg	

Preheat oven to 400°. In a mixing bowl combine cornmeal, baking soda, salt, egg, oil and buttermilk. Mix well; pour into an oiled preheated 8" cast iron skillet. Bake for 30 minutes until golden. Makes 8 servings.

SOUTHERN BUTTERMILK SPIDER CORNBREAD #4

1 1/2 c. cornmeal	2 egg yolks, well beaten
3/4 t. baking soda	2 egg whites, stiffly beaten
1 t. salt	1/4 c. shortening, melted
1 1/3 c. buttermilk	

Sift cornmeal, baking soda and salt in a mixing bowl. In another bowl add buttermilk to egg yolks. Add cornmeal mixture; beat well. In the oven, heat shortening in an 8" cast iron skillet. Add to cornmeal mixture. Fold in egg whites; pour batter into hot skillet. Bake at 450° for 30 minutes. Makes 8 servings.

SOUTHERN BUTTERMILK SPIDER CORNBREAD #5

2 T. bacon drippings	1 t. salt
2 c. cornmeal	1 egg
1 t. baking soda	1 1/4 c. buttermilk

Preheat oven to 375°. Heat bacon drippings in a 9" cast iron skillet over low heat. Sift cornmeal, baking soda and salt into a mixing bowl. In another bowl mix together egg and buttermilk. Add to cornmeal mixture, combining well. Pour batter into hot skillet; bake for 35 minutes. Makes 8 servings.

SOUTHERN BUTTERMILK SPIDER CORNBREAD #6

1 c. self-rising cornmeal	1 egg
1 c. self-rising flour	Vegetable oil for skillet
1 c. buttermilk	

Preheat oven to 450°. In a mixing bowl combine cornmeal, flour, buttermilk and egg. Heat an oiled 8" cast iron skillet in oven. Pour batter into hot skillet and bake for 15 minutes. Makes 8 servings.

SOUTHERN BUTTERMILK PAN CORNBREAD #1

2 c. cornmeal	1 1/4 c. buttermilk
1 t. salt	2 T. butter, melted
1/2 t. baking soda	2 beaten eggs
1 t. baking powder	Vegetable oil for baking pan

Preheat oven to 450°. Sift cornmeal, salt, baking soda and baking powder into a mixing bowl. Stir in buttermilk and butter. Add eggs; mix until smooth. Heat an oiled 9x9x2" baking pan in oven. Pour batter into hot pan and bake for 20 minutes. Makes 8 servings.

SOUTHERN BUTTERMILK PAN CORNBREAD #2

Vegetable oil for baking pan	1 t. baking soda
2 eggs	2 c. cornmeal
2 c. buttermilk	1 t. salt

Preheat oven to 450°. Heat an oiled 9x9x2" baking pan in oven. In a small bowl beat eggs and add buttermilk. In another bowl, combine baking soda, cornmeal and salt. Add egg mixture; stir until smooth. Pour batter into the hot pan and bake for 25 minutes. Makes 9 servings.

SOUTHERN BUTTERMILK PAN CORNBREAD #3

2 c. cornmeal	2 c. buttermilk
1 t. baking soda	1/4 c. shortening, melted
1 t. salt	Vegetable oil for baking pan
1 beaten egg	

Preheat oven to 500°. In a mixing bowl combine cornmeal, baking soda and salt. In another bowl mix together egg, buttermilk and shortening. Pour batter into an oiled preheated 8x12x2" baking pan. Bake for 25 minutes. Makes 12 servings.

SOUTHERN BUTTERMILK PAN CORNBREAD #4

1/2 t. baking soda
1 c. buttermilk
1 beaten egg
2/3 c. cornmeal

3/4 t. salt
3 T. butter, melted
Vegetable oil for baking pan

In a mixing bowl add baking soda to buttermilk; mix well. Add egg, cornmeal, salt and butter. Blend well; pour into an oiled preheated 8x8x2" baking pan. Bake at 425° for 15 minutes. Makes 8 servings.

SOUTHERN BUTTERMILK PAN CORNBREAD #5

2 c. cornmeal
2 t. baking powder
1 t. baking soda
1 t. salt

1 c. buttermilk
1 beaten egg
1/4 c. shortening, melted
Vegetable oil for baking pan

In a mixing bowl combine cornmeal, baking powder, baking soda and salt. Add buttermilk, egg and shortening; stir just until moistened. Pour batter into an oiled 8x8x2" baking pan dusted with cornmeal. Bake at 425° for 20 minutes. Makes 8 servings.

SOUTHERN BUTTERMILK PAN CORNBREAD #6

2 c. cornmeal
1 c. flour
2 t. baking soda
1 t. salt

2 1/2 c. buttermilk
2 eggs
1/4 c. butter, melted
Vegetable oil for baking pan

In a mixing bowl combine cornmeal, flour, baking soda and salt. In another bowl stir together buttermilk, eggs and butter. Add to cornmeal mixture; stir just to blend. Pour batter into an oiled 9x9x2" baking pan; bake at 450° for 25 minutes until golden. Makes 12 servings.

SOUTHERN BUTTERMILK PAN CORNBREAD #7

2 c. cornmeal
1 t. salt
1 t. baking soda
1 beaten egg

2 c. buttermilk
4 T. butter, melted
Vegetable oil for baking pan

Preheat oven to 475°. Sift cornmeal, salt and baking soda into a mixing bowl. Stir in egg and buttermilk. Fold in butter. Pour batter into an oiled preheated 8x8x2" baking pan; bake for 25 minutes. Makes 8 servings.

SOUTHERN BUTTERMILK PAN CORNBREAD #8

1/2 c. sifted flour
2 c. cornmeal
3 t. baking powder
1/2 t. salt
1/2 c. milk

2 beaten eggs
2/3 t. baking soda
1 1/2 c. buttermilk
5 T. shortening, melted
Vegetable oil for baking pan

Preheat oven to 475°. Sift flour, cornmeal, baking powder and salt into a mixing bowl. In a small bowl add milk to eggs. Add to cornmeal mixture; beat well. In another bowl mix baking soda with buttermilk; add to batter. Add shortening; mix well. Pour batter into an oiled preheated 9x13x2" baking pan. Bake for 30 minutes. Makes 12 servings.

SOUTHERN BUTTERMILK PAN CORNBREAD #9

2 c. cornmeal
1/2 t. baking soda
2 t. baking powder
1 t. salt

2 eggs
2 c. buttermilk
2 T. shortening, melted
Vegetable oil for baking pan

Preheat oven to 475°. Sift cornmeal, baking soda, baking powder and salt into a mixing bowl. Add eggs and buttermilk; stir to combine. Add shortening; mix into batter. Pour batter into an oiled preheated 8x8x2" baking pan; bake for 30 minutes. Makes 8 servings.

SOUTHERN BUTTERMILK PAN CORNBREAD #10

1 c. cornmeal	2 eggs
1 c. floor	1 1/4 c. buttermilk
1 1/2 t. baking powder	1/4 c. butter, melted and cooled
1/2 t. baking soda	Vegetable oil for baking pan
1/2 t. salt	

Preheat oven to 425°. In a mixing bowl combine cornmeal, flour, baking powder, baking soda and salt. In another bowl stir together eggs, buttermilk and butter. Add to cornmeal mixture and stir just until combined. Pour batter into an oiled preheated 9x9x2" baking pan. Bake for 15 minutes until golden. Makes 9 servings.

SOUTHERN SKILLET CORNBREAD #1

1 1/2 c. cornmeal	1 1/2 c. milk
3 T. flour	1 beaten egg
1 1/2 t. baking powder	2 T. shortening
1 t. salt	

Preheat oven to 425°. In a mixing bowl combine cornmeal, flour, baking powder and salt. Add milk, egg and shortening to cornmeal mixture; mix well. Melt shortening in a 9" cast iron skillet. Pour batter into hot skillet; bake for 25 minutes. Makes 9 servings.

SOUTHERN SKILLET CORNBREAD #2

2 c. cornmeal	6 T. butter, melted
1 1/2 t. baking powder	1 egg
1/4 t. salt	Vegetable oil for skillet
1 c. milk	

In a mixing bowl combine cornmeal, baking powder and salt. Add milk, butter and egg, stirring to mix well. Pour into an oiled 8" cast iron skillet and bake at 400° for about 25 minutes. Makes 8 servings.

SOUTHERN SKILLET CORNBREAD #3

2 c. self-rising cornmeal   1 1/4 c. milk
1/2 c. vegetable oil   Vegetable oil for skillet

Preheat oven to 450°. In a mixing bowl combine cornmeal, oil and milk, stirring to blend well. Pour batter into an oiled preheated 8" cast iron skillet. Bake for 20 minutes. Makes 8 servings.

SOUTHERN SKILLET CORNBREAD #4

2 1/2 c. milk, divided   1 t. salt
2 t. vinegar   1 2/3 c. cornmeal
2 beaten eggs   1/3 c. flour
1 t. baking soda   2 T. melted butter

Preheat oven to 375°. In a mixing bowl combine 1 cup milk with vinegar to make sour milk. In another bowl combine sour milk, 1 cup milk, baking soda and salt. Mix in cornmeal and flour, stirring until smooth. Pour batter into a 9" cast iron skillet, tilting to coat sides and bottom; pour remaining 1/2 cup of milk over top. Bake for 35 minutes until golden. Makes 10 servings.

SOUTHERN PAN CORNBREAD #1

4 T. melted butter, divided   1 1/4 c. cornmeal
3/4 c. flour   1 beaten egg
1 T. baking powder   3/4 c. milk
3/4 t. salt

Preheat oven to 425°. Heat 1 tablespoon butter in an 8x8x2" baking pan. Sift flour, baking powder and salt into a mixing bowl. Stir in cornmeal. In another bowl stir together egg, remaining 3 tablespoons of butter and milk. Add to cornmeal mixture, stirring just until combined. Pour batter into hot pan; bake for 20 minutes. Makes 8 servings.

SOUTHERN PAN CORNBREAD #2

2 c. self-rising flour

1 c. self-rising cornmeal

2 eggs

1 1/2 c. milk

3 T. butter, melted

Vegetable oil for baking pan

Preheat oven to 425°. In a mixing bowl combine flour and cornmeal. In another bowl, mix eggs and milk together; add to cornmeal mixture. Add butter and mix. Pour batter into an oiled 8x8x2" baking pan. Bake for 30 minutes. Makes 8 servings.

SOUTHERN PAN CORNBREAD #3

1 c. cornmeal

1 t. baking powder

3 eggs

2 c. milk

2 T. butter

Preheat oven to 350°. Sift cornmeal and baking powder into a mixing bowl. In another bowl mix together eggs and milk; stir into cornmeal mixture. Melt butter in an 8x8x2" baking pan in oven. Pour into batter; stir to mix. Pour batter into pan; bake for 35 minutes. Makes 8 servings.

SOUTHERN PAN CORNBREAD #4

2 c. self-rising cornmeal

1 egg

Milk

Vegetable oil for baking pan

In a mixing bowl combine cornmeal and egg. Stir in enough milk to make a thick batter. Pour into an oiled 8x8x2" baking pan. Bake at 425° for 30 minutes. Makes 8 servings.

SWEET NORTHERN CORNBREAD #1

1 c. cornmeal	1/2 c. milk
2 T. flour	1 egg
1 T. sugar	1 T. shortening, melted
2 t. baking powder	Vegetable oil for baking pan
1/2 t. salt	

Preheat oven to 425°. In a mixing bowl combine cornmeal, flour, sugar, baking powder and salt. In another bowl mix together milk, egg and shortening. Pour into cornmeal mixture; stir quickly to combine. Pour into an oiled 8x8x2" baking pan; bake for 25 minutes. Makes 8 servings.

SWEET NORTHERN CORNBREAD #2

1 1/2 c. cornmeal	6 T. butter, melted and cooled
1 c. flour	8 T. shortening,
1/3 c. sugar	melted and cooled
1 t. salt	1 1/2 c. milk
1 T. baking powder	Vegetable oil for baking pan
2 eggs	

Preheat oven to 400°. Sift cornmeal, flour, sugar, salt and baking powder into a mixing bowl. In another bowl beat eggs and add butter and shortening. Stir in milk. Add to cornmeal mixture; beat until smooth. Pour into an oiled 8x12x2" baking pan; bake for 30 minutes until golden. Makes 12 servings.

SWEET NORTHERN CORNBREAD #3

1 1/2 c. cornmeal	1 t. salt
1/2 c. flour	2 eggs
1 T. sugar	1 1/2 c. buttermilk
2 t. baking powder	3 T. butter
1 t. baking soda	

Preheat oven to 425°. Sift cornmeal, flour, sugar, baking powder, baking soda and salt into a mixing bowl. in another bowl, mix eggs and buttermilk together. In oven, melt butter in a 9" cast iron skillet. Stir into buttermilk mixture. Add to cornmeal mixture, stirring to combine well. Pour mixture into hot skillet; bake for 30 minutes until golden. Makes 9 servings.

SWEET NORTHERN CORNBREAD #4

1 c. sifted flour	1 egg, beaten
3/4 c. cornmeal	1 c. milk
1/2 t. salt	1/2 c. vegetable oil
2 1/2 t. baking powder	Vegetable oil for baking pan
2 T. sugar	

Preheat oven to 425°. Sift flour, cornmeal, salt, baking powder and sugar into a mixing bowl. Add egg, milk and oil. Stir lightly to mix. Pour into an oiled 9x9x2" baking pan. Bake 30 minutes until golden. Makes 9 servings.

SWEET NORTHERN CORNBREAD #5

1 c. cornmeal	1/2 c. butter
2 c. flour	2 eggs
3 T. baking powder	1 c. milk
1 t. salt	Vegetable oil for baking pan
3/4 c. sugar	

In a mixing bowl combine cornmeal, flour, baking powder and salt. Set aside. In another bowl cream sugar and butter together. Add eggs, one at a time, beating well. Alternately add milk and cornmeal mixture; mix until smooth. Pour into an oiled 9x13x2" baking pan; bake at 350° for 30 minutes. Makes 10 servings.

SWEET NORTHERN CORNBREAD #6

4 T. butter	1 c. flour
1/3 c. sugar	1 1/4 t. baking powder
1 egg	1/8 t. salt
1 c. water	Vegetable oil for baking pan
1 c. cornmeal	

In a mixing bowl cream butter, sugar and egg. Add water, cornmeal, flour, baking powder and salt. Mix until smooth. Pour into an oiled 9" pie pan. Bake at 400° for 25 minutes. Makes 8 servings.

SWEET NORTHERN CORNBREAD #7

1 c. flour	1 egg, beaten
3/4 c. cornmeal	1 c. milk
1 T. sugar	2 T. vegetable oil
2 t. baking powder	Vegetable oil for baking pan
1/8 t. salt	

In a mixing bowl combine flour, cornmeal, sugar, baking powder and salt. In another bowl stir together egg, milk and oil. Mix into cornmeal mixture. Pour into an oiled 8x8x2" baking pan. Bake at 450° for 30 minutes until golden. Makes 9 servings.

SWEET NORTHERN CORNBREAD #8

3/4 c. cornmeal	1 t. baking powder
1/4 c. sifted flour	1 1/2 c. plus 1 T. milk, divided
1/2 T. sugar	1 egg, beaten
1/2 t. salt	2 T. butter

Preheat oven to 400°. In a mixing bowl combine cornmeal, flour, sugar, salt and baking powder. Mix in 1 cup plus 1 tablespoon milk. In oven melt butter in a 9x9x2" baking dish. Pour batter into pan and pour remaining half cup milk over top. Bake for 30 minutes. Makes 8 servings.

SWEET NORTHERN CORNBREAD #9

1 c. sifted flour	1 egg, beaten
2 t. baking powder	1 c. milk
3 T. sugar	1/4 c. shortening, melted
1 t. salt	Vegetable oil for baking pan
1 c. cornmeal	

Sift flour, baking powder, sugar and salt into a mixing bowl. Add cornmeal. In another bowl mix together egg, milk and shortening. Add to cornmeal mixture; stir just until moistened. Pour into an oiled 9x9x2" baking pan; bake at 400° for 30 minutes. Makes 8 servings.

SWEET NORTHERN CORNBREAD #10

1 c. sifted flour	1 c. cornmeal
1/4 c. sugar	1 c. milk
1 t. baking powder	1 egg, beaten
1/2 t. baking soda	5 T. shortening, melted
3/4 t. salt	Vegetable oil for baking pan

In a mixing bowl combine flour, sugar, baking powder, baking soda, salt, cornmeal, milk, egg and shortening. Mix well; pour into an oiled 8x8x2" baking pan. Bake at 425° for 20 minutes. Makes 8 servings.

SWEET NORTHERN CORNBREAD #11

1 c. cornmeal	1/3 c. sugar
1 c. flour	1 t. salt
2 c. milk, divided	1/2 c. butter
1 egg	

Preheat oven to 400°. In a mixing bowl combine cornmeal and flour. Mix in 1 1/2 cups of milk, egg, sugar and salt. In oven melt butter in an 8x12x2" baking pan. Pour into cornmeal mixture. Add remaining milk; mix in. Pour batter into hot baking pan and bake for 30 minutes. Makes 10 servings.

SWEET NORTHERN CORNBREAD #12

3/4 c. milk, scalded	1 t. baking powder
1/2 c. cornmeal	1/4 t. salt
1 T. shortening	1 T. sugar
1 egg, beaten	Vegetable oil for baking pan

In a mixing bowl pour hot milk over cornmeal and shortening. Allow to cool; add egg, baking powder, salt and sugar. Mix well; pour into an oiled 8x8x2" baking pan. Bake at 400° for 30 minutes. Makes 8 servings.

SWEET NORTHERN CORNBREAD #13

1 c. flour	1 c. cornmeal
2 t. baking powder	3 T. vegetable oil
1/2 t. baking soda	2 eggs
1/2 t. salt	1 c. buttermilk
1 T. sugar	Vegetable oil for baking pan

In a mixing bowl combine flour, baking powder, baking soda and salt, mixing well. Mix in sugar and cornmeal. In another bowl mix oil and eggs. Add to cornmeal mixture, mixing just until moistened. Pour into an oiled 8x8x2" baking pan; bake at 400° for 30 minutes until golden. Makes 8 servings.

SWEET NORTHERN CORNBREAD #14

1 c. cornmeal	2 eggs
1 c. flour	5 T. butter, melted
4 t. baking powder	1 c. buttermilk
2 t. sugar	Vegetable oil for baking pan
3/4 t. salt	

Preheat oven to 425°. In a mixing bowl combine cornmeal, flour, baking powder, sugar and salt. In another bowl beat eggs with butter, then mix in buttermilk. Add to cornmeal mixture, stirring just until moistened. Pour into an oiled 8x8x2" baking pan; bake for 25 minutes until golden. Makes 8 servings.

SWEET NORTHERN CORNBREAD #15

1 1/2 c. self-rising cornmeal	1/2 c. vegetable oil
2/3 c. self-rising flour	1 egg, beaten
1 1/2 c. milk	1/4 c. sugar
1 1/2 c. buttermilk	Vegetable oil for skillet

Preheat oven to 450°. In a mixing bowl combine cornmeal, flour, milk, buttermilk, oil, egg and sugar. Mix well; pour into an oiled preheated 9" cast iron skillet; bake for 25 minutes. Makes 12 servings.

SWEET NORTHERN CORNBREAD #16

2 T. butter	1 1/4 t. salt
1 1/3 c. cornmeal	2 c. milk, divided
1/3 c. sifted flour	2 eggs
1 t. baking soda	1 c. buttermilk
3 T. sugar	

Preheat oven to 400°. Melt butter in a 9" cast iron skillet in oven. Stir cornmeal, flour, baking soda, sugar and salt into a mixing bowl. Stir in one cup milk and eggs. Add buttermilk; stir to blend. Pour mixture into hot skillet. Pour the additional cup of milk over top of cornmeal mixture. Bake for 35 minutes. Cornbread will have a layer of custard. Makes 6 servings.

Cornmeal Sides and Miscellaneous

CORNMEAL BANANA BREAD

2 beaten eggs	6 T. cornmeal
4 T. water	1/2 t. baking soda
2/3 c. dry milk	10 t. sugar
1/2 t. salt	1/2 t. vanilla
2 overripe bananas, cut up	Vegetable oil for loaf pan

Place eggs, water, dry milk, salt, bananas, cornmeal, baking soda, sugar and vanilla in an electric blender. Blend on high speed until well mixed. Pour batter into an oiled 8x8x2" baking pan. Bake at 350° for 40 minutes. Makes 10 servings.

RYE BREAD BISCUITS

1 c. whole-wheat flour	3 T. shortening
1 c. rye flour	Buttermilk
1/2 c. cornmeal	Baking soda
1 t. salt	Vegetable oil for baking sheet
1 t. baking powder	

Sift whole-wheat flour, rye flour, cornmeal, salt and baking powder into a mixing bowl. Cut in shortening. Add enough buttermilk to make a firm dough, adding 1/2 teaspoon baking soda per cup of buttermilk. Stir to mix well; roll out on a lightly floured board to 1/2" thickness. Cut with a biscuit cutter and place on an oiled baking sheet. Bake at 450° for 12 minutes. Makes 24 biscuits.

CORNMEAL BLUEBERRY BREAD

1 1/2 c. sifted flour	1/2 c. molasses
1 c. cornmeal	1 2/3 c. milk
1/2 t. baking powder	2 T. melted shortening
1/2 t. baking soda	1 c. blueberries
1/4 t. salt	Vegetable oil for baking pan
1 beaten egg	

Sift flour, cornmeal, baking powder, baking soda and salt into a mixing bowl. Add egg, molasses and milk; beat until smooth. Add shortening and fold in blueberries. Pour into an oiled 9x9x2" baking pan. Bake at 450° for 20 minutes. Makes 10 servings.

CORNMEAL BREADSTICKS

1 pkg. dry yeast	2 t. salt
1 c. warm water	1 T. rosemary, crumbled
2 1/2 c. flour	4 T. olive oil
2/3 c. cornmeal	

Dissolve yeast in warm water. Combine with flour and knead for 5 minutes. Place in a floured bowl; cover with a damp towel for 2 hours. Combine cornmeal, salt and rosemary; add olive oil. Mix these ingredients into flour mixture; knead for 6-7 minutes. Let this dough stand again in a floured bowl for 2 hours until doubled in bulk. Knead again for a few minutes; divide into 3 equal parts. Divide each part into 12 to make 36 pieces. Roll each piece of dough on a bread board and between palms of hands, into a long thin roll. Place them an inch apart on greased baking sheets; press the edges down to anchor them lightly to baking sheets. Bake at 400° for 12 minutes until golden. Makes 36 servings.

CORNMEAL BRIOCHES

1 c. cornmeal	6 egg yolks, at room temperature
4 1/2 c. flour, divided	3 eggs, at room temperature
1/3 c. sugar	2 t. salt
3 pkgs. dry yeast	Vegetable oil for brioche mold
1/4 c. dry milk	Egg wash, made by beating
3/4 c. hot water	1 egg with 1 T. water
10 T. butter, cut into bits and softened	

In a large mixing bowl, combine cornmeal, 1 cup flour, sugar, yeast and dry milk. Mix in hot water, butter, egg yolks, eggs and salt. Stir to combine well. Add enough remaining flour, a little bit at a time, to make a soft slightly sticky dough. Turn out onto lightly floured board; knead about 10 minutes. Place dough in oiled bowl, turning to oil top. Cover with plastic wrap; let dough rise in warm place for 30 minutes. Punch down dough; divide into 2 parts. Work with half of dough at a time, placing remaining part under inverted bowl. Pinch off a lemon-size piece of dough; form into ball. Form larger piece of dough into ball and place in oiled 8" brioche mold, seam side down. Make an indentation in center of top; put small ball in it, seam side down. Repeat with second half of dough. Cover loosely with waxed paper; let brioches rise in warm place for 15 minutes. Brush with egg wash. Preheat oven to 375°; bake for 35 minutes until golden. Cool in molds for 1 hour. Makes 2 servings.

CORNMEAL CRACKERS

1 c. cornmeal	1/2 c. milk
1/2 c. flour	3 T. vegetable oil
3/4 t. salt	1/4 t. Worcestershire sauce
1/4 t. baking soda	

Preheat oven to 350°. Combine cornmeal, flour, salt and baking soda. Mix well. Combine milk, oil and Worcestershire sauce. Add to dry ingredients; mix well. Turn dough out onto a lightly floured board; knead for 5 minutes. Divide the dough in half and roll out each half in 12" squares. Cut into 2" squares and, if desired, prick the tops with a 3-tined fork. Place squares on a lightly greased baking sheet. Bake 15 minutes or until edges are golden. Allow to cool on baking sheet. Makes 6 dozen.

CORNMEAL CHEESE CRACKERS #1

2/3 c. yellow cornmeal	2/3 c. cold water
1/3 c. flour	2 T. melted butter, cooled
1/2 t. salt	1 egg
1 t. sugar	1 c. grated sharp Cheddar cheese
1 1/2 t. baking powder	

Preheat oven to 400°. Combine the cornmeal, flour, salt, sugar and baking powder. Add the water, butter and egg; stir until thoroughly mixed. Add the cheese, mix until well combined. Drop the batter by quarter cupfuls onto a lightly buttered baking sheet. Bake for 6 minutes. Turn crackers and bake 5 minutes longer until they are crisp. Makes 24 servings.

CORNMEAL CHEESE CRACKERS #2

1 c. unbleached flour	1/4 t. cayenne pepper
1/4 c. whole-wheat flour	1 c. finely grated Cheddar cheese
3/4 c. cornmeal	1 egg
1/4 t. baking powder	1/4 c. vegetable oil
1/2 t. salt	1/4 c. water

Preheat oven to 375°. Combine flours, cornmeal, baking powder, salt and cayenne pepper. Mix well; add the cheese. Combine well. Beat together the remaining ingredients; add to the dry mixture. Mix until dough sticks together. Roll dough out on lightly floured board about 1/8" thick. Cut into 2" squares, prick tops if desired and place on an ungreased baking sheet. Bake for 15 minutes until crisp and golden. Makes 36 crackers.

CORNMEAL CRISPS #1

1 c. cornmeal	Salt to taste
1 c. boiling water	Vegetable oil for baking sheet
4 stiffly beaten egg whites	

In a mixing bowl scald cornmeal with boiling water. Allow to cool. When cold, fold in egg whites and season with salt. Drop by teaspoonfuls onto an oiled baking sheet. Bake at 325° for 30 minutes. Makes 12 servings.

CORNMEAL CRISPS #2

1 c. boiling water	3 T. melted butter
1 c. minus 2 T. cornmeal	Vegetable oil for baking sheet
1 t. salt	

In a mixing bowl pour boiling water over cornmeal. Add salt and butter; mix well. Drop by teaspoonfuls onto an oiled baking sheet. Flatten them with a spatula dipped in cold water. Bake at 350° for 20 minutes or until edges are brown. Makes 12 servings.

CORNBREAD CROUTONS #1

1 T. olive oil	Salt and pepper to taste
2 cornbread muffins	

In a medium skillet heat oil over medium-high heat. Cut muffins into 1/3" cubes. Toast cubes in skillet until golden brown and crisp. Salt and pepper to taste. Makes 4 servings.

CORNBREAD CROUTONS #2

1/2 c. yellow cornmeal	1 beaten egg
1/2 c. flour	1 T. melted butter or margarine
1/2 t. baking soda	Vegetable cooking spray
1/4 t. salt	1 T. honey
1/2 c. buttermilk	

Preheat oven to 400°. In a bowl combine cornmeal, flour, baking soda and salt. Combine buttermilk, egg and butter. Add to cornmeal mixture, stirring just until moistened. Spray an 8x8x2" pan with cooking spray. Spread batter evenly into pan; bake for 10-12 minutes until lightly browned. Cool to room temperature. If desired, spread with honey. Cut cornbread into 1/2" cubes. Put cubes in a single layer on a baking sheet and spray with cooking spray. Lower oven temperature to 350°; bake cubes for 12-15 minutes or until lightly browned. Makes 6 servings.

CORNMEAL PIZZA CRUST

1 pkg. dry yeast	2/3 c. cornmeal
1/2 t. sugar	1 1/2 c. flour, divided
2/3 c. lukewarm water, divided	1/2 t. salt
2 T. olive oil	Vegetable oil for bowl

In a large mixing bowl dissolve yeast and sugar in 1/3 cup of warm water. Let it sit for 10 minutes until it is foamy. Stir in remaining 1/3 cup warm water, olive oil, cornmeal, 1 1/4 cups flour and salt. Stir mixture until it forms a dough. Turn out onto floured board; knead, incorporating as much of remaining flour as needed to prevent dough from sticking, until smooth and elastic, about 10 minutes. Place dough in an oiled bowl, turning to oil top. Cover with plastic wrap; let dough rise in a warm place until doubled in bulk, about 1 hour. Punch down dough; form into a 14"crust. Makes 1 crust.

CORNMEAL QUICHE CRUST

2 c. fresh corn kernels	1 t. salt
4 T. melted butter	1/4 t. pepper
2 egg yolks, divided	1 c. cornmeal

Preheat oven to 375°. Place corn kernels and butter in electric blender. Process until smooth. Add 1 egg yolk, salt and pepper; process until well mixed. Add cornmeal; process until barely mixed. Press the mixture into a greased 9" pie plate. Beat remaining egg yolk; brush it onto crust. Bake crust for 20 minutes until it is firm and set. Makes 1 crust.

CORNMEAL DOUGHNUTS #1

3/4 c. milk	1 1/2 c. flour
1 1/2 c. cornmeal	2 t. baking powder
1/2 c. butter	1/4 t. cinnamon
3/4 c. sugar	1 t. salt
2 beaten eggs	Vegetable oil for frying

In a saucepan heat milk and stir in cornmeal. Cook, stirring constantly, for 10 minutes. Remove from heat; add butter and sugar. Stir in eggs. Sift flour with baking powder, cinnamon and salt. Stir into cornmeal mixture. Roll dough out on a lightly floured board. Cut out with a doughnut cutter. Let doughnuts stand while heating deep oil in a Dutch oven. Fry doughnuts until brown; drain well. If desired, roll in additional sugar. Makes 36 donuts.

CORNMEAL DOUGHNUTS #2

1 1/2 c. milk	1 1/2 c. sugar
2 c. cornmeal	1 T. cinnamon
2 c. flour	1 c. melted butter
3 t. baking powder	3 beaten eggs
1 t. salt	Vegetable oil for frying

Heat milk to boiling. Pour over cornmeal; allow to cool. Sift together flour, baking powder, salt, sugar and cinnamon. Add to cornmeal mixture; blend well. Add butter and eggs. Mix well and, if necessary, add more flour to make dough firm enough to handle. Roll out on a lightly floured board, cut with a doughnut cutter. Allow to rest while heating oil. Fry in deep hot oil in a Dutch oven until brown. Makes 48 donuts.

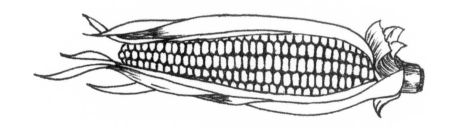

CORNMEAL DUMPLINGS

Cornmeal dumplings are often served cooked on top of collard or turnip greens or used to rim the pots of chowders, soups or stews. They may also be simmered in beef, chicken or pork stock and served as a side dish.

CORNMEAL DUMPLINGS #1

3 c. self-rising cornmeal
1 egg
1 T. finely chopped onion

Pepper to taste
1 1/2 c. country ham hock stock

Combine cornmeal, egg, onion and pepper in a bowl. Pour enough boiling broth over mixture to make a stiff dough that is easy to handle and will hold together when shaped into balls. Drop on top of turnip greens as they cook. Cook for 10 minutes, or until dumplings rise to the top. Makes 8 servings.

CORNMEAL DUMPLINGS #2

1 c. cornmeal
1 T. flour

1/2 t. salt
1/2 c. water

In a bowl, combine cornmeal, flour and salt. Add just enough water to make a stiff dough. Form into small patties or cakes. Drop around the sides of the pot of chowder, greens or stew for the last 15 minutes of cooking. The dumplings will float to the top when done. Makes 4 servings.

EGGS AND CORNBREAD

3/4 c. crumbled cornbread
1 1/2 c. shredded extra sharp
　　Cheddar cheese
6 beaten eggs
1 1/2 c. milk

1 t. hot sauce
1 t. Pickapeppa sauce
1/4 t. pepper
1/4 t. seasoned salt
Vegetable oil for baking dish

Spread cornbread in the bottom of an oiled 13x9x2" baking dish. Cover with cheese. In a mixing bowl combine eggs, milk, hot sauce, Pickapeppa sauce, pepper and seasoned salt. Pour mixture over cheese. Bake at 375° for 25 minutes until golden. Makes 6 servings.

EGGS AND CORNMEAL

1/2 c. butter	Salt and pepper to taste
Cornmeal	4 eggs

In a 10" cast iron skillet melt butter. Sprinkle in enough cornmeal to cover bottom of skillet. Add salt and pepper. When cornmeal starts to brown, break eggs into skillet. When edges begin to brown, turn, cover and brown on the other side until eggs puff up. Serve at once. Makes 4 servings.

CORNMEAL FOCCACIA

1 T. dry yeast	1/4 c. finely chopped garlic
1 c. very warm water	1/4 c. chopped fresh rosemary
2 c. flour, divided	leaves
3/4 c. cornmeal	1/3 c. grated Parmesan cheese
1 T. salt, divided	Black pepper
1/3 c. olive oil, divided	
1/2 c. white vinegar	

In a medium bowl dissolve yeast in water. Stir in 1 cup of flour. Cover with plastic wrap; set aside for 3 hours until bubbly. In a mixing bowl using an electric mixer, beat together the remaining 1 cup flour, cornmeal, 1 teaspoon salt and 3 tablespoons olive oil. Add yeast mixture and vinegar; mix well. Add garlic and rosemary; mix again. Turn out onto a very lightly floured board; knead until dough is smooth and elastic, about 10 minutes. Place in a bowl; cover with a damp cloth. Let rise in warm place until doubled in bulk, about 1 1/2 hours. Preheat oven to 475°. Punch down; let it rise for 2 minutes. Remove from bowl; pat into large circle, about 1/4" thick. Place it on baking sheet sprinkled with cornmeal. Make dents on top with fingers. Sprinkle with remaining oil, salt, cheese and pepper. Bake for 15 minutes; serve warm. Makes 1 foccacia.

Gnocchi is made from a basis of cornmeal mush and is an Italian special-ty. It is generally served with cheese or cheese sauce, a highly seasoned tomato sauce or any sauce similar to that used for spaghetti.

CORNMEAL GNOCCHI #1

1/2 c. cornmeal
2 c. boiling salted water
1 c. scalded milk

1/2 c. grated Parmesan cheese
Salt and pepper

Sift cornmeal into water. Stir constantly over direct heat until mixture thick-ens and boils. In a double boiler gradually add milk, stirring constantly for 30 minutes. Pour into a wet 8x8x2" pan and chill until firm. Cut into diamond shaped pieces and arrange alternately with cheese in an oiled baking dish, sea-soning each layer with salt and pepper. Pour some milk or tomato sauce over layers, cover and bake at 400° for 35 minutes. Uncover and bake until light-ly browned. Makes 4 servings.

CORNMEAL GNOCCHI #2

5 c. milk
1 1/4 c. cornmeal
1 t. salt

1/2 c. melted butter
1/4 c. grated Parmesan cheese

Bring milk to a boil and gradually pour cornmeal into milk, stirring constant-ly until mixture thickens. Remove from heat, stir in salt; pour mixture into a pan to a depth of 1/4". Chill until firm. Cut into desired shapes and arrange in a baking dish with edges slightly overlapping. Pour butter over all; sprinkle with cheese. Bake at 350° for 15 minutes or until lightly browned on top. Makes 6 servings.

CORNMEAL GRAVY #1

1/4 c. bacon drippings
1 c. cornmeal

3 c. milk

Heat bacon drippings in skillet over medium-high heat. Stir in cornmeal; cook until it is browned. Stir in milk, all at once, and stir constantly until it is as thick as desired. Makes 4 servings.

CORNMEAL GRAVY #2

1 T. shortening	1 egg
1 heaping T. cornmeal	2/3 t. salt
2 c. milk	1/2 t. pepper

Heat shortening in a skillet over medium-high heat. Stir in cornmeal, but do not brown. Combine milk, egg, salt and pepper; add to cornmeal in skillet. Stir constantly over medium heat until gravy is as thick as desired. Makes 4 servings.

HASTY PUDDING

1/2 c. cornmeal	1/2 t. salt
1 c. cold water	2 c. boiling water

In a small bowl combine cornmeal and cold water. Add to salted boiling water in a saucepan. Reduce heat; cook 15 minutes, stirring constantly. Serve with syrup. Makes 2 servings.

CORNMEAL MEAT PIE TOPPING

1 1/2 c. cornmeal	1 beaten egg
1/2 c. sifted flour	1/4 c. melted butter
1 T. baking powder	1 c. milk
1 t. salt	Vegetable oil for baking pan
1 T. sugar	

Sift cornmeal, flour, baking powder, salt and sugar into a mixing bowl. In another bowl mix egg, butter and milk. Add to cornmeal mixture; stir just until blended. Pour over meat pie or pour into an oiled 8x8x2" baking pan. Bake at 425° for 25 minutes until golden. Makes 4 servings.

CORNMEAL MERINGUES

5 T. cornmeal	4 egg whites, stiffly beaten
1 1/2 c. boiling water	with a pinch of salt
1/4 t. salt	Vegetable oil for baking sheet

In a mixing bowl combine cornmeal and boiling water, stirring until smooth. Pour into a saucepan; boil for 3 minutes, stirring constantly. Add salt; let cool slightly. Fold in egg whites, mixing well. Drop by tablespoonfuls onto a baking sheet covered with an oiled sheet of waxed paper. Bake at 300° for 30 minutes until golden brown. Remove with a spatula and serve hot with soups or salads. Makes 8 servings.

CORNMEAL MUFFIN RING #1

1 c. self-rising cornmeal	1 beaten egg
1 t. sugar	3 T. melted shortening
1 c. buttermilk	Vegetable oil for ring mold

In a mixing bowl combine cornmeal and sugar. In a small bowl mix together buttermilk and egg; add to cornmeal mixture. Add shortening; mix well. Pour into an oiled ring mold; bake at 450° for 20 minutes. Let stand 5 minutes and unmold onto a platter. Fill with creamed chicken or other filling. Makes 8 servings.

CORNMEAL MUFFIN RING #2

6 whole cloves,	3/4 c. cornmeal
heads removed	Salt, pepper, nutmeg,
1 med. onion	mixed to taste
2 c. milk	3 beaten eggs
1 c. cold water	Vegetable oil for ring mold
1/8 t. salt	

Stick cloves into onion; place in a saucepan. Add milk, water and salt. Bring to a boil; gradually sprinkle in cornmeal. Cook for 20 minutes, stirring frequently. Remove from heat; beat until thoroughly blended with onion. Season with salt, pepper and nutmeg mixture. Beat in eggs. Spoon into an oiled ring mold; bake at 350° for 20 minutes. Let stand 5 minutes and unmold onto a platter. Fill with creamed chicken or other filling. Makes 8 servings.

CORNMEAL NOODLES

2 c. cornmeal	3/4 t. salt
Boiling salted water	1 beaten egg
1 c. bread flour	1 rounded T. butter
1 T. baking powder	

Scald cornmeal with enough water to make a smooth and moderately stiff mush. Sift flour with baking powder and salt. Add to cornmeal mush and stir well. Beat in egg and butter. Roll out as thin as possible on a lightly floured board. Let stand 20 minutes and cut to desired size. Cook, uncovered, in boiling water or broth for 10 minutes or until done. Makes 2 servings.

CORNMEAL PUDDING #1

1 pt. milk	4 egg yolks
1 1/2 t. salt	4 stiffly beaten egg whites
1 T. sugar	Vegetable oil for baking dish
2/3 c. cornmeal	

In a saucepan heat milk. Add salt and sugar; when milk is hot, gradually add cornmeal. Cook, stirring constantly, until almost thick. Remove from heat; add egg yolks, beating constantly. Fold in egg whites; spoon into an oiled 8x8x2" baking dish. Bake at 350° for 30 minutes until golden. Makes 8 servings.

CORNMEAL PUDDING #2

1 qt. milk	1 egg, beaten
3 T. cornmeal	1/2 c. floured raisins
3 T. sifted flour	1/2 t. ginger
1 T. butter	1/2 t. cinnamon
1/2 c. sugar	1/8 t. baking soda
1/4 c. molasses	Vegetable oil for baking dish

In a saucepan heat milk and stir in cornmeal, flour and butter. Allow mixture to cool; add sugar, molasses, egg, raisins, ginger, cinnamon and baking soda. Spoon into an oiled 1 1/2-quart baking dish. Bake at 350° for 2 hours. Serve with cream and sugar. Makes 8 servings.

PENNSYLVANIA DUTCH SOFT CORNMEAL PRETZELS

1 1/2 c. warm water, 105°-115°	Additional cornmeal
2 envelopes dry yeast	12 c. water
1 T. plus 1 t. sugar, divided	2 T. baking soda
1/2 c. cornmeal	1 egg yolk beaten with
2 1/2 t. salt, divided	1 T. water for glaze
4 3/4 c. bread flour, divided	Coarse salt

Pour water into a large bowl. Sprinkle yeast and 1 tablespoon sugar over water; stir to blend. Let stand 10 minutes until yeast foams. Mix in cornmeal and 2 teaspoons salt. Using an electric mixer on low speed, mix in 4 1/2 cups flour, 1 cup at a time. Beat 3 minutes. Dough will be sticky. Turn dough out onto a board sprinkled with 1/4 cup of flour. Knead dough about 8 minutes until smooth and slightly sticky. Add more flour, a tablespoon at a time, if it is too sticky. Form dough into a ball; place in a buttered bowl, turning to coat. Cover bowl with a towel; let rise in a warm place until doubled in bulk, about 1 hour. Punch dough down; turn out onto a floured board. Knead briefly until smooth. Divide dough into 16 pieces. Roll 1 piece into a 15" rope. To form pretzel, pick up each end of rope and curve center of rope into circle. Cross ends twice, fold up over center of circle; press into opposite side of circle to adhere. (See diagram below.) Place pretzel on a baking sheet sprinkled with cornmeal. Repeat with remaining pieces of dough. Let pretzels rise, uncovered, about 20 minutes until almost doubled in bulk. Bring water to boil in a large pot. Place one rack in center and one in top third of oven; preheat to 375°. Butter two clean baking sheets; sprinkle with cornmeal. Add baking soda, remaining 1 teaspoon sugar and remaining 1/2 teaspoon salt to boiling water which will bubble up. Using a spatula, transfer four pretzels to boiling water; cook 30 seconds per side. Transfer pretzels to baking sheets. Brush with egg glaze; sprinkle with coarse salt. Bake 20 minutes, switching and turning baking sheets after 10 minutes. Pretzels should be golden brown. Transfer baking sheets to racks to cool. Makes 16 pretzels.

CORNMEAL PUFFS #1

1/2 c. cornmeal	2 stiffly beaten egg whites
1/2 c. boiling water	Vegetable oil for baking sheet
1/2 t. salt	

In a mixing bowl combine cornmeal, boiling water and salt. Cook and stir until mixture is consistency of thick mush. Fold in egg whites; drop by tablespoonfuls onto an oiled baking sheet. Bake at 350° for 30 minutes until puffed and golden. Makes 4 servings.

CORNMEAL PUFFS #2

2 c. boiling water	1 t. salt
1 c. cornmeal	2 beaten egg yolks
1 T. sugar	2 stiffly beaten egg whites
2 T. butter	Vegetable oil

In a mixing bowl pour boiling water over cornmeal. Add sugar, butter and salt. Cook and stir until mixture is consistency of thick mush. Cool and beat in egg yolks. Fold in egg whites. Heat oil in a Dutch oven. Drop cornmeal mixture by tablespoonfuls into hot oil. Cook until golden. Remove and allow to cool slightly. Makes 12 servings.

Cornmeal rolls have a delicious crunchiness and a delightful color. They are crisp on the outside and light and fluffy on the inside. They are especially good served with pork dishes.

CORNMEAL ROLLS #1

1/2 c. cornmeal	1 cake compressed yeast
1/4 c. shortening	1 egg
1 T. sugar	3 c. sifted flour
1 1/2 t. salt	1 egg white
1/2 c. scalded milk	Extra cornmeal
1/2 c. water	

Combine cornmeal, shortening, sugar and salt. Add milk cooled to lukewarm by adding water. Add yeast; mix well. Blend egg into mixture. Gradually add flour; mix until well blended. Let stand, covered for 15 minutes. On a well floured board, shape dough into 18 medium rolls. Dip rolls in egg white and then in cornmeal; place in oiled muffin pans. Let rise in a warm place, 85°-90°, until doubled in bulk, about 1 hour. Bake in a 400° oven for 20 minutes. Makes 18 servings.

CORNMEAL ROLLS #2

1 pkg. active dry yeast	2 3/4 c. flour
Pinch of sugar	2 t. coarse salt
1 1/4 c. water, lukewarm,	1 beaten egg
divided	Caraway seeds for sprinkling
1 c. cornmeal	Coarse salt for sprinkling

Combine yeast and sugar in 1/4 cup of water. Let stand for 10 minutes until mixture is foamy. Beat in remaining water, cornmeal, 2 1/4 cups flour and salt. Knead dough for 5 minutes; knead in remaining 1/2 cup flour. Dough should pull away from bowl but remain sticky. Place dough in a large bowl, dusted with flour; cover with plastic wrap. Let it rise in a warm place until it is doubled in bulk, about 1 1/2 hours. Punch down dough and let rise again in warm place about 1 1/2 hours. Punch down dough, knead it lightly on a lightly floured board; divide into 16 pieces. Form into rolls; place on greased baking sheet. Let rolls rise, uncovered, in a warm place until they are almost double in bulk, about 30 minutes. Brush rolls with egg and sprinkle with caraway seeds and salt. Preheat oven to 450°. Bake rolls in upper third of oven for 10-12 minutes or until they are golden brown. Makes 16 servings.

CORNMEAL ICE BOX ROLLS

1/2 c. shortening	1 cake yeast
2 c. scalded milk	1/4 c. warm water
1/2 c. cornmeal	2 beaten eggs
1/2 c. sugar	4 c. flour
1 t. salt	

Add shortening to milk. Sift cornmeal, sugar and salt; stir into milk. Allow to cool. Dissolve yeast in water; add to eggs. Add to cornmeal mixture and stir in flour. You may let it rise but it is not necessary. Put in refrigerator overnight. When ready to cook, roll out dough, cut into rolls; let rise until doubled. Bake in 400° oven on a lightly greased baking sheet for 15-20 minutes. Makes 24 servings.

CORNMEAL PARKER HOUSE ROLLS

1 1/4 c. flour	4 t. baking powder
1/2 c. milk	1/2 t. salt
3/4 c. cornmeal	2 T. melted shortening
2 eggs	

Combine flour, milk, cornmeal, eggs, baking powder and salt in a large mixing bowl. Turn out onto a floured board; roll or pat to 1/2" thickness. Cut with a biscuit cutter. Brush half each round with shortening. Fold over remaining half to make a half moon shape. Bake on a lightly greased baking sheet in a 450° oven for 15 minutes or until lightly browned. Makes 10 rolls.

CORNBREAD SALAD #1

12 cornbread muffins	2 diced tomatoes
1 c. chopped celery	Salt and pepper to taste
1 c. chopped green pepper	1/4 lb. bacon,
1 c. chopped onion	cooked and crumbled
1 c. mayonnaise	

In a large mixing bowl break up cornmeal muffins into pieces. Add celery, green peppers, onion and mayonnaise. Stir in tomatoes, salt and pepper. Sprinkle with bacon pieces. Makes 6 servings.

CORNBREAD SALAD #2

12 cornbread muffins	1/4 lb. bacon,
1 c. chopped onion	cooked and crumbled
1 c. chopped green pepper	3/4 c. sweet pickle relish
1 c. chopped celery	1 1/2 c. mayonnaise
5 chopped tomatoes	1 T. sugar

In a large mixing bowl break up cornbread muffins. Add onion, green pepper, celery, tomatoes and bacon. Mix together gently. In a separate bowl combine pickle relish, mayonnaise and sugar. Add to vegetable mixture; toss gently to combine. Chill overnight. Makes 12 servings.

CORNMEAL CHICKEN SALAD CASSEROLE

3 lbs. chicken breasts,
   skinless and boneless
6 c. water
1 t. salt
6 peppercorns

1 can cream of mushroom soup
1/4 c. mayonnaise
1 c. diced celery
1/4 c. minced onion
1/4 t. pepper
3/4 c. cornbread crumbs

Put chicken in a large stew pot with just enough water to cover. Add salt and peppercorns; bring to a boil. Lower heat, cover and simmer until chicken is cooked through, about 30 minutes. Remove from liquid. When cool enough to handle, dice meat. Mix chicken with soup, mayonnaise, celery, onion and pepper; place in a 1 1/2-quart casserole dish. Bake at 325° for 40 minutes. Cover with the cornbread crumbs; bake for 10 minutes longer. Makes 4 servings.

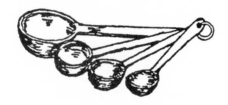

CORNMEAL FRIED CHICKEN SALAD

2 beaten eggs
1 T. Worcestershire sauce
1 T. Tabasco sauce
1 c. cornmeal
4 chicken breasts,
   skinless and boneless

Salt and pepper to taste
Vegetable oil for frying
2 red bell peppers
2 yellow bell peppers
4 c. mixed salad greens
Vinaigrette salad dressing

In a bowl combine eggs, Worcestershire sauce and Tabasco sauce. Put cornmeal on a shallow plate. Season chicken with salt and pepper. Dip chicken in egg mixture; coat with cornmeal. Heat oil in a deep skillet to 375°. Fry chicken until brown on both sides. Char peppers over flame of a gas burner or under a broiler. Remove skins, seeds and cut into strips. Arrange salad greens on 4 plates; add pepper strips. Slice chicken into strips; arrange on greens. Serve with vinaigrette dressing. Makes 4 servings.

CORNMEAL, OKRA AND POTATO SALAD

2 lbs. potatoes
1/2 lb. okra
1/2 c. cornmeal
Salt and pepper to taste
Vegetable oil for frying

1 1/2 T. cider vinegar
1 1/2 T. honey
3/4 c. mayonnaise
1 T. water
1 tomato

Quarter potatoes lengthwise and cut crosswise into 3/4" pieces. Cover with salted water in a saucepan. Bring to a boil; cook just until tender, about 30 minutes. Drain and return to pan over heat to dry out. Put in a large bowl and let them cool to room temperature. Trim okra; cut crosswise into 1/4" thick slices. In a bowl toss okra with cornmeal, salt and pepper. Heat 1" deep oil to 375° in a deep skillet. Fry okra, stirring, for 2 minutes or until golden brown. Drain on paper towels. Stir together vinegar, honey, mayonnaise, water, salt and pepper. Seed tomatoes; chop coarsely. Combine potatoes, okra, tomato and dressing. Makes 6 servings.

CORNMEAL SOUFFLÉ #1

1 c. milk
3/4 c. cornmeal
2 T. butter

1 t. salt
4 eggs, separated
Vegetable oil for baking dish

Preheat oven to 400°. In a saucepan bring milk to a simmer. Gradually pour in cornmeal and cook, stirring constantly, until thickened. Mix in butter and salt. Stir in egg yolks; set aside. In a small mixing bowl whip egg whites to soft-peak stage. Fold into cornmeal mixture. Spoon mixture into an oiled 2-quart soufflé dish. Bake for 25 minutes. Makes 6 servings.

CORNMEAL SOUFFLÉ #2

28-oz. pkg. frozen whole
    kernel corn, thawed
6 T. softened butter
2 eggs, separated
1/2 c. whipping cream
1 1/2 c. cornmeal

1 c. flour
1/3 c. sugar
1 T. baking powder
1 1/2 t. salt
Vegetable oil for skillet

Place corn in an electric blender and process until juicy. Put corn through a wire strainer into a 2-cup glass measuring cup to get 1 1/4 cups corn liquid. If you don't have enough liquid, add milk to get desired amount. In a mixing bowl use an electric mixer and beat butter and egg yolks on medium speed. Add corn liquid and whipping cream; mix well. In a mixing bowl combine cornmeal, flour, sugar, baking powder and salt. Add to corn liquid mixture; stir to blend. Whip egg whites to soft peaks and fold into batter. Preheat oven to 375°. Heat an oiled 10" cast iron skillet in hot oven. Pour cornmeal mixture into skillet; bake for 25 minutes until golden. Makes 8 servings.

CORNBREAD BUTTERMILK SOUP

4 c. crumbled cornbread	1/2 sm. red chili pepper, minced
5 c. buttermilk	1 1/2 t. vegetable oil
1/2 sm. onion, finely chopped	Milk
1 c. shredded cooked greens	Salt and pepper to taste

Combine cornbread and buttermilk in batches in electric blender. Process until as smooth as possible. Place in a saucepan; bring to a simmer. Cover and set aside. In a skillet cook onion, greens and chili in oil 5 minutes until well mixed. Reheat soup; add some milk if it is too thick. Season with salt and pepper; garnish with greens mixture. Makes 6 servings.

CORNMEAL, GARLIC AND SPINACH SOUP

6 c. chicken broth	2 c. chopped spinach leaves
3/4 c. cornmeal	1 c. milk
Salt and pepper to taste	1/4 t. grated nutmeg
4 cloves garlic, finely chopped	1 c. grated Gruyere cheese

Bring chicken broth to a boil; gradually stir in cornmeal until smooth. Add salt and pepper; cook over medium heat until it begins to thicken, about 20 minutes. Add garlic; when mixture thickens to mush, add spinach. Thin with milk. Sprinkle with nutmeg and serve with a bowl of cheese. Makes 6 servings.

CORNMEAL POTATO SOUP

1 qt. water	1 lge. onion, finely diced
1 qt. milk	1/2 c. cornmeal
6 lge. potatoes,	4 T. butter
pared and diced	Salt and pepper to taste
2 stalks celery, finely diced	

In a large soup pot combine water and milk over medium-high heat. Add potatoes, celery and onions. Add cornmeal; stir occasionally until potatoes are done and soup is as thick as you like. Season soup with butter, salt and pepper. Makes 8 servings.

SOFTSHELL TACO

1 c. flour	1 1/2 c. cold water
1/2 c. cornmeal	1 egg
1/2 t. salt	Vegetable oil for griddle

Combine flour, cornmeal, salt, water and egg. Pour batter onto a hot griddle brushed with oil. Cook until brown on the bottom; turn to cook on the other side. Serve with cooked ground beef, taco seasoning, grated cheese, lettuce and taco sauce. Makes 4 servings.

TORTILLAS #1

1 t. salt	1 c. cornmeal
1 c. boiling water	

Pour salted water over cornmeal; stir to combine. When batter is cool enough to handle, shape into thin flat cakes. Cook on an ungreased griddle, turning once until brown on both sides. Makes 8 servings.

TORTILLA #2

1 c. flour, sifted
1/2 c. cornmeal
1/4 t. salt

1 egg
1/2 c. cold water

Combine flour and cornmeal. Add salt and egg. Gradually add water, beating constantly. Drop batter by tablespoonfuls onto a hot unoiled griddle. Turn when edges start to curl. Cook on the other side. Do not brown. Makes 12 servings.

CORNMEAL TURNOVERS

1 1/2 c. sifted flour
1 T. sugar
1/2 t. salt
1/4 t. baking soda
2 t. baking powder
3/4 c. cornmeal

1 beaten egg
2 T. melted shortening
1/2 c. buttermilk
Melted butter
Vegetable oil for baking sheet

Sift flour, sugar, salt, baking soda and baking powder into a mixing bowl. Add cornmeal and mix. Add egg, shortening and buttermilk; mix well. Turn out onto a lightly floured board and pat into a half inch thickness. Cut out with a round cookie cutter. Brush with melted butter; fold over. Place on an oiled baking sheet and bake at 450° for 10 minutes. Makes 8 servings.

CORNMEAL WAFERS #1

3/4 c. boiling water
1 t. salt
2/3 c. cornmeal
1 t. sugar

2 T. butter
Grated sharp Cheddar cheese
Vegetable oil for baking sheet

Pour boiling salted water over cornmeal, sugar and butter in a medium mixing bowl. Stir to blend well. Drop by teaspoonfuls onto an oiled baking sheet, leaving room for batter to spread. Sprinkle with cheese; bake at 425° for 10 minutes until golden. Let stand to crisp; remove to a wire rack to cool. Makes 12 wafers.

CORNMEAL WAFERS #2

1/4 c. softened butter	3 T. cornmeal
2 t. sugar	1 T. flour
1 egg white	2 T. grated Parmesan cheese
1/2 t. salt	Vegetable oil for baking sheet

Preheat oven to 425°. In a mixing bowl cream butter and sugar until fluffy with an electric mixer. Add egg white and salt; beat on low speed until mixture is just combined, about 5 seconds. Add cornmeal, flour and Parmesan cheese; stir until just combined. Cover and chill overnight. Drop by teaspoonfuls 3" apart on an oiled baking sheet. Flatten with a fork to make 2" rounds. Bake for 6 minutes until edges are golden. Cool on a wire rack. Makes 12 wafers.

CORNMEAL WAFERS #3

1/4 c. cornmeal	1 beaten egg
1/4 c. flour	6 T. milk
3/4 t. baking powder	1 T. shortening, softened
1/2 t. sugar	Vegetable oil for baking sheet
1/2 t. salt	

Preheat oven to 450°. In a mixing bowl, combine cornmeal, flour, baking powder, sugar and salt. Mix in egg, milk and shortening. Stir until well combined. Spread mixture in an oiled 9" cake pan and bake for 15 minutes until golden. Invert onto a cutting board and cut into wedges. Makes 12 servings.

Made with all natural ingredients, pets love these homemade dog biscuits. Even better, they are good for your canine and your canine's canines. A tin of these, along with a recipe, makes an excellent gift for a fellow dog owner. Specialty cooking stores have cookie cutters shaped like bones for sale.

CORNMEAL DOG BISCUITS #1

3 1/2 c. flour	1 T. salt
2 c. whole-wheat flour	1 pkg. dry yeast dissolved in
1 c. rye flour	1/4 c. warm water
1 c. cornmeal	1 pint warmed chicken stock
2 c. cracked wheat	1 beaten egg mixed with
1/2 c. nonfat dry milk	1 T. milk

Preheat oven to 300°. Combine flour, whole-wheat flour, rye flour, cornmeal, cracked wheat, dry milk and salt. Add yeast, stock and egg mixture; mix well. Knead about 3 minutes to make a stiff dough. Roll out on a lightly floured board to 1/4" thickness. Use a cookie cutter or knife to cut out biscuits. Place on baking sheet sprayed with vegetable cooking spray. Bake for 35 minutes. Turn off oven and leave in oven overnight. Makes 50.

CORNMEAL DOG BISCUITS #2

5 1/2 c. whole-wheat flour	2 c. chicken stock
1 c. cornmeal	1 1/2 c. nonfat dry milk, recon-
2 c. cracked wheat	stituted
1 T. salt	6 eggs, beaten
1 pkg. dry yeast dissolved in	1 c. chicken fat
1/2 c. warm water	

Preheat oven to 300°. Combine flour, cornmeal, cracked wheat and salt in a mixing bowl. Put dissolved yeast in a medium bowl; add stock, milk, eggs and chicken fat. Pour into flour mixture. Knead into a stiff dough, about 3 minutes. Roll out on a lightly floured board to 1/4" thick. Cut out with a cookie cutter or knife. Place on baking sheets sprayed with vegetable cooking spray. Bake for 45 minutes. Turn off oven and leave biscuits in oven overnight to harden. Makes 50.

HOW TO MAKE SELF-RISING CORNMEAL

4 c. cornmeal   2 t. salt
2 T. baking powder

Combine cornmeal, baking powder and salt and store in a tightly covered container. Use in any recipe that calls for self-rising cornmeal.

Cornbread Specialties

BACON CORNBREAD #1

2 slices bacon, diced
1 c. flour
3 t. baking powder
1/2 t. salt
1 c. cornmeal

1 t. sugar
1 beaten egg
1 c. milk
Vegetable oil for baking pan

Preheat oven to 450°. In a cast iron skillet cook bacon until crisp. Remove and drain on paper towels. Sift flour, measure and sift again with baking powder and salt. Add cornmeal and sugar. In a mixing bowl combine egg, milk and bacon pieces. Add cornmeal mixture; stir to combine. Pour batter into an oiled 8x8x2" baking pan; bake for 20 minutes. Makes 10 servings.

BACON CORNBREAD #2

1/4 lb. sliced bacon, diced
1 c. flour
1 c. cornmeal
1/2 t. salt
1 t. sugar

2 t. baking powder
2 beaten eggs
1 c. milk, divided
1 c. fresh corn kernels

Preheat oven to 425°. Using a cast iron skillet fry bacon over medium heat until it is crisp. Remove to paper towels, leaving drippings in skillet. In a mixing bowl combine flour, cornmeal, salt, sugar and baking powder. Add eggs and half cup milk; stir mixture until smooth. Add remaining half cup milk, corn and bacon pieces. Stir to combine; pour into skillet on top of bacon drippings. Bake for 20 minutes. Makes 8 servings.

CAMPSTYLE CORNBREAD

These recipes can be used if you are cooking on an open fire. They can be used for baking cakes also.

CORNBREAD COOKED IN A DUTCH OVEN

2 c. cornmeal
1 c. flour
1 c. buttermilk

1 t. salt
1 t. baking soda
Vegetable oil for oven

Preheat the Dutch oven and lid over the coals of an open fire. When hot, carefully oil the entire inside of oven. Sprinkle bottom and sides of oven with cornmeal. Mix batter by combining cornmeal, flour, buttermilk, salt and baking soda; pour batter into Dutch oven. Make sure that it is level over fire, and using tongs, place lid on oven. Cover lid with some hot coals. Bake for 20 minutes; time will depend on how hot the coals are. When cornbread is brown, remove by turning oven on its side and sliding cornbread out. It may also be cut right in the oven. Makes 6 servings.

CORNBREAD COOKED IN A HOMEMADE OVEN

To Make An Outdoor Oven you will need:

1-case cardboard liquor box
Heavy duty aluminum foil
Duct tape

4 wire coat hangers
Charcoal briquettes
A shovel

To make oven, remove the top lid flaps of the box and discard. Cut out bottom of the box in one piece and save. Cover inside of box with foil, making sure it is completely covered. Tape foil to edges with duct tape. Bend coat hangers to make a rack that will hold a skillet in the middle of the oven. Cover the bottom piece of the box with foil to make a lid for the oven. Seal edges with tape. Using a shovel, place several hot charcoal briquettes on a piece of foil. Put oven over fire; put in rack and place skillet on rack. Cover with lid.

To make outdoor cornbread you will need:

3/4 c. milk	2 beaten eggs
1/4 c. vegetable oil,	1 T. salt
preheated in outdoor oven	1 c. self-rising cornmeal

In a bowl combine milk, oil, eggs, salt and cornmeal. Pour into hot oiled 8"
cast iron skillet. Place skillet on rack, cover with foil-covered oven. Put foil-
covered lid on top of box. Bake for 20 minutes until brown. Do not remove
lid before this time is up or heat will escape from oven. Makes 6 servings.

CORNMEAL BISCUITS #1

1/2 c. flour	3/4 c. yellow cornmeal
1 t. salt	2 T. shortening
1/2 t. baking powder	1 beaten egg
1/2 t. baking soda	3/4 c. milk

Preheat oven to 425°. Sift together flour, salt, baking powder and baking soda.
Stir in cornmeal. Using a pastry blender cut in shortening. Add egg and milk.
Mix just until flour is moistened. Drop from a spoon onto a greased baking
sheet. Bake for 15 minutes until golden brown. Makes 6 servings.

CORNMEAL BISCUITS #2

3/4 c. scalded milk	1 t. salt
1 c. cornmeal	3/4 c. sifted flour
2 1/2 T. shortening	4 t. baking powder

Preheat oven to 425°. Pour milk over cornmeal. Cut in shortening and salt.
Allow mixture to cool. Add sifted flour and baking powder. Stir to combine;
roll out on a floured board. Cut with a floured biscuit cutter and bake on a
greased baking sheet for 15 minutes until golden brown. Makes 8 servings.

CORNMEAL CHEESE BISCUITS #1

1 1/4 c. flour
1/2 c. yellow cornmeal
3 t. baking powder
1/2 t. salt

1/3 c. grated sharp cheese
1/4 c. shortening
1/2 c. milk

Preheat oven to 450°. Sift flour into a bowl. Add cornmeal, baking powder and salt; combine. Cut in cheese and shortening until mixture resembles coarse meal. Add milk; stir until well mixed. If dough is too dry, add an additional 1/4 cup milk. Gather into a ball; place dough on a floured board. Knead 6 times and roll out 1/2" thick. Cut with a floured biscuit cutter; place on an ungreased baking sheet. Bake for 12 minutes or until golden brown. Makes 6 biscuits.

CORNMEAL CHEESE BISCUITS #2

1 c. self-rising flour
1 c. self-rising cornmeal
1/3 c. butter or margarine

1 c. shredded Monterey Jack cheese
   with peppers
3/4 c. buttermilk
Melted butter or margarine

Preheat oven to 425°. Combine flour and cornmeal. Cut butter and cheese into dry mixture until it is crumbly. Add buttermilk; stir until mixture is moistened. Gather into a ball, turn out onto a lightly floured board. Knead 4 times and roll dough to 3/4" thickness. Cut out with floured biscuit cutter; place on an ungreased baking sheet. Bake for 14 minutes until golden brown. Brush with melted butter. Makes 10 biscuits.

CORNMEAL CHEESE BISCUITS #3

5 T. sesame seeds, divided	1 1/4 sticks cold butter,
2 1/2 c. unbleached flour	cut into small pieces
4 t. baking powder	1 1/2 c. buttermilk
1 T. sugar	1 1/2 t. dried rubbed sage
3/4 t. salt	1 t. dried thyme
1/2 t. baking soda	2 c. grated extra sharp cheese
1/2 c. yellow cornmeal	Additional buttermilk

Preheat oven to 450°. In a small cast iron skillet stir sesame seeds over medium heat for 2 minutes or until golden. Cool. Sift flour, baking powder, sugar, salt and baking soda into a large bowl. Add cornmeal and three tablespoons sesame seed. Stir to blend. Cut in butter until mixture resembles coarse meal. In a medium bowl mix buttermilk, sage and thyme. Add to dry mixture; stir to blend well. Mix in cheese. Gather dough into a ball. It will be sticky. Turn dough out onto a generously floured board. Knead 8 times, adding more flour if dough is too sticky. Roll out dough to 3/4" thickness; cut out with a floured biscuit cutter. Place on an ungreased baking sheet. Brush with buttermilk and sprinkle with sesame seeds. Bake in middle of oven for 16 minutes until golden brown. Makes 24 biscuits.

CORNMEAL CHILI BISCUITS

1 c. fresh corn kernels	1/2 t. salt
1 clove garlic, minced	1/4 c. sour cream
6 T. butter, divided	4-oz. can whole,
1 1/2 c. flour	roasted, peeled chilies
1/4 c. yellow cornmeal	1 1/2 c. Monterey Jack cheese,
4 t. baking powder	chilled and grated
1 T. sugar	1 beaten egg

In a small pan over low heat sauté corn and garlic in two tablespoons of the butter for 5 minutes. Set aside. Preheat oven to 425°. Using a large mixing bowl sift flour, cornmeal, baking powder, sugar and salt. Cut the remaining 4 tablespoons butter into pieces. Using a pastry blender cut the butter into the dry mixture until it resembles coarse meal. Seed, rinse and drain the chilies.

Stir in the sour cream, chilies, cheese, corn and garlic. Turn dough out onto a lightly floured board. Working quickly, roll out dough to 1/2" thickness. Cut out with a floured biscuit cutter; place on a lightly greased baking sheet. Brush tops with beaten egg and bake on the middle rack of the oven for 12 minutes until golden brown. Makes 24 biscuits.

CORNMEAL SAGE BISCUITS

1 1/4 c. flour	3/4 t. dried sage
3/4 c. yellow cornmeal	1/4 c. butter
2 t. baking powder	2/3 c. apple juice
1/4 t. baking soda	1 lightly beaten egg white
1/8 t. pepper	

Preheat oven to 425°. Combine flour, cornmeal, baking powder, baking soda, pepper and sage. Cut in butter with a pastry blender until the size of peas. Gradually stir in apple juice until dough is moistened and pulls away from the sides of the bowl. Dough will be sticky. Turn dough out onto a generously floured board; pat gently until 3/4" thick. Fold in thirds, pat out and fold in thirds again. Roll out dough 1/2" thick. Cut with a floured biscuit cutter. Arrange biscuits, barely touching, on an ungreased baking sheet. Brush tops with egg white. Bake for 16 minutes until lightly browned. Makes 14 biscuits.

CHEESE CORNBREAD #1

Vegetable oil for mold	2 beaten eggs
1 c. flour	1 c. milk
1 c. cornmeal	2 c. shredded sharp Cheddar cheese
1 T. baking powder	
2 T. salt	

Preheat oven to 425°. Place an oiled 1 1/2-quart ring mold in oven. Sift flour, cornmeal, baking powder and salt into a mixing bowl. Add eggs, milk and cheese; stir just until blended. Pour batter into hot mold; bake for 20 minutes. Let cool slightly; unmold onto a platter. Center may be filled with creamed chicken or vegetables. Makes 6 servings.

CHEESE CORNBREAD #2

1 1/4 c. cornmeal	2 beaten eggs
3/4 c. flour	1/4 c. melted butter, cooled
1 T. baking powder	3/4 c. milk
1/2 t. baking soda	1/2 c. sour cream
1 t. salt	1/2 c. grated Cheddar cheese
Pinch of cayenne pepper	1 1/4 c. fresh corn kernels
2 t. honey	Vegetable oil for baking dish

Preheat oven to 400°. In a mixing bowl combine cornmeal, flour, baking powder, baking soda, salt and cayenne pepper. In another bowl stir together honey, eggs, butter, milk and sour cream. Add to cornmeal mixture; mix well. Fold in cheese and corn. Spoon batter into an oiled 13x9x2" baking dish; bake for 30 minutes. Makes 10 servings.

CHEESE CORNBREAD #3

1/3 c. cornmeal	1 t. salt
1 T. butter	1/4 t. paprika
2 c. scalded milk	Pinch of cayenne pepper
2 T. grated sharp	3 beaten egg yolks
Cheddar cheese	3 egg whites

In a saucepan, stir cornmeal and butter into hot milk. Reduce heat and stir in cheese. Cook until mixture is the consistency of mush. Stir in salt, paprika and cayenne pepper. Add egg yolks, one at a time, beating well after each addition to prevent curdling. Cook and stir 1 minute longer to permit the yolks to thicken. Remove from heat; cool. Whip egg whites until stiff; fold into batter. Pour batter into a 8" square ungreased baking dish. Bake at 350° for 25 minutes until crusty. Bits of ham or seafood may be added to batter. Serve as a main dish with egg, tomato, mushroom or brown sauce. Makes 6 servings.

CHEESE CORNBREAD #4

1 c. self-rising cornmeal
1 c. sour cream
1/2 c. grated
   Cheddar cheese

1/2 c. vegetable oil
2 beaten eggs
1 c. cream-style corn
Vegetable oil for baking pan

Preheat oven to 400°. Combine cornmeal, sour cream and cheese. Add oil, eggs and corn. Spoon batter into an oiled 8x8x2" pan; bake for 30 minutes until golden. Makes 8 servings.

CHEESE CORNBREAD #5

3/4 c. flour
1/2 c. cornmeal
1 1/4 t. baking powder
1 t. sugar
1/2 t. salt
Pinch of cayenne pepper
3 T. cold butter, cut into bits

3/4 c. plus 2 T. grated sharp
   Cheddar cheese, divided
1 egg, separated
1/2 c. milk
Vegetable oil for baking sheet

Preheat oven to 425°. In a mixing bowl combine flour, cornmeal, baking powder, sugar, salt and cayenne pepper. Stir in butter until mixture resembles coarse meal. Add 3/4 cup cheese; mix well. In another bowl mix together egg yolk and milk. Add to cornmeal mixture; stir until it forms a soft dough. Turn dough out onto a lightly floured board; knead gently 8 times. Pat dough into a 6" round and cut into 6 wedges. Arrange wedges 2" apart on an oiled baking sheet; brush with lightly beaten egg white. Sprinkle each wedge with 1 teaspoon cheese; bake for 15 minutes until golden. Makes 6 servings.

CHEESE CORNBREAD #6

2 c. water
1 1/4 t. salt
1 1/2 c. cornmeal

1 c. grated Edam cheese
Vegetable oil for frying

In a saucepan combine water and salt; heat to boiling. Gradually stir in cornmeal; cook 5 minutes, stirring constantly. When mixture separates from the bottom and sides of pan remove from heat; stir in cheese. When mixture is cool enough to handle, shape into balls, 1 heaping tablespoon at a time. Roll each ball into a small cylinder about 1/2" thick. Heat oil to 375° in a heavy skillet. Drop sticks into hot oil and cook until golden; drain on paper towels. Makes 10 servings.

CHEESE CORNBREAD #7

2 c. cornmeal	1/2 c. sour cream
3/4 c. flour	2 beaten eggs
2 t. baking powder	2 c. milk
1/2 t. baking soda	6 T. melted butter
1/2 t. sugar	Vegetable oil for baking dish
3 c. crumbled Feta cheese	

Preheat oven to 375°. Sift cornmeal, flour, baking powder, baking soda and sugar into a mixing bowl. In another bowl mix together cheese, sour cream, eggs, milk and butter. Add to cornmeal mixture; combine well. Cover bowl with plastic wrap and set aside for 15 minutes. Spoon batter into an oiled 13x9x2" baking dish; bake for 40 minutes until golden brown. Makes 8 servings.

CHEESE CORNBREAD #8

2 T. bacon drippings	1 c. milk
1 c. flour	1 egg
1 c. cornmeal	5 oz. grated Gouda cheese
1 T. baking powder	1/4 c. finely chopped green onions
1 T. salt	

Preheat oven to 375°. Heat bacon drippings in a 10" cast iron skillet for 10 minutes. In a mixing bowl stir together flour, cornmeal, baking powder and salt. In another bowl combine milk and egg, mixing well. Add to cornmeal mixture, stirring just until moistened. Fold in cheese and onions, Add drippings from skillet to batter; stir to blend. Spoon batter into skillet; bake for 20 minutes. Makes 8 servings.

CHEESE CORNBREAD #9

1/2 c. cornmeal
1 1/4 t. baking powder
1/2 t. salt
1/4 c. vegetable oil
1/2 c. sour cream
1/2 c. fresh corn kernels

4-oz. can chopped mild green
   chilies, drained
1 beaten egg
1/2 c. grated Monterey Jack cheese
1 T. vegetable oil for skillet

Preheat oven to 400°.   In a mixing bowl combine cornmeal, baking powder and salt. Add oil, sour cream, corn, chilies, egg and cheese. Stir just until blended. Heat oil in a 9" cast iron skillet until hot. Pour into batter; stir to combine. Spoon batter into hot skillet; bake for 30 minutes until golden brown. Makes 4 servings.

CHEESE CORNBREAD #10

1 c. cornmeal
1/2 c. flour
1 T. sugar
2 t. baking powder
1 t. baking soda
1/2 t. salt
Pinch of cayenne pepper

1 c. buttermilk
4 T. melted butter
1 egg
1/2 c. diced Munster cheese
1/2 c. fresh corn kernels
1 T. grated Parmesan cheese
Vegetable oil for baking pan

Preheat oven to 375°. Sift cornmeal, flour, sugar, baking powder, baking soda, salt and cayenne pepper into a mixing bowl. In another bowl, combine buttermilk, butter and egg. Add to cornmeal mixture, stirring just until moistened. Stir in Munster cheese and corn. Spoon batter into an oiled 9x9x2" baking pan. Sprinkle with Parmesan cheese; bake for 25 minutes until golden. Makes 8 servings.

CORNMEAL BATTER BREAD #1

1 c. cornmeal	2 beaten eggs
1 1/4 c. boiling water	1 c. buttermilk
1/2 t. salt	1/2 t. baking soda
1 T. butter	Vegetable oil for baking dish

Place cornmeal in a mixing bowl. Scald cornmeal by slowly pouring boiling water over. Stir constantly to prevent lumps. Add salt and butter. When butter has melted, mix well; allow to cool slightly. In another bowl stir eggs with buttermilk and baking soda. Add to cornmeal mixture and stir well. Pour mixture into an oiled baking dish. Bake at 450° for 40 minutes until mixture is set. Makes 6 servings.

CORNMEAL BATTER BREAD #2

1/2 c. cornmeal	1 t. salt
2 c. milk	3 beaten eggs
3 T. butter	Vegetable oil for baking dish

In a saucepan cook cornmeal and milk together to the boiling point, stirring constantly. Mix in butter and salt; allow to cool. Add eggs and mix well. Pour into an oiled baking dish; bake at 350° for 40 minutes. Makes 6 servings.

BOURBON CORNBREAD

2 c. milk	1/8 t. rosemary
1 c. cornmeal	1/8 t. oregano
1 c. softened butter	5 eggs, separated
1/2 t. salt	1 1/2 T. bourbon
1 T. sugar	Vegetable oil for loaf pan
1/8 t. thyme	

Preheat oven to 350°. In a saucepan scald the milk. Add cornmeal; cook over low heat, stirring constantly, until thick. Remove from heat. Add butter, salt, sugar, thyme, rosemary and oregano; stir until butter has melted. Allow to cool. In another bowl beat egg yolks; stir into cornmeal mixture with bourbon. In a small bowl whip egg whites until stiff peaks form. Fold into corn-meal mixture. Spoon into an oiled loaf pan; bake for 40 minutes until gold-en. Makes 8 servings.

BRAN FLAKES CORNBREAD

1 c. sifted flour	3/4 c. bran flakes
1/2 c. sifted cornmeal	1 beaten egg
3 T. sugar	1 c. milk
1 T baking powder	3 T. butter
1/2 t. salt	

Preheat oven to 425°. Sift flour, cornmeal, sugar, baking powder and salt into a mixing bowl. Mix in bran flakes. In another bowl combine egg and milk. Add to cornmeal mixture; stir just to blend. Melt butter in oven in an 8x8x2" baking pan. Add butter to batter. Pour batter into pan; bake for 20 minutes. Makes 8 servings.

BROWN SUGAR CORNBREAD #1

1 c. sifted flour	1/4 c. melted shortening
3/4 t. baking soda	2 T. brown sugar
1 t. salt	2 beaten eggs
1 t. baking powder	1 1/2 c. buttermilk
1 c. cornmeal	Vegetable oil for baking pan

Preheat oven to 425°. Sift flour, baking soda, salt and baking powder into a mixing bowl. Add cornmeal; stir to mix. In another bowl combine shorten-ing, brown sugar and eggs. Add buttermilk; stir to combine. Add to cornmeal mixture and beat until smooth. Pour into an oiled 9x9x2" baking pan; bake for 30 minutes. Makes 8 servings.

BROWN SUGAR CORNBREAD #2

1 c. self-rising cornmeal
1 c. self-rising flour
1 1/2 c. milk
1/4 c. buttermilk

2 beaten eggs
2 T. brown sugar
Vegetable oil for skillet

In a mixing bowl combine cornmeal, flour, milk, buttermilk, eggs and brown sugar. Mix well; pour into an oiled 9" cast iron skillet. Bake at 450° for 25 minutes. Makes 9 servings.

CARAWAY CORNBREAD

1 c. flour
3/4 c. cornmeal
1 T. sugar
2 t. baking powder
1 t. salt
1/4 t. baking soda

2 t. caraway seeds, divided
2 eggs
1 c. milk
1/3 c. sour cream
5 T. melted butter, cooled
Vegetable oil for baking pan

Preheat oven to 425°. In a mixing bowl combine flour, cornmeal, sugar, baking powder, salt, baking soda and 1 teaspoon caraway seeds. In another bowl mix together eggs, milk, sour cream and butter. Add to cornmeal mixture; stir until just combined. Spread batter in an oiled 8x8x2" pan; sprinkle with remaining caraway seeds. Bake for 20 minutes. Cool in pan on a wire rack for 5 minutes. Makes 6 servings.

COTTAGE CHEESE CORNBREAD

1 c. cornmeal
3/4 c. milk
1/2 c. creamed cottage cheese
2 eggs

1 t. salt
1 t. baking powder
1/2 t. baking soda
Vegetable oil for baking pan

Preheat oven to 425°. In a mixing bowl combine cornmeal, milk, cottage cheese, eggs, salt, baking powder and baking soda. Mix well; pour batter into an oiled 8x8x2" baking pan and bake for 20-25 minutes until golden. Makes 16 servings.

COUSH-COUSH #1

2 c. cornmeal	3 beaten eggs
2 t. baking powder	1 1/2 c. scalded milk
1/2 t. salt	1 T. bacon drippings

In a mixing bowl combine cornmeal, baking powder and salt. Add eggs; mix well. Add scalded milk; stir to combine. Heat an 8" cast iron skillet; melt bacon drippings until hot but not smoking. Pour cornmeal mixture into hot skillet; cook 5 minutes. Scrape from the bottom with a spatula, reduce heat and invert another hot skillet on top and steam 10 minutes longer until completely cooked. Serve with bacon or hash. Makes 8 servings.

COUSH-COUSH #2

2 c. cornmeal	2 t. salt
1/2 c. flour	1 1/2 c. water
1 T. baking powder	8 T. shortening
2 T. sugar	

In a mixing bowl combine cornmeal, flour, baking powder, sugar and salt. Add water; stir until smooth and thick. Melt shortening in a 10" cast iron skillet over medium heat until hot but not smoking. Spoon cornmeal mixture into hot skillet and pat it flat. Increase heat to high and fry cornmeal mixture until it is brown and crusty on bottom, about 10 minutes. Stir the cornmeal mixture, reduce heat to low, cover skillet; cook for 15 minutes longer. Serve with milk and sugar or syrup. Makes 10 servings.

Cracklings are the crisp, brown pork bits that are left after pork has been rendered. Cooked crisp bacon, crumbled, may be substituted in the recipes. They may be cooked in baked cakes or in skillet cornbread. Good to serve with a "mess of greens."

CRACKLIN' CORNBREAD #1

3 c. boiling water	1/4 t. salt
1 1/2 c. cornmeal	1 c. cracklings

Pour water over cornmeal; add salt. Set aside to cool. When mixture is cool enough to handle, mix in cracklings. Shape into cakes and place on a well oiled baking pan. Bake at 400° for 25-30 minutes. Makes 6 servings.

CRACKLIN' CORNBREAD #2

Vegetable oil for skillet	2 beaten eggs
1 c. cornmeal	1 c. buttermilk
1 c. flour	1/4 c. vegetable oil
1 t. baking soda	1 c. cracklings
1 t. salt	

Preheat oven to 450°. Place a well oiled 10" cast iron skillet in oven and heat until hot. Combine cornmeal, flour, baking soda and salt. Add eggs, buttermilk and oil to cornmeal mixture. Stir just until moistened. Stir in cracklings. Pour batter into hot skillet; bake 35 minutes until golden brown. Makes 8 servings.

CRANBERRY CORNBREAD

1 c. dried cranberries, packed
1/4 c. orange juice
Vegetable oil for baking pan
1 c. flour
1 c. cornmeal
2 t. baking powder
1 1/4 t. salt
1 t. ground cardamon

1/2 t. baking soda
2 beaten eggs
1 1/2 c. sour cream
1/3 c. maple syrup
6 T. melted butter, cooled
2 t. orange peel, grated and packed
1/2 c. chopped pecans

In a small bowl combine cranberries and orange juice. Let stand for 30 minutes until cranberries soften slightly. Drain and discard juice. Preheat oven to 400°. Oil a 10" springform pan and wrap outside with foil wrap. In a mixing bowl combine flour, cornmeal, baking powder, salt, cardamon and baking soda. In another bowl mix together eggs, sour cream, maple syrup, butter and orange peel. Add sour cream mixture to cornmeal mixture; stir just until blended. Fold in pecans and cranberries. Spoon batter into prepared pan. Bake for 35 minutes Cool completely on a wire rack in pan. Makes 12 servings.

CORNMEAL CRANBERRY BREAD

1 c. coarsely chopped cranberries
1/2 c. plus 2 T. sugar, divided
1 1/2 c. flour
1 c. cornmeal
2 t. baking powder
1 t. baking soda

1/2 t. salt
2 beaten eggs
1 c. sour cream
3 T. melted butter
1 T. fresh lime juice
Vegetable oil for baking pan

Preheat oven to 375°. In a small bowl combine cranberries and 2 tablespoons sugar; set aside for 20 minutes. In a medium bowl combine flour, cornmeal, 1/2 cup sugar, baking powder, baking soda and salt. In a large bowl combine eggs, sour cream, butter and lime juice. Add cornmeal mixture; stir just until combined. Fold in cranberry mixture. Pour batter into an oiled 9x9x2" baking pan. Bake 35 minutes; cool on a wire rack for 10 minutes. Remove from pan. Makes 16 servings.

CUMIN CORNBREAD #1

3/4 c. flour	1 c. milk
1 c. cornmeal	1 beaten egg
1 T. sugar	1 T. melted butter, cooled
1 1/2 t. baking powder	2 t. cumin seed
1/2 t. salt	Vegetable oil for baking pan

Preheat oven to 425°. In a mixing bowl combine flour, cornmeal, sugar, baking powder and salt. Add milk, egg, butter and cumin seed; stir to combine. Spoon batter in an even layer in an oiled 8x8x2" pan. Bake for 25 minutes until golden. Makes 6 servings.

CUMIN CORNBREAD #2

1 1/2 c. cornmeal	1 c. thinly sliced green onion
1 c. flour	2 eggs
2 t. baking powder	1 c. milk
1/2 t. baking soda	2 T. sugar
1 t. salt	1/4 c. olive oil
2 t. ground cumin	Vegetable oil for baking pan
1 1/2 c. crumbled Feta cheese	

Preheat oven to 350°. Using a large mixing bowl sift together cornmeal, flour, baking powder, baking soda, salt and cumin. Add cheese and green onion; mix thoroughly. In another bowl combine eggs, milk, sugar and oil; add to cornmeal mixture. Stir just until combined. Pour batter into an oiled 9x5x3" loaf pan; bake for 50 minutes. Cool in pan on a wire rack for 5 minutes. Turn out onto the rack and cool completely. Makes 8 servings.

CUSTARD CORNBREAD

1 c. flour	2 beaten egg yolks
1/2 t. salt	1 1/2 c. buttermilk
1 t. baking powder	1/4 c. melted butter, cooled
1/2 t. baking soda	2 egg whites, at room temperature
1 c. cornmeal	1 3/4 c. milk
2 T. brown sugar, firmly packed	Vegetable oil for baking dish

Preheat oven to 425°. Sift flour, salt, baking powder and baking soda into a mixing bowl. Mix in cornmeal and brown sugar. In another bowl mix together egg yolks and buttermilk just until combined. Add to cornmeal mixture. Stir in butter just until combined. In a small bowl whip egg whites until stiff peaks form. Stir in one fourth the egg whites, then fold in remaining egg whites into the cornmeal mixture. Pour batter into an oiled 8x8x2" baking dish. Carefully pour milk over the top, stirring slightly on top of mixture. Bake for 30 minutes until set. Makes 8 servings.

CORNMEAL FRITTERS #1

1 c. flour	3 eggs
1 c. cornmeal	1/2 c. milk
2 t. baking powder	Powdered sugar
1/4 t. salt	Vegetable oil for Dutch oven
1/4 c. molasses	

Sift flour, cornmeal, baking powder and salt into a mixing bowl. Add molasses, eggs and milk; mix well. Drop by tablespoonfuls into hot oil in a Dutch oven. Cook until golden brown, turning once. Drain on paper towels and roll in powdered sugar. Makes 8 servings.

CORNMEAL FRITTERS #2

1 c. flour	1 beaten egg
1 c. cornmeal	1 c. milk
2 t. baking powder	Vegetable oil for Dutch oven
3/4 t. salt	

In a mixing bowl combine flour, cornmeal, baking powder and salt. Stir in egg and milk to make a stiff batter. Drop by tablespoonfuls into hot oil in a Dutch oven. Cook until golden brown, turning once. Drain on paper towels. Makes 8 servings.

HOMINY CORNBREAD

1 c. canned hominy, drained
1 T. melted shortening
2 beaten eggs
1 c. milk

1/2 c. cornmeal
1/2 t. salt
1 t. baking powder
Vegetable oil for baking pan

In a mixing bowl combine hominy, shortening, eggs and milk. Add cornmeal, salt and baking powder. Stir to mix; let stand for 5 minutes. Pour batter into an oiled 9x9x2" pan; bake at 425° for 35 minutes until golden. Makes 6 servings.

BAKED CORNMEAL JOHNNYCAKES #1

1/4 c. shortening
1/4 c. sugar
1 c. flour
1/2 c. cornmeal
4 t. baking powder

1/2 t. baking soda
1 beaten egg
1 c. sour cream
Vegetable oil for baking pan

Preheat oven to 375°. Cream shortening and sugar. Sift together flour, cornmeal, baking powder and baking soda. In another bowl combine egg and sour cream. Add to cornmeal mixture, then add shortening mixture. Mix only until moistened. Spoon batter into an oiled 8x8x2" baking pan. Bake for 25 minutes. Cool in pan on a wire rack. Makes 12 servings.

BAKED CORNMEAL JOHNNYCAKES #2

2 c. cornmeal
1/2 t. salt
1 t. baking soda
1/2 c. butter, chilled
   and cut into pieces

1 c. buttermilk
1/2 c. molasses
Vegetable oil for baking pan

Preheat oven to 400°. Sift cornmeal, salt and soda together until well blended. Cut butter into cornmeal mixture with a pastry blender until mixture resembles coarse meal. Mix together buttermilk and molasses; stir into cornmeal mixture. Pour batter into an oiled and floured 8x8x2" baking pan. Bake for 30 minutes. Makes 8 servings.

CORN KERNEL CORNBREAD #1

3 eggs
1 c. sour cream
1/2 c. vegetable oil
8 1/4-oz. can cream-style corn

1/2 t. salt
1 T. baking powder
1 c. cornmeal
Vegetable oil for skillet

Preheat oven to 375°. In a mixing bowl combine eggs, sour cream, oil and corn. Add salt, baking powder and cornmeal. Mix well; pour into an oiled 9" cast iron skillet and bake for 35 minutes. Makes 8 servings.

CORN KERNEL CORNBREAD #2

2 beaten eggs
8-oz. can cream-style corn
1 c. sour cream

1/2 c. vegetable oil
1 c. self-rising cornmeal
Vegetable oil for skillet

Preheat oven to 400°. In a mixing bowl combine eggs, corn, sour cream, oil and cornmeal. Pour batter into an oiled preheated 8" cast iron skillet. Bake for 20 minutes until golden. Makes 6 servings.

MAPLE SYRUP CORNBREAD

1 1/8 c. cornmeal
1 1/8 c. whole-wheat flour
3 t. baking powder
1/2 t. salt
1 beaten egg

1/2 c. maple syrup
3/4 c. milk
3 T. melted shortening
Vegetable oil for baking pan

In a mixing bowl combine cornmeal, whole-wheat flour, baking powder and salt. Add egg, maple syrup, milk and shortening. Stir to blend. Pour into an oiled 9x9x2" baking pan. Bake at 400° for 20 minutes. Makes 9 servings.

MAYONNAISE CORNBREAD #1

Vegetable oil for skillet   1/2 c. milk
1 c. self-rising cornmeal   1 egg
1 c. self-rising flour   1 T. mayonnaise

Preheat oven to 425°. Heat an oiled 10" cast iron skillet in oven until hot. In a mixing bowl mix together cornmeal, flour, milk, egg and mayonnaise. Pour batter into hot skillet and bake for 20 minutes until golden. Makes 6 servings.

MAYONNAISE CORNBREAD #2

Vegetable oil for skillet   1 c. milk
1/2 c. self-rising cornmeal   1/4 c. plus 2 T. mayonnaise
1 1/2 c. self-rising flour   1/2 t. cornmeal

Preheat oven to 400°. Heat an oiled 10" cast iron skillet in oven until hot. In a mixing bowl combine cornmeal, flour, milk and mayonnaise, stirring just until moistened. Sprinkle hot skillet with cornmeal and spread batter evenly over it. Bake for 25 minutes until golden brown. Makes 6 servings.

MOLASSES CORNBREAD

3/4 c. cornmeal   3/4 c. buttermilk
1 c. flour   1 beaten egg
1 t. salt   2 T. melted shortening
3/4 t. baking soda   Vegetable oil for baking pan
1/2 c. molasses

Preheat oven to 425°. Sift cornmeal, flour, salt and baking soda into a mixing bowl. Add molasses, buttermilk, egg and shortening. Stir just until blended. Pour batter into an oiled 8x8x2" pan and bake for 20 minutes until golden brown. Makes 6 servings.

OATMEAL CORNBREAD

1 c. oatmeal	2 T. bacon drippings
1 c. self-rising cornmeal	2 beaten eggs
1 c. milk	Vegetable oil for skillet

In a mixing bowl, combine oatmeal, cornmeal, milk, bacon drippings and eggs. Pour into an oiled 9" cast iron skillet dusted with cornmeal. Bake at 400° for 25 minutes until golden. Makes 9 servings.

ONION CORNBREAD #1

4 t. baking powder	1 1/2 c. diced celery
1 1/2 c. flour	1 t. thyme
2 T. sugar	2 t. sage
2 1/2 t. salt	1/3 c. melted shortening
1/4 c. chopped pimiento	3 beaten eggs
1 1/2 c. chopped onion	1 1/2 c. milk
1 1/2 c. cornmeal	Vegetable oil for skillet

Sift baking powder, flour, sugar and salt into a mixing bowl. Add pimiento, onion, cornmeal, celery, thyme and sage; mix thoroughly. Add shortening, eggs and milk; stir well. Pour into a 10" skillet lined with oiled foil wrap. Bake at 400° for 45 minutes. Makes 12 servings.

ONION CORNBREAD #2

1 c. flour	2 beaten eggs
2 T. sugar	3/4 c. milk
1 T. baking powder	1/4 c. heavy cream
1/2 t. salt	1/4 c. melted shortening
1 c. cornmeal	Vegetable oil for skillet
1/2 c. finely chopped onion	

Preheat oven to 425°. Sift flour, sugar, baking powder and salt into a mixing bowl. Add cornmeal and stir. Blend in onion. In another bowl combine eggs, milk and cream. Add to cornmeal mixture. Blend in shortening just until moistened. Spoon batter into a 9" cast iron skillet; bake for 20 minutes. Makes 8 servings.

PECAN CORNBREAD #1

1 1/2 c. cornmeal	1 1/2 c. half & half
1 c. flour	3/4 c. melted butter
1/4 c. sugar	2 beaten eggs
1 T. baking powder	1/2 c. chopped pecans
1 t. salt	Vegetable oil for baking pan

In a mixing bowl, combine cornmeal, flour, sugar, baking powder and salt. Make a well in the center. In another bowl, combine half & half, butter, eggs and pecans. Add to cornmeal mixture; stir just until moistened. Pour batter into an oiled 9x5x3" pan. Bake at 375° for 50 minutes until golden. Remove from pan and cool on a wire rack. Makes 9 servings.

PECAN CORNBREAD #2

1 c. flour	2 T. brown sugar
1 c. cornmeal	2 beaten eggs
1 t. salt	1/3 c. maple syrup
1 t. baking soda	3/4 c. buttermilk
1 t. baking powder	1/2 c. chopped pecans
3 T. softened butter	Vegetable oil for baking pan

Preheat oven to 350°. In a medium bowl combine flour, cornmeal, salt, baking soda and baking powder. In a large mixing bowl mix together butter and brown sugar. Add eggs; mix well. Stir in maple syrup and buttermilk. Add cornmeal mixture and pecans. Stir just until combined. Pour batter into an oiled 9x5x3" pan. Bake for 50 minutes until a skewer comes out clean. Cool in pan on a wire rack for 10 minutes. Turn loaf out and cool bread for 2 hours. Makes 9 servings.

PECAN CORNBREAD ROUNDS

14 T. softened butter	3/4 t. salt
1 1/2 c. flour	1 beaten egg
1/2 c. cornmeal	3/4 c. chopped pecans
2 T. sugar	

Cream butter until light and fluffy. Add flour, cornmeal, sugar, salt and egg; combine well. Stir in pecans, wrap in waxed paper and chill 1 hour. Turn out dough onto a lightly floured board and roll to 1/2" thickness. Cut with a 3" cookie cutter; place rounds on a cookie sheet. Bake at 350° for 25 minutes until lightly browned. Cool on a wire rack. Serve topped with creamed chicken or shrimp. Makes 8 servings.

RICE CORNBREAD #1

1 c. cold cooked rice	1 c. milk
2 beaten eggs	1 t. salt
2 T. melted butter	1 t. sugar
1 c. cornmeal	Vegetable oil for baking pan

Place rice in a mixing bowl. Stir in eggs and butter. Add cornmeal, milk, salt and sugar; mix thoroughly. Pour batter into an oiled 9x9x2" baking pan; bake at 350° for 20 minutes. Makes 9 servings.

RICE CORNBREAD #2

2 c. cornmeal	1 T. sugar
1 t. salt	1 c. cold cooked rice
1 t. baking soda	3 beaten eggs
2 1/2 t. baking powder	2 c. buttermilk
1 T. butter	Vegetable oil for baking pan

Preheat oven to 400°. In a mixing bowl combine cornmeal, salt, baking soda and baking powder. In another bowl mix together butter, sugar and rice. Stir in eggs and buttermilk. Add cornmeal mixture; stir just until combined. Pour batter into an oiled 8x8x2" baking pan; bake for 35 minutes. Let bread cool in pan for 10 minutes. Makes 8 servings.

SAGE CORNBREAD

1 c. flour	1 c. buttermilk
3/4 c. cornmeal	2 beaten eggs
1 1/2 t. baking powder	1/4 c. melted butter, cooled
1/2 t. baking soda	1/2 t. crumbled dried sage
1/2 t. salt	Vegetable oil for baking pan

Preheat oven to 425°. Sift flour, cornmeal, baking powder, baking soda and salt into a mixing bowl. Add buttermilk, eggs, butter and sage. Stir just until combined. Pour into an oiled 8x8x2" baking pan; bake for 45 minutes. Let cool in pan and invert onto a wire rack. Makes 8 servings.

SOUR CREAM CORNBREAD #1

1 1/2 c. cornmeal	1 beaten egg
1 t. baking soda	1/2 c. milk
1 t. salt	2 T. melted butter
3 T. brown sugar	Vegetable oil for baking pan
1 c. sour cream	

Preheat oven to 375°. Combine cornmeal, baking soda, salt and brown sugar in a mixing bowl. In a second bowl mix together sour cream, egg, milk and butter. Gradually add to cornmeal mixture. Pour batter into an oiled 9x9x2" baking pan; bake for 20 minutes. Makes 8 servings.

SOUR CREAM CORNBREAD #2

Vegetable oil for skillet	8-oz. carton sour cream
1 c. self-rising cornmeal	2 beaten eggs
8-oz. can cream-style corn	1/4 c. vegetable oil

Preheat oven to 400°. Heat a lightly oiled 8" cast iron skillet in oven until hot. Combine cornmeal, corn, sour cream, eggs and oil. Stir just until moistened. Pour batter into hot skillet; bake for 20 minutes. Makes 6 servings.

SUNFLOWER SEED CORNBREAD

1 c. cornmeal	1 egg
1/2 c. whole-wheat flour	1/4 c. vegetable oil
1/2 c. sunflower seeds	2 T. honey
3 t. baking powder	1 c. buttermilk
1/2 t. salt	

Preheat oven to 375°. In a mixing bowl combine cornmeal, whole-wheat flour, seeds, baking powder and salt. In another bowl, mix egg with oil, honey and buttermilk. Add to cornmeal mixture, stirring just until moistened. Spoon into an oiled 8x8x2" baking pan; bake for 30 minutes until browned. Makes 6 servings.

SWEET POTATO CORNBREAD

2 c. cooked sweet potato chunks	1 T. baking powder
4 T. melted butter	1 T. ground ginger
1 beaten egg	1 t. cinnamon
1/2 c. milk	1 t. salt
3 T. brown sugar	1/2 t. pepper
1 1/2 c. cornmeal	Vegetable oil for skillet

Preheat oven to 400°. In an electric blender process sweet potato chunks, butter, egg and milk until smooth. Sift brown sugar, cornmeal, baking powder, ginger, cinnamon, salt and pepper into a mixing bowl. Add to puree in blender; process until well mixed. Spoon mixture into an oiled preheated 10" cast iron skillet. Cover skillet and bake for 15 minutes. Uncover and bake for 15 minutes longer. Makes 8 servings.

Spoonbread

Spoonbread, the most elegant cornmeal preparation, is a cross between a soufflé and cornbread. It is a very old Southern regional dish and is at its best served piping hot from the baking dish with a spoon, hence its name. It is often served with roasts and game at formal dinners. Also, it is excellent with fried chicken, country ham and red-eye gravy, seafoods, vegetable dishes and salads. It is a last-minute dish and should be served straight from the oven. It should be hot enough to fog your glasses and served with lots of butter. It is customary, when preparing this dish, to use white cornmeal.

KENTUCKY SPOONBREAD #1

1 1/4 c. cornmeal	1 3/4 t. baking powder
3 c. milk	2 T. melted butter
3 beaten eggs	Vegetable oil for baking dish
1 t. salt	

In a saucepan stir cornmeal into boiling milk. Cook, stirring constantly, until very thick. Remove from heat; set aside to cool. Add eggs, salt, baking powder and butter. Using an electric mixer, beat until well mixed, about 15 minutes. Spoon into an oiled 1 1/2-quart casserole dish. Bake at 375° for 30 minutes. Makes 6 servings.

This is the famous recipe for spoonbread from Boone Tavern in Berea.

KENTUCKY SPOONBREAD #2

1 c. cornmeal	1 t. salt
3 c. milk, divided	3 t. sugar
3 beaten eggs	2 T. melted butter
3 t. baking powder	Vegetable oil for baking dish

In a saucepan stir cornmeal into 2 cups of milk. Cook over medium-high heat, stirring constantly, until thick and mushy. Add remaining milk, eggs, baking powder, salt, sugar and butter. Mix well; pour into an oiled 1 1/2-quart casserole dish. Bake at 350° for 30 minutes. Makes 6 servings.

KENTUCKY SPOONBREAD #3

2 1/2 c. milk	4 beaten egg yolks
1 c. cornmeal	1 t. baking powder
1 t. salt	4 stiffly beaten egg whites
1 1/2 T. melted butter	Vegetable oil for baking dish

In the top of a double boiler combine milk and cornmeal. Add salt; stir until smooth. Cook over hot water, stirring constantly, until thick. Add butter and allow to cool for 10 minutes. Add egg yolks and baking powder; mix well. Fold in egg whites and spoon into an oiled 1 1/2-quart casserole dish; bake at 325° for 1 hour. Makes 6 servings.

KENTUCKY SPOONBREAD #4

1 c. cornmeal	2 beaten eggs
2 c. water	2 T. melted butter
1 t. salt	Vegetable oil for baking dish
1 c. cold milk	

Preheat oven to 400°. In a saucepan combine cornmeal, water and salt. Bring to a boil. Reduce heat and cook, stirring constantly, until mixture is very thick, about 5 minutes. Remove from heat; stir in milk, eggs and butter. Blend well. Turn mixture into an oiled preheated 1 1/2-quart casserole dish. Bake for 40 minutes. Makes 6 servings.

FLORIDA SPOONBREAD

1 1/2 c. water	2 T. melted butter
2 c. milk	5 eggs
1 1/2 c. cornmeal	1 T. baking powder
1 1/4 t. salt	Vegetable oil for baking dish
1 1/2 t. sugar	

Preheat oven to 350°. In a saucepan combine water and milk; heat to a simmer. Add cornmeal, salt, sugar and butter. Stir over medium heat until thickened, about 5 minutes. Remove from heat; set aside. In another bowl beat eggs with baking powder until light and fluffy. Stir into cornmeal mixture. Turn into an oiled 1 1/2-quart soufflé dish; bake for 50 minutes. Makes 8 servings.

ILLINOIS SPOONBREAD

2 c. cornmeal	1 1/2 c. buttermilk
2 1/2 c. boiling water	1 t. baking powder
2 T. melted shortening	2 stiffly beaten egg whites
1 1/2 t. salt	Vegetable oil for baking dish
2 egg yolks	

In a saucepan gradually add cornmeal to boiling water, stirring constantly. Remove from heat; allow mixture to cool. Add shortening, salt, egg yolks, buttermilk and baking soda. Beat for 2 minutes until well blended. Fold in egg whites; pour into an oiled 1 1/2-quart casserole dish. Bake at 425° for 40 minutes. Makes 6 servings.

INDIANA SPOONBREAD #1

1 c. boiling water	3 T. butter
1 c. cornmeal	2 eggs
1 t. salt	2 c. milk
1 t. sugar	Vegetable oil for baking dish

Preheat oven to 425°. In a saucepan pour boiling water over cornmeal. Stir to make a soft mush. Mix in salt, sugar, butter and eggs. Blend in milk; pour into an oiled preheated 1 1/2-quart casserole dish. Bake for 40 minutes. Makes 6 servings.

INDIANA SPOONBREAD #2

2 c. milk	1 c. cold milk
1 c. cornmeal	1 t. baking powder
1 T. brown sugar	3 beaten egg yolks
1 t. salt	3 stiffly beaten egg whites
3 T. butter	Vegetable oil for baking dish

In a saucepan heat milk to scalding stage. Gradually stir in cornmeal, brown sugar, salt and butter. Remove from heat and blend in cold milk and baking powder. Add egg yolks; mix well. Fold in egg whites; pour into an oiled 2-quart casserole dish. Bake at 325° for 50 minutes. Makes 8 servings.

MISSISSIPPI SPOONBREAD

3 c. milk, divided	2 t. baking powder
1 1/2 c. cornmeal	4 egg yolks
1/4 c. butter	4 stiffly beaten egg whites
1 t. salt	Vegetable oil for baking dish

Preheat oven to 350°. In a small saucepan heat 2 cups of the milk. Gradually stir into cornmeal in the top of a double boiler over boiling water. Add butter; bring to a boil, stirring constantly and cook for 10 minutes. Remove from heat, stir in salt and allow to cool to lukewarm. In a mixing bowl dissolve baking powder in the remaining milk. Add egg yolks; beat into cornmeal mixture. Fold in egg whites and pour mixture into an oiled 1 1/2-quart casserole dish. Bake for 40 minutes. Makes 6 servings.

NORTH CAROLINA SPOONBREAD

1 c. cornmeal	2 T. shortening, melted
3 c. milk, divided	3 beaten egg yolks
1 t. salt	3 stiffly beaten egg whites
1 t. baking powder	Vegetable oil for baking dish

In a saucepan cook cornmeal and 2 cups of the milk until consistency of mush. Remove from heat; cool slightly. Add salt, baking powder, shortening and remaining cup of milk. Stir in egg yolks and fold in egg whites. Pour mixture into an oiled 2-quart casserole dish. Bake at 325° for 1 hour. Makes 6 servings.

SOUTH CAROLINA SPOONBREAD

3/4 c. cornmeal	2 beaten eggs
2 T. shortening	1 c. milk
1 t. salt	2 1/4 t. baking powder
1 c. boiling water	Vegetable oil for baking dish

Sift cornmeal into a mixing bowl. Add shortening and salt. Pour boiling water over cornmeal mixture; stir until smooth. Allow to cool and beat in eggs and milk. Mix in baking powder. Pour into an oiled 1 1/2-quart casserole dish; bake at 350° for 40 minutes. Makes 6 servings.

TENNESSEE SPOONBREAD #1

1 c. cornmeal	1 1/2 c. milk
1 t. salt	1 1/2 t. baking powder
1 c. boiling water	2 stiffly beaten egg whites
2 T. melted butter	Vegetable oil for baking dish
2 egg yolks	

In a mixing bowl combine cornmeal and salt. Pour boiling water over corn-meal mixture, stir and allow to cool. Stir in butter and egg yolks. Add milk and baking powder; stir vigorously. Fold in egg whites and pour into an oiled 1 1/2-quart casserole dish; bake at 400° for 40 minutes. Makes 6 servings.

TENNESSEE SPOONBREAD #2

3 c. milk, divided	2 T. butter
1 c. cornmeal	1 t. sugar
1 t. salt	3 beaten eggs
1 t. baking powder	Vegetable oil for baking dish

In a saucepan heat 2 cups of the milk and add cornmeal. Stir until mixture has the consistency of mush. Add salt, baking powder, butter, sugar, eggs and remaining cup of milk. Mix well; pour into an oiled 2-quart casserole dish. Bake at 325° for 1 hour. Makes 6 servings.

VERMONT SPOONBREAD

3/4 c. cornmeal	1 c. milk
1 t. salt	2 beaten eggs
3 T. butter, melted	2 t. baking powder
1 c. boiling water	Vegetable oil for baking dish

In a mixing bowl combine cornmeal, salt, butter, boiling water and milk. In another bowl beat eggs with baking powder. Add to cornmeal mixture. Pour mixture into an oiled 1 1/2-quart casserole dish. Bake at 350° for 40 minutes. Makes 6 servings.

VIRGINIA SPOONBREAD #1

1 1/2 c. cornmeal	5 eggs
1 1/3 t. salt	2 c. milk
1 t. sugar	1 T. baking powder
1 1/2 c. boiling water	Vegetable oil for baking dish
4 T. melted butter	

In a mixing bowl combine cornmeal, salt and sugar. Scald with boiling water. Add butter; stir to mix. In another bowl beat eggs and milk together. Add to cornmeal mixture; stir in baking powder. Pour into an oiled 1 1/2-quart casserole dish; bake at 350° for 40 minutes. Makes 6 servings.

VIRGINIA SPOONBREAD #2

1 1/2 c. boiling water	1 t. sugar
1 c. self-rising cornmeal	1/4 t. baking soda
1 T. butter	3 stiffly beaten egg whites
3 egg yolks	Vegetable oil for baking dish
1 c. buttermilk	

In a mixing bowl stir boiling water into cornmeal. Allow to cool slightly. Add butter and egg yolks; stir to blend well. Mix in buttermilk, sugar and baking soda. Fold in egg whites; pour into an oiled 2-quart casserole dish. Bake at 375° for 50 minutes. Makes 6 servings.

SHAKER SPOONBREAD

1 qt. milk	3 stiffly beaten egg whites
1 c. cornmeal	1/2 t. baking powder
3 beaten egg yolks	1 3/4 t. salt
2 T. butter	Vegetable oil for baking dish

In a saucepan scald milk. Gradually add cornmeal and cook, stirring constantly, until thick. Pour a small amount over egg yolks and then add egg yolks to cornmeal mixture. Return to heat; cook 3 minutes longer. Add butter and fold in egg whites. Stir in baking powder and salt. Pour into an oiled 1 1/2-

quart casserole dish; bake at 325° for 1 1/2 hours stirring once after first 15 minutes of baking. Makes 8 servings.

BROCCOLI SPOONBREAD

3 c. broccoli florets	2 stiffly beaten egg whites
1/2 c. cornmeal	2 T. butter
2 1/2 c. milk, divided	1 T. cornstarch
2 beaten egg yolks	1 c. grated Parmesan cheese
2 t. baking powder	1/2 t. salt
1 t. salt	1/8 t. pepper
1 T. sugar	1/4 t. nutmeg
	Vegetable oil for baking pan

In a saucepan parboil broccoli. Drain and reserve half cup liquid. Place broccoli in an oiled 2-quart soufflé dish. In a saucepan combine cornmeal and 1 1/2 cups of milk. Cook over medium heat until thickened, about 5 minutes. Allow to cool slightly. Add egg yolks, baking powder, salt and sugar to cornmeal mixture; stir to blend. Fold in egg whites; pour batter over broccoli. Place soufflé dish in a pan containing one inch of warm water. Bake at 375° for 45 minutes until golden. In a saucepan blend together butter and cornstarch. Add broccoli liquid, remaining milk, cheese, salt, pepper and nutmeg. Stir to blend until sauce has thickened. Spoon over spoonbread. Makes 6 servings.

BROWN SUGAR SPOONBREAD

1 c. sifted cornmeal	1 c. butter
1 T. brown sugar	6 beaten egg yolks
1 t. salt	6 stiffly beaten egg whites
2 c. scalded milk	Vegetable oil for baking dish

In a saucepan slowly stir cornmeal, brown sugar and salt into scalded milk. Stir vigorously, gradually adding butter. Allow mixture to cool; add egg yolks, stirring constantly. Fold in egg whites; spoon mixture into a 1-quart soufflé dish. Bake at 400° for 25 minutes. Makes 6 servings.

CHEESE SPOONBREAD #1

3 c. milk, divided	3 T. butter, cut into pieces
1 c. cornmeal	7 beaten eggs
1 T. sugar	3 T. grated sharp Cheddar cheese
1 t. salt	Vegetable oil for baking pan

Preheat oven to 400°. In a saucepan bring 2 1/2 cups of milk to a boil over medium heat. In a mixing bowl combine cornmeal, sugar and salt. Stir in remaining 1/2 cup milk. Gradually stir mixture into boiling milk. Cook, stirring constantly, until mixture thickens, about 3 minutes. Remove from heat; stir in butter. In another bowl gradually stir 1/4 cup cornmeal mixture into eggs, then stir in another 1/2 cupful. Add egg mixture to remaining cornmeal; stir until well blended. Spoon batter into an oiled 1 1/2-quart soufflé dish. Sprinkle with cheese; bake for 40 minutes. Makes 8 servings.

CHEESE SPOONBREAD #2

1/2 lb. bacon, crisply cooked and crumbled	8 T. butter
	1/2 t. salt
1 clove garlic, finely chopped	1 c. milk
1 T. bacon drippings	4 egg yolks
3/4 c. cornmeal	4-oz. jar pimientos, drained and chopped
1/2 c. hominy grits	
2 1/2 c. water	4 stiffly beaten egg whites
2 c. shredded sharp Cheddar cheese	Vegetable oil for baking dish

Preheat oven to 325°. In a skillet sauté garlic in bacon drippings until soft; set aside. In a saucepan mix together cornmeal, hominy grits and water. Bring to a boil, stirring constantly; cook for 1 minute. Remove from heat; stir in cheese and butter until both are melted. Add salt, milk, egg yolks, bacon, garlic and pimientos. Fold egg whites into cornmeal mixture. Spoon into an oiled 3-quart soufflé dish; bake for 1 1/4 hours. Makes 8 servings.

CHICKEN SPOONBREAD

3/4 c. cornmeal
2 T. flour
1 t. salt
4 c. chicken broth
1/4 c. butter

4 beaten egg yolks
3 c. chopped cooked chicken
4 stiffly beaten egg whites
Vegetable oil for baking dish

In a saucepan combine cornmeal, flour and salt. Add broth; cook until thickened. Stir in butter; allow to cool. Stir in egg yolks and blend in chicken. Fold in egg whites. Spoon into an oiled 1 1/2-quart casserole dish. Bake at 375° for 40 minutes. Makes 6 servings.

CORN SPOONBREAD #1

2 c. milk
3/4 c. cornmeal
1 T. sugar
1/2 t. baking powder
1/4 t. salt

Pepper to taste
4 eggs, separated
1 c. frozen corn kernels, thawed
Vegetable oil for baking dish

Preheat oven to 350°. In a saucepan scald milk to near boiling; gradually stir in cornmeal. Stir until very thick, about 2 minutes. Remove from heat; stir in sugar, baking powder and salt. Sprinkle with pepper. Add egg yolks and corn; blend well. In another bowl whip egg whites until stiff. Fold into cornmeal mixture. Spoon batter into an oiled 1 1/2-quart soufflé dish; bake for 40 minutes. Makes 6 servings.

CORN SPOONBREAD #2

1 1/2 c. milk
3/4 c. cornmeal
2 c. fresh corn kernels
3 T. butter
1 t. salt

1 t. baking powder
4 egg yolks
4 stiffly beaten egg whites
Vegetable oil for baking dish

Preheat oven to 350°. In a saucepan scald milk. Add cornmeal, stirring constantly until thick. Add corn, butter, salt, baking powder and egg yolks. Stir to blend well. Fold in egg whites. Spoon batter into an oiled 1-quart casserole dish. Bake for 30 minutes. Makes 6 servings.

HAM SPOONBREAD

2 1/2 c. milk	2 T. melted butter
1/2 c. cornmeal	Vegetable oil for baking dish
1 c. ground cooked ham	

In a saucepan combine milk and cornmeal. Cook, stirring constantly, until thick. Remove from heat; blend in ham and butter. Spoon into an oiled 1-quart casserole dish. Bake at 375° for 1 hour. Makes 6 servings.

HOMINY GRITS SPOONBREAD #1

1 c. cornmeal	2 T. baking powder
1 1/2 t. salt	1 T. butter
1 c. boiling water	1 c. milk
1 c. cooked hominy grits	Vegetable oil for baking dish
2 beaten eggs	

Preheat oven to 375°. Sift cornmeal and salt into a mixing bowl. Pour boiling water over cornmeal mixture. Stir and allow to cool. Mix in grits. Stir in eggs, baking powder, butter and milk. Spoon into an oiled 1 1/2-quart soufflé dish; bake for 45 minutes. Makes 8 servings.

HOMINY GRITS SPOONBREAD #2

1 c. cornmeal	1 c. heavy cream
1/4 c. uncooked regular hominy grits	1 t. salt
2 1/2 c. water	3 beaten egg yolks
1/4 c. butter, cut into pieces	3 stiffly beaten egg whites
	Vegetable oil for baking pan

In a saucepan stir cornmeal and hominy grits into water. Cook over low heat, stirring often, until thick and grits are tender. Reduce heat; stir in butter, cream, salt and egg yolks. Fold in egg whites. Spoon batter into an oiled 8x8x2" baking pan. Bake at 375° for 40 minutes. Makes 6 servings.

HOMINY GRITS SPOONBREAD #3

2 c. cooked hominy grits	1 c. milk
2 eggs beaten	2 T. butter, melted
2 T. cornmeal	Vegetable oil for baking dish
1/2 t. salt	

In a mixing bowl mash hominy grits with a fork. Add eggs and stir until well blended and free of lumps. Add cornmeal and salt and beat. Add milk and butter and stir to combine well. Spoon into an oiled 1-qt. carrerole dish. Bake at 300° for 1 1/2 hours. Makes 6 servings.

HOMINY GRITS SPOONBREAD #4

1T. butter	1/2 t. salt
2 c. cooked hominy grits	1/2 t. pepper
3 egg yolks, beaten	1/2 t. Tobasco sauce
3 egg whites, stiffly beaten	1 1/2 c. milk
1/2 c. cornmeal	Vegetable oil for baking dish
2 t. baking powder	

In a mixing bowl, combine butter, hominy grits, egg yolks, cornmeal, baking powder, salt, pepper, Tobasco sauce and enough milk to make custard like batter. Fold in egg whites and spoon into an oiled 2-qt. souffle dish. Bake at 350° for 1 hour. Makes 6 servings.

OYSTER SPOONBREAD

3 c. milk, divided
1 1/2 c. cornmeal
1/2 c. butter
2 t. salt
2 fresh jalapeño peppers,
    seeded and minced
16 oysters, drained
1/2 t. minced garlic

1/2 c. grated sharp Cheddar cheese
1 red bell pepper,
    roasted and finely chopped
6 slices bacon,
    crisply cooked and crumbled
4 beaten egg yolks
2 t. baking powder
4 stiffly beaten egg whites
Vegetable oil for baking dish

In a saucepan bring 2 cups milk to a boil. Gradually stir in cornmeal; add butter and salt. Cook over low heat, stirring constantly, until mixture forms a ball. Stir in jalapeño peppers, oysters, garlic, cheese, bell pepper, bacon and egg yolks. In another bowl mix together remaining 1 cup milk and baking powder. Stir into cornmeal mixture. Fold egg whites into cornmeal mixture. Spoon batter into an oiled 2 1/2-quart casserole dish. Cover with a piece of buttered parchment paper. Put baking dish in a large baking pan; fill with enough water to come halfway up sides of dish. Bake at 350° for 40 minutes. Makes 10 servings.

RICE SPOONBREAD

1/4 c. cornmeal
1 T. flour
1 t. salt
2 T. sugar
1 c. boiling water
2 beaten egg yolks

1 c. milk
1 c. cooked rice
2 T. melted butter
2 stiffly beaten egg whites
Vegetable oil for baking dish

In a mixing bowl combine cornmeal, flour, salt and sugar. In a saucepan stir cornmeal mixture into boiling water; cook, stirring constantly, until thick. Add egg yolks and milk; stir in. Blend in rice and butter. Fold in egg whites. Spoon mixture into an oiled 1-quart baking dish. Bake at 350° for 40 minutes. Makes 6 servings.

TOMATO SPOONBREAD

1 c. cornmeal	1 t. baking powder
1 c. tomato juice	3/4 t. salt
2 c. scalded milk	3 beaten egg yolks
1/4 c. butter	3 stiffly beaten egg whites
1 sm. onion, grated	Vegetable oil for baking dish

In a small bowl mix cornmeal and tomato juice together. In a saucepan gradually stir cornmeal mixture into milk and cook, stirring constantly, until thick. Remove from heat; add butter, onion, baking powder and salt. Add egg yolks gradually, stirring hard to blend. Fold egg whites into cornmeal mixture. Spoon into an oiled 1 1/2-quart casserole dish. Bake at 375° for 45 minutes. Makes 6 servings.

VEGETABLE SPOONBREAD

1 c. cornmeal	5 slices bacon,
1 1/2 t. salt	crisply cooked and crumbled
1 c. cold milk	4 beaten egg yolks
1 1/2 c. scalded milk	4 stiffly beaten egg whites
1 T. butter	Vegetable oil for baking dish
1-lb. can mixed vegetables, drained	

Preheat oven to 350°. In a mixing bowl combine cornmeal, salt and cold milk. In a saucepan add cornmeal mixture to scalded milk; cook, stirring constantly, until thickened, about 5 minutes. Remove from heat; add butter, vegetables and bacon. Blend well. Slowly stir egg yolks into batter; mix well. Fold in egg whites. Spoon into an oiled 2-quart casserole dish; bake for 1 hour. Makes 8 servings.

WINTER SQUASH SPOONBREAD

1 1/2 c. winter squash,
   peeled and finely diced
1/3 c. maple syrup
2 c. milk
1 c. cornmeal
3/4 t. salt

1/8 t. nutmeg
4 T. butter, cut into pieces
5 egg yolks
5 stiffly beaten egg whites
Vegetable oil for baking dish

Preheat oven to 375°. In a saucepan with plenty of water, add squash and cover. Bring to a boil; simmer until squash is soft, about 20 minutes. Drain and place in an electric blender with maple syrup. Puree; set aside. Pour milk into large pot; gradually stir in cornmeal. Cook on medium-high, stirring constantly, until slightly thickened, about 5 minutes. Reduce heat; cook, stirring until it is very thick. Mix in salt, nutmeg, butter and squash puree. Remove from heat; stir in egg yolks. Fold in egg whites. Spoon into an oiled 2-quart baking dish; bake for 35 minutes. Makes 8 servings.

Vegetables

Some vegetables, such as okra, onions and tomatoes lend themselves particularly well to being cooked with a coating of cornmeal. Here are some old and some new combinations.

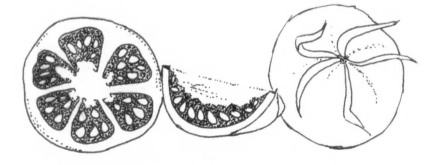

CORNBREAD-BEAN CASSEROLE

5 T. vegetable oil, divided
1 c. chopped onion
1 c. chopped green pepper
2 minced garlic cloves
16-oz. can kidney beans,
    drained
16-oz. can pinto beans,
    drained
16-oz. can tomatoes,
    undrained; chopped
8-oz. can tomato sauce
1 t. chili powder
1 1/2 t. salt

1/2 t. pepper
1/2 t. prepared mustard
1/8 t. Tabasco sauce
1 c. cornmeal
1 c. flour
2 1/2 t. baking powder
1/2 t. salt
1 T. sugar
1 1/4 c. milk
2 eggs
8 1/2-oz. can cream-style
    corn

In a large skillet heat 2 tablespoons vegetable oil. Cook onion, green pepper and garlic over medium-high heat until tender, stirring constantly. Stir in kidney beans, pinto beans, tomatoes, tomato sauce, chili powder, salt, pepper, mustard and Tabasco sauce. Cover; cook for 5 minutes. Pour into a lightly oiled 13x9x2" baking dish. Set aside. Preheat oven to 375°. In a medium bowl combine cornmeal, flour, baking powder, salt and sugar. In a separate bowl combine milk, eggs, 3 tablespoons oil and corn. Add to dry ingredients; stir until dry mixture is moistened. Spoon over bean mixture. Bake for 35 minutes until cornbread is done and golden brown. Makes 8 servings.

CHEESE AND BLACK BEAN FRITTERS

1/2 c. yellow cornmeal
1/4 c. flour
1/4 t. baking powder
1/4 t. cayenne pepper
1/2 t. salt
1/2 t. ground cumin
1/3 c. milk
1 egg yolk

1 c. extra-sharp Cheddar
    cheese, cut into 1/4" cubes
1 c. canned black beans,
    rinsed, drained and patted
    dry
2 egg whites
Vegetable oil for frying

In a medium bowl combine cornmeal, flour, baking powder, cayenne, salt and cumin. Stir in milk and egg yolk. Stir in the cheese and beans. In a small bowl beat egg whites until they make soft peaks; fold into cheese mixture. Over medium-high heat, heat 1/8" oil in a cast iron skillet. Drop batter by heaping tablespoons into skillet, spreading them slightly. Fry fritters 1 minute on each side until golden brown; drain on paper towels. If desired, top with sour cream and tomato salsa. Makes 18 servings.

CORNBREAD AND BROCCOLI PIE

2 onions, chopped
3 T. olive oil
4-oz. jar sliced mushrooms, drained
2 minced garlic cloves
28-oz. can plum tomatoes, drained and chopped, juice reserved
1/4 c. chicken broth
7 c. broccoli flowerets
Salt and pepper to taste
1 c. cornmeal

1 c. flour
2 t. baking powder
1/2 t. baking soda
1 t. salt
2 beaten eggs
1/4 c. melted butter, cooled
1/2 c. milk
1/2 c. sour cream
2 t. honey
4 oz. grated sharp Cheddar cheese

In a large skillet over medium-low heat, stir onions in oil until they are soft. Add mushrooms; stir until mixture is fairly dry. Add garlic, cook for 2 minutes. Add tomatoes, reserved juice, broth, broccoli, salt and pepper to taste. Bring to a boil, cover; reduce heat. Simmer, stirring occasionally, for 15 minutes. Strain the liquid into a pan. Place the mixture in an 11 1/2x8x2" baking pan. Boil the liquid until it is reduced to about 3/4 cup. Pour over the broccoli mixture. Preheat oven to 400°. In a medium bowl combine cornmeal, flour, baking powder, baking soda and salt. Add eggs, butter, milk, sour cream, honey and cheese Stir batter just until combined. Spread batter evenly over broccoli mixture. Bake pie for 30 minutes until a toothpick inserted in cornbread comes out clean. Makes 8 servings.

FRIED CARROT STICKS #1

2 med. carrots
1 beaten egg
1/2 t. salt

1/4 c. flour
1 c. cornmeal
Vegetable oil for frying

Peel and cut carrots into 2" lengths. Cut pieces lengthwise into 8 sticks. Blanch in boiling water for 2 minutes; drain. In a shallow bowl combine egg with salt. Dip carrot sticks in flour, then in egg mixture, then in cornmeal. In a deep-fryer heat 3" oil to 375°. Using a slotted spoon, lower a few carrot sticks at a time into fryer basket. Fry 1 minute or until golden and crispy. Remove from basket; drain on paper towels. If desired, sprinkle with salt and serve hot. Makes 2 servings.

FRIED CARROT STICKS #2

3/4 c. cornmeal
3/4 c. flour
1 t. onion powder
1 t. Old Bay seasoning
1/2 t. salt
1/2 t. pepper

2 1/2 T. chopped fresh parsley
1 egg white
2/3 c. buttermilk
1/2 t. Tabasco sauce
4 large carrots
Vegetable oil for frying

Combine cornmeal, flour, onion powder, Old Bay seasoning, salt, pepper and parsley. Set aside. In a small bowl beat egg white until foamy. Stir in buttermilk and Tabasco sauce. Peel carrots and cut into 2" lengths. Cut pieces lengthwise into 8; dip in buttermilk mixture. Drain off excess; dip in cornmeal mixture. Pour oil to depth of 1" in Dutch oven. Heat to 350°. Fry carrots for 2 minutes until golden brown; serve hot. Makes 4 servings.

CORN CASSEROLE #1

Two 16-oz. cans cream-style corn
2 c. shredded Cheddar cheese
4-oz. can chopped green
    chilies, drained
1/2 c. finely chopped onion
1 c. milk
2 beaten eggs
1 c. cornmeal
1 1/2 t. garlic salt
1/2 t. baking soda

Preheat oven to 350°. Combine corn, cheese, chilies, onion, milk and eggs in large bowl. Combine cornmeal, garlic salt and baking soda; stir into corn mixture. Pour into lightly greased 11x7x1 1/2" baking dish. Bake for 50 minutes until knife inserted in center comes out clean. Makes 8 servings.

CORN CASSEROLE #2

1/2 c. sifted flour
1 c. cornmeal
1 1/2 t. chili powder
2 t. salt
1/4 t. pepper
3 c. canned cream-style corn
8-oz. can tomato sauce
1 c. milk
1/2 c. vegetable oil
2 beaten eggs
2 T. grated onion
1 c. sliced black olives

Preheat oven to 325°. Sift together flour, cornmeal, chili powder, salt and pepper. In a separate bowl combine corn, tomato sauce, milk, oil and eggs. Blend dry ingredients into corn mixture, mixing well. Add onion and black olives. Pour mixture into lightly greased casserole dish. Bake for 2 hours. Makes 8 servings.

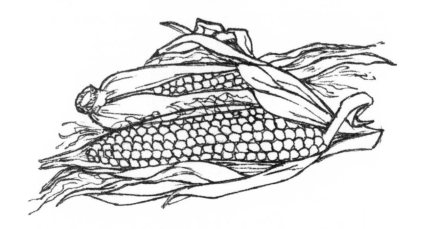

CORN PUDDING

1/2 c. cornmeal	1/2 c. buttermilk
1 t. salt	2 T. butter
1/4 t. baking soda	2 beaten eggs
1/2 t. baking powder	1/2 t. Worcestershire sauce
17-oz. can cream-style corn	

Preheat oven to 400°. Sift cornmeal with salt, baking soda and baking powder. Add corn, buttermilk, butter, eggs and Worcestershire sauce. Pour into lightly greased 2-quart casserole dish; bake for 45 minutes. Makes 8 servings.

FRIED CORNMEAL WITH COLLARD GREENS

2 1/2 c. cold water	3/4 c. yellow cornmeal
1/2 t. butter	1/2 c. olive oil
3/4 t. salt	1 large garlic clove, slivered
1/4 t. pepper	
1 c. loosely packed, finely shredded collard greens	

In a heavy pan combine water, butter, salt, pepper, collard greens and cornmeal. Simmer, stirring constantly, for 8 minutes or until mixture is consistency of mush. Reduce heat; continue stirring an additional 5 minutes. Spoon mixture into buttered 8x8x2" baking pan. Smooth mixture into corners; put pan on a rack. Let stand for 1 hour until firm enough to cut. Heat oil in a large cast iron skillet; add garlic for 2 minutes until golden. Remove garlic with slotted spoon. Cut cornmeal mixture into 12 squares. Fry cornmeal squares over medium-high heat 5 minutes on each side until brown. Serve warm. Makes 6 servings.

TURNIP GREENS AND CORNMEAL DUMPLINGS

1 lb. ham hock	2 T. minced onion
2 c. water	1/2 t. salt
1 t. salt	1/2 t. pepper
3 lbs. turnip greens,	1/2 t. baking soda
washed and drained	1/4 c. buttermilk
1 c. cornmeal	

Simmer meat in water for 45 minutes. Add salt and greens. Cover; cook for 30 minutes until tender. Meanwhile, mix cornmeal, onion, salt and pepper. Dissolve soda in buttermilk; add to cornmeal mixture to make stiff dough. Beat well and form dough into patties. Drop on top of greens the last 15 minutes of cooking time. Makes 4 servings.

CARIBBEAN CORNMEAL AND OKRA CAKE

1/2 lb. fresh okra,	1 c. cornmeal
cut into 1/4" rounds	2 T. butter
2 c. water	2 T. minced onion
1 t. salt	2 T. softened butter

Bring okra, water and salt to a boil in heavy 1 1/2-quart saucepan. Reduce heat, cover. Simmer for 10 minutes until okra is tender. Stirring constantly, pour in cornmeal in thin stream. Cook, stirring over medium heat until mixture is thick, about 5 minutes. Mixture should be smooth and thick. Meanwhile, in separate pan, melt butter and sauté onion for 5-8 minutes until very soft. Add to cornmeal mixture; mix well. Spoon onto serving plate. With spatula, shape into round "cake" 1" thick and 8" round. Spread with softened butter; let stand for 10 minutes. Serve warm. Makes 4 servings.

FRIED OKRA #1

2 lbs. okra
Salt and pepper to taste

1/2 c. cornmeal
Vegetable oil for frying

Cut okra into 1/2" rounds, discarding stems and tips. Sprinkle with salt and pepper; place in a bowl. Add cornmeal and toss the okra to coat thoroughly. Heat 1" oil in cast iron skillet. When oil is hot, fry okra in batches, stirring occasionally, for 5 minutes until light brown and crispy. Remove with slotted spoon and drain on paper towels. When all okra is fried, heat briefly in hot oven and serve immediately. Makes 4 servings.

FRIED OKRA #2

2 lbs. okra
2 beaten eggs
1/4 c. milk or buttermilk

1 c. cornmeal
Salt and pepper to taste
Vegetable oil for frying

Cut okra into 1/2" rounds, discarding stems and tips. Combine eggs and milk. Add okra; let stand 15 minutes. In bowl season cornmeal with salt and pepper. Place okra in cornmeal; toss to cover completely. Heat 1" oil in cast iron skillet. Fry okra until golden brown. Drain on paper towels; serve at once. Makes 4 servings.

OKRA FRITTERS

1/4 c. cornmeal
1/4 c. flour
1/2 c. finely chopped onion
1/2 c. evaporated milk
1 beaten egg
3 T. chopped fresh parsley

2 T. grated Parmesan cheese
1/2 t. salt
1/4 t. red pepper
1 lb. okra
Vegetable oil for frying
Coarse salt, optional

Combine cornmeal, flour, onion, milk, egg, parsley, cheese, salt and red pepper. Cut okra into 1/4" rounds; stir into cornmeal mixture. Heat 2" oil in a Dutch oven. Drop batter by tablespoonfuls into hot oil. Cook until golden brown, turning once. Drain on paper towels and, if desired, sprinkle with coarse salt. Makes 4 servings.

CARIBBEAN CORNMEAL WITH OKRA

6 pods okra	1/2 t. salt
2 c. water	1/2 c. butter
1 c. cornmeal	

Trim ends and stems from okra. Place in gently boiling water; cook for 10 minutes. Remove from water and set aside. Raise heat to a brisk boil; add cornmeal in thin stream, stirring constantly. Add okra and salt; continue stirring for 10 minutes. Remove from heat and stir in butter, a piece at a time. Serve hot. Makes 4 servings.

ONION CORNMEAL CAKE

2 c. chopped onions	2 beaten eggs
1/4 c. melted butter	1/4 c. milk
1 1/2 c. self-rising cornmeal	1/4 c. vegetable oil
2 T. sugar	8-oz. carton sour cream
1/4 t. dillweed	1 can cream-style corn
1 c. shredded sharp Cheddar cheese, divided	Dash of Tabasco sauce

Preheat oven to 400°. Using a 10" cast iron skillet, sauté onion in butter until tender. Set aside. In large bowl combine cornmeal, sugar and dillweed. Add onion, half cup cheese, eggs, milk, oil, sour cream, corn and Tabasco sauce. Stir just until moistened. Spoon cornmeal mixture into lightly greased iron skillet. Bake for 20 minutes. Sprinkle with remaining half cup cheese; bake 5 minutes longer. Makes 8 servings.

FRIED ONION RINGS #1

3 large Bermuda onions
3 1/2 c. flour, divided
1 1/2 c. cornmeal

2 c. evaporated milk
Vegetable oil for frying

Slice onions in 1/4" rings; cover with iced water. Chill in refrigerator for 30 minutes. Combine 1 1/2 cups flour and cornmeal. Dredge onion rings in 2 cups flour, then in milk, then in cornmeal mixture. Heat oil to 375° in Dutch oven. Fry onions in batches for 3 minutes until golden and crisp. Drain on paper towels and sprinkle with salt if desired. Makes 6 servings.

FRIED ONION RINGS #2

3 large Spanish onions
1 3/4 c. flour
1/2 c. self-rising cornmeal
1 T. onion powder
1 1/2 t. salt

3/4 t. sugar
2 c. milk
1 beaten egg
Vegetable oil for frying

Slice onions into 1/4" rings. Combine flour, cornmeal, onion powder, salt, sugar, milk and egg. Beat until smooth. Heat 3" oil in Dutch oven to 375°. Dip onion rings in batter; fry 2 minutes until golden brown. Drain on paper towels and sprinkle with salt if desired. Makes 6 servings.

CORNMEAL AND ONION MINI MUFFINS

1/4 c. minced shallots
2 T. butter, divided
1/3 c. cornmeal
1/3 c. flour
3/4 t. baking powder
1 lightly beaten egg

1/4 c. sour cream
3 T. water
Salt and pepper to taste
Additional sour cream for top-
    ping
2 oz. caviar

Preheat oven to 400°. In a skillet cook shallots in 1 tablespoon butter over medium heat until soft. Cool completely. In a medium bowl combine cornmeal, flour, baking powder and shallots. Add remaining 1 tablespoon butter, cut into pieces. Blend until mixture resembles coarse meal. Stir in egg, sour cream, water, salt and pepper. Stir batter until well blended. Heat mini muffin tins in oven for 2 minutes. Spoon 1 1/2 teaspoons batter into each cup of tins. Bake for 6 minutes. Turn out onto wire rack to cool. Top each muffin with sour cream and caviar. Serve as a canapé. Makes 16 servings.

FRIED BANANA PEPPERS

12 banana peppers	1 1/2 c. cornmeal
1 beaten egg	1/3 c. cracker crumbs
3/4 c. milk	Vegetable oil for frying

Cut peppers in half lengthwise. Remove stems and seeds. In a deep bowl combine egg and milk. Add peppers; set aside for 1 hour. Combine cornmeal and cracker crumbs. With slotted spoon remove pepper slices from milk mixture. Coat them heavily in cornmeal mixture. Repeat, coating peppers twice. Refrigerate. When ready to fry, put enough oil in cast iron skillet to cover peppers. Heat oil until drop of water sizzles. Fry peppers until golden brown. Do not turn. Remove from oil with slotted spoon; drain on paper towels. Makes 4 servings.

FRIED STUFFED ROASTED PEPPERS

2 green peppers	1/2 t. ground cumin
1/2 c. Monterey Jack cheese, grated	Salt and pepper
	1 beaten egg
1/2 c. Cheddar cheese, grated	1/3 c. cornmeal
1/2 c. corn kernels, cooked	Vegetable oil for frying
2 T. onion, minced	Sour cream for topping
1 1/2 T. pickled jalapeno peppers, minced*	*Wear rubber gloves

Char the green peppers by putting them on rack over an electric stove burner on high or by putting them on long-handled fork over an open flame. Turn them for 3-10 minutes or until skins are blackened. Seal them in a plastic bag; let them steam for 15 minutes. Meanwhile, combine cheeses, corn, onion, jalapeño peppers, cumin and salt and pepper to taste. After green peppers have steamed, peel, cut out stem ends, discard seeds and ribs. Stuff them with cheese mixture; pat to make even thickness. Place egg in a bowl and cornmeal in another bowl. Coat the peppers thoroughly with egg, then cornmeal, then egg again. In cast iron skillet, heat 1/4" deep oil over medium-high heat. Fry peppers for 2 minutes on each side until golden brown. Drain on paper towels. Serve hot and top with sour cream if desired. Makes 2 servings.

STUFFED PEPPERS

2 c. canned Italian tomatoes	1 clove garlic, finely minced
1/2 c. cornmeal	1 c. chopped cooked ham
Salt and pepper to taste	1 c. cooked whole kernel corn
1 T. chili powder	6 green peppers
1/2 t. ground cumin	1 c. grated sharp Cheddar cheese
1 T. olive oil	Boiling water
1/2 c. finely chopped onion	

Preheat oven to 350°. In heavy skillet heat tomatoes, cornmeal, salt, pepper, chili powder and cumin. Combine well; cook 10 minutes. In separate skillet heat oil; cook onion and garlic until onion is wilted. Add to tomato mixture with ham and corn. Core and seed green peppers. Parboil for 3-5 minutes. Drain and cool. Fill with tomato mixture; top with the cheese. Place them upright in deep baking dish. Pour boiling water around to a depth of 1/2". Bake 45 minutes to 1 hour depending on size of peppers. Makes 6 servings.

CORNMEAL POTATO CAKES

4-5 medium potatoes	1/2 t. baking powder
2 beaten eggs	2 T. finely chopped onions
1 1/2 c. cornmeal	Vegetable oil for frying

Pare and cut potatoes into chunks. Cook in boiling salted water for 30 minutes until barely done. Drain and return to pan. Shake over low heat until dry. In large bowl combine potatoes, eggs, cornmeal, baking powder and onion. Mash until well mixed. If mixture is too dry, add a little milk. Form into small cakes. Heat oil to depth of 1/4" in cast iron skillet over medium-high heat. Fry cakes until golden brown, turning once. Makes 4 servings.

CORNMEAL FRIED POTATOES

1 large potato	3 T. butter or margarine
3 T. cornmeal	Salt and pepper to taste

With skin left on, slice potato very thinly. In cast iron skillet melt butter over medium-low heat. Dust potato slices with cornmeal. Fry a few at a time, turning once. If necessary, add more butter. Salt and pepper; serve hot. Makes 2 servings.

CORNMEAL POTATO MADELEINES

3 lbs. potatoes	3 egg yolks
3/4 c. butter, softened	1/4 t. salt
1/2 c. cornmeal	1/8 t. white pepper
1/4 c. heavy cream or half & half	2 T. chopped fresh chives

Grease Madeleine molds. Peel and quarter potatoes. Place in a 3-quart saucepan with enough cold water to cover. Heat to boiling; cook until fork tender, about 20 minutes. Drain potatoes and return to pan, stirring constantly. Cook over medium-high heat until potatoes are dry, about 1-2 minutes. Preheat oven to 500°. With electric mixer on medium speed, beat potatoes 2 minutes. Add butter, cornmeal, cream, egg yolks, salt and pepper.

Continue beating until smooth, 2-3 minutes. Scrape down pan often. Add chives; stir in well. Fill molds with mixture. Bake 12-15 minutes until Madeleines are golden brown. Invert onto baking sheet and serve immediately. Makes 40 servings.

CORNMEAL BAKED ACORN SQUASH RINGS

2 beaten eggs	Salt and pepper
1/4 c. milk	2 acorn squash, seeded,
2 t. honey	sliced 1/2" thick
3/4 c. cornmeal	3 T. melted butter
1 1/2 c. fine bread crumbs	

Preheat oven to 400°. In shallow bowl mix together eggs, milk and honey. In another bowl combine cornmeal, bread crumbs, salt and pepper to taste. Dip squash rings into egg mixture, then into cornmeal mixture. Coat them well, patting on the crumbs. Arrange in single layer on buttered baking sheet. Bake for 30 minutes, turning once, until tender. If desired, sprinkle with salt and pepper. Serve hot. Makes 6 servings.

CORNMEAL FRIED SUMMER SQUASH

8 small summer squash	1/2 t. pepper
1 c. cornmeal	Vegetable oil
1 t. salt	

Slice squash into 1/4" rounds, discarding end pieces. Combine cornmeal, salt and pepper. Roll squash pieces in cornmeal mixture. Heat 1/4" deep oil over medium-high heat. Fry squash in one layer about 5 minutes, turning once, until brown and crisp. Remove from skillet; drain on paper towels. If desired, you can fry green tomatoes and okra rolled in cornmeal at the same time. Makes 4 servings.

FRIED GREEN TOMATOES #1

6 green tomatoes	1/4 t. pepper
1 c. cornmeal	Vegetable oil or bacon drip
1/2 t. salt	pings for frying

Wash tomatoes and slice 1/4" thick. Discard stem and end pieces. Combine cornmeal, salt and pepper in shallow bowl. Coat both sides of tomato slices with cornmeal mixture. In large cast iron skillet heat enough oil to coat bottom of pan. Fry slices slowly until lightly browned and tender, about 3 minutes, turning once. Cook tomatoes in batches, adding oil as needed. Drain on paper towels. Keep tomatoes warm in low oven until all are cooked. Serve hot. Makes 6 servings.

FRIED GREEN TOMATOES #2

6 green tomatoes	1 t. brown sugar
1 c. cornmeal	Butter, oil or bacon drippings
1/2 t. salt	for frying
1/4 t. pepper	

Wash tomatoes, slice 1/4" thick. Discard stem and end pieces. In shallow dish combine cornmeal, salt, pepper and brown sugar. Coat both sides of tomato slices with cornmeal mixture. In large cast iron skillet heat enough butter to coat bottom of skillet. Fry slices over medium heat until lightly browned and tender, about 3 minutes each side. Turn once. Drain on paper towels. Cook tomatoes in batches, adding more butter as needed. Keep warm on heated platter. Serve hot. Makes 6 servings.

OVEN-FRIED GREEN TOMATOES

1/3 c. cornmeal	1/2 t. brown sugar
1/3 c. flour	4 green tomatoes
1/2 t. salt	Vegetable cooking spray
1/2 t. pepper	1 T. grated Parmesan cheese

Preheat oven to 400°. In shallow bowl combine cornmeal, flour, salt, pepper and brown sugar. Wash tomatoes; cut into 1/2" slices. Discard stem and end pieces. Dip slices in water letting excess drip off. Coat slices with cornmeal mixture. Coat a baking sheet with vegetable spray. Place tomato slices on baking sheet; spray with oil. Bake for 15 minutes. Sprinkle with cheese and bake 5 more minutes. Serve hot. Makes 4 servings.

Yeast Breads

Cornmeal yeast breads have more texture and flavor than regular flour bread. They have a hearty, full-bodied character.

"Anna, damn her" must have been quite a baker since the breads named for her have lasted since New England Pre-Revolutionary days. They all call for cornmeal and molasses and are as delicious today as they were then.

ANADAMA BREAD

1/2 c. cornmeal	2 1/2 t. salt
2 c. boiling water	2 cakes yeast
2 T. shortening	1/2 c. warm water
1/2 c. molasses	7 c. flour

Slowly stir cornmeal into boiling water. Add shortening, molasses and salt. Let stand to lukewarm. Dissolve yeast in warm water; add to cornmeal mixture. Sift flour and stir into cornmeal mixture until dough is smooth and rather thick. Knead on floured board 8-10 minutes until smooth and elastic. Place in greased bowl; turn once to grease surface. Cover and let rise in warm place for about 1 1/2 hours until doubled in bulk. Punch dough, cover and let rise again for 20 minutes. Form into 2 loaves and place in greased loaf pans. Cover; let rise for about 1 hour until doubled in bulk. Bake at 400° for 50 minutes. Remove from pans; cool on rack. If desired, loaves can be brushed with a mixture of 1 tablespoon each melted butter and milk while hot. Makes 2 loaves.

ANADAMA BREADSTICKS

1 3/4 to 2 1/4 c. flour	2 T. shortening
1/4 c. cornmeal	1 egg white
1 pkg. dry yeast	1 T. water
2/3 c. milk	Sesame seeds or poppy seeds
3 T. molasses	

Combine 3/4 c. flour, cornmeal and yeast in mixing bowl. Heat milk, molasses, shortening and salt in saucepan until warm, stirring constantly. Add to flour mixture. Using electric mixer, beat on low speed for 30 seconds, scraping down sides. Beat on high speed for 3 minutes. Stir in as much of remaining flour as possible. Turn out dough onto lightly floured board; knead in enough of remaining flour to make stiff dough, about 8-10 minutes, until smooth and elastic. Form into ball; place in greased bowl, turning once. Cover and let rise in warm place for 1 hour until nearly doubled in bulk. Punch down dough; turn out onto lightly floured board. Divide dough into 2 pieces, cover and let rest for 10 minutes. Roll each portion to make 10" square. Cut into 36 strips of dough about 10" long and 1/4" wide. Using 3 strips for each breadstick, braid strips and pinch ends to secure. Place on greased baking sheet. Repeat with remaining dough. Cover and let rise in warm place about 30 minutes until double. Brush with mixture of egg white and water. Sprinkle with seeds, if desired. Bake at 375° for 10-15 minutes until golden brown. Makes 24 servings.

ANADAMA ROLLS

2 c. milk	2 t. salt
3/4 c. cornmeal, divided	2 1/2 c. flour
1/3 c. molasses	2 T. butter, at room temperature
1 pkg. dry yeast	1 beaten egg
1 c. whole-wheat flour	

Using small saucepan slowly stir milk into 1/2 cup cornmeal. Bring to boil over low heat, stirring constantly. Pour into mixing bowl and stir in molasses. Cool to warm; stir in yeast. Let stand 5 minutes. Add whole-wheat flour and salt. Mix in white flour, 1/2 cup at a time, to make a sticky but kneadable dough. Turn out onto floured board and knead until soft, elastic and slightly sticky, about 10 minutes. Add more white flour if too sticky. Form dough into ball and place in bowl coated with butter, turning once to cover entire surface. Cover with a towel; let rise in warm place until doubled in bulk, about 2 hours. Punch down dough and knead on lightly floured board until smooth. Return to bowl, cover and let rise again until doubled in bulk, about another 2 hours. Sprinkle baking sheet with 1/4 cup cornmeal. Punch down dough; cut into 16 pieces. Form each piece into ball. Place on baking sheet about 1 1/2" apart; cover with a towel. Let rise until almost doubled in bulk, about 30 minutes. Preheat oven to 375°. Brush tops of rolls with egg; bake in middle of oven for 20 minutes until brown and crisp. Cool on wire rack. Makes 16 servings.

CORNMEAL BREAD

2 1/2 T. cornmeal	1 beaten egg
1/4 c. white corn syrup	2 c. sifted flour
1 1/3 c. lukewarm milk, divided	1 cake yeast
4 T. butter, melted	2 T. warm water
1/2 t. salt	Vegetable oil for loaf pans

In saucepan mix together cornmeal and corn syrup. In mixing bowl combine 2/3 cups of the milk and butter. Add salt; add to cornmeal mixture. Bring to a boil, stirring constantly. Reduce heat to low and cook until mixture has consistency of mush, about 4 minutes. Set aside and allow to cool to lukewarm. Add egg, remaining warm milk and flour. Dissolve yeast in warm water; add to cornmeal mixture. Cover with a towel and let rise in warm place for 1 hour. Turn dough out onto floured board; roll smooth incorporating as little extra flour into dough as possible. Dough should be soft but manageable. Divide dough into 2 parts; roll each part into a loaf. Place in oiled loaf pans, pressing to fill all of pans. Brush each loaf with vegetable oil; let rise in warm place until dough is light, about 1-2 hours. Preheat oven to 400°. Bake loaves for 25 minutes, reduce heat to 375° and bake 25 minutes longer. Brush with additional melted butter; leave in oven for 10 minutes. Turn loaves out onto wire rack to cool. Makes 2 loaves.

ENGLISH MUFFINS #1

1 pkg. dry yeast	1/4 c. shortening
1 c. warm water	3 c. flour
2 t. salt	2 T. cornmeal, divided
1 t. sugar	

Dissolve yeast in warm water. Add salt, sugar, shortening and flour; mix until smooth. Roll out dough on floured board to 1/4" thickness. Cut with a 4" cookie cutter. Sprinkle an ungreased baking sheet with 1 T. cornmeal. Place rounds on baking sheet and sprinkle with remaining tablespoon of cornmeal. Cover and let rise in warm place for 1 hour. Heat an electric skillet to 375°. Place rounds in skillet. Cook about 7 minutes on each side. Transfer rounds to platter and cool slightly. Makes 10 muffins.

ENGLISH MUFFINS #2

1 t. sugar	3/4 t. salt
1/4 c. lukewarm water	3 T. melted shortening
1 pkg. dry yeast	4 c. sifted flour
1 1/4 c. milk	3 T. cornmeal

Add sugar to water; sprinkle with yeast to dissolve, about 10 minutes. Scald milk with salt; cook to lukewarm. Combine water and milk. Add shortening; mix in 2 cups flour until smooth. Stir in remaining flour. Form dough into ball and place in large oiled bowl. Turn to cover ball with oil. Cover with a towel; let rise in warm place until doubled, about 2 hours. Turn out onto floured board; knead about 5 minutes. Roll out dough to 1/4" thickness. Cut out 3" rounds with a cookie cutter. Place on baking sheet; sprinkle with cornmeal. Cover and let rise for 45 minutes. Cook in ungreased electric skillet for 10 minutes each side. Makes 12 muffins.

FRENCH BREAD

1 pkg. dry yeast	5-6 c. flour
1 1/4 T. salt	Vegetable oil
1 T. sugar	Cornmeal
2 c. lukewarm water	Boiling water

In mixing bowl add yeast, salt and sugar to warm water; stir until yeast dissolves. Using a wooden spoon beat in flour, a cup at a time, to make a smooth dough. Turn out onto floured board and knead until elastic. Put dough in a bowl; brush top and sides with oil. Cover with a towel and let stand in warm place to rise until double in bulk, at least 1 hour. Turn out onto floured board; divide into 2 parts. Roll each piece into a rectangle, then roll each up into a long loaf, smoothing ends. Place loaves on a greased baking sheet sprinkled with cornmeal. Sprinkle loaves with cornmeal. Let stand to rise for 5 minutes. Cut slashes in tops and brush with water. Place loaves in a cold oven. Place a pan of boiling water in oven with loaves and bake at 400° for 40-45 minutes until crusty. Makes 2 loaves.

SALLY LUNN CORNBREAD #1

2 pkgs. dry yeast	4 eggs, at room temperature
1/4 t. sugar	1 t. salt
1/3 c. lukewarm water	1 1/4 c. sifted cornmeal
2/3 c. milk	3 c. sifted flour
1/2 c. butter, at room temperature	Vegetable oil for muffin tins
1/4 c. light brown sugar, firmly packed	

In small bowl sprinkle yeast and sugar on water. Stir well; let stand until bubbly. Scald milk and let cool to lukewarm. Combine with yeast mixture; set aside. In a mixing bowl cream butter until light. Add brown sugar; beat until fluffy. Add eggs, one at a time, beating after each addition. Stir in salt. In another bowl combine cornmeal and flour. Alternately add with the yeast mixture to the butter mixture, beginning and ending with the cornmeal mixture. Beat until smooth and elastic. Place dough in a buttered bowl, turn to coat and cover with a towel. Set aside in warm place to rise until double in bulk, about 1 hour. Stir dough down and beat hard, about 100 strokes. Place dough in 12 oiled 2" muffin tin cups. Cover; let rise again until doubled, about 30 minutes. Preheat oven to 350°. Bake bread 20 minutes until rolls are nicely browned. Cool in tins on wire rack for 5 minutes. Turn out onto a plate. Makes 24 rolls.

SALLY LUNN CORNBREAD #2

1 c. flour	3 beaten eggs
3 c. cornmeal	1 pkg. dry yeast
1 T. sugar	3 c. lukewarm milk
1 t. salt	Vegetable oil for skillet
1 T. shortening	

Combine flour, cornmeal, sugar and salt in mixing bowl. Cut in shortening with a pastry blender. Beat in eggs. Stir yeast in milk until dissolved. Add to cornmeal mixture. Pour batter into an oiled cast iron skillet. Let it rise in warm place for 30 minutes. Bake in preheated 375° oven for 30-40 minutes until golden. Makes 10 servings.

YEAST CORNBREAD #1

1 pkg. dry yeast	1 T. salt
1/4 c. warm water	7 c. sifted flour, divided
2 c. scalded milk	2 beaten eggs
1/3 c. sugar	1 c. cornmeal
1/3 c. softened shortening	Oil for bowl

In a small bowl dissolve yeast in warm water. In a mixing bowl, combine milk, sugar, shortening and salt. Mix in 3 cups of flour. Add yeast, eggs and cornmeal; stir to mix. Add remaining flour and combine well. Turn out onto lightly floured board; knead until smooth, about 10 minutes. Place in an oiled bowl, turning to oil top. Let rise in warm place until doubled in bulk, about 1 hour. Divide dough and place in two loaf pans; let rise about 20 minutes. Bake at 375° for 35 minutes. Makes 2 loaves.

YEAST CORNBREAD #2

4 c. self-rising flour, divided	2 T. vegetable oil
2 pkgs. dry yeast	1 egg
2 c. milk	2 c. self-rising cornmeal
1/4 c. water	Vegetable oil
1/4 c. sugar	

In a mixing bowl mix together two cups of the flour and yeast. In a saucepan heat milk, water, sugar and oil over low heat until warm. Stir to blend; add to flour mixture. Using an electric mixer on medium speed beat until smooth, about 2 minutes. Blend in egg; stir in cornmeal. Add enough flour to make a medium stiff dough. Turn out onto lightly floured board; knead until smooth, about 8 minutes. Shape into a ball and place in oiled bowl, turning to oil top. Refrigerate for 24 hours. Punch down dough; divide into 2 parts and shape into balls. Let rest for 10 minutes. Shape into loaves; place in 2 oiled loaf pans, brush with oil. Let rise in warm place until doubled in bulk, about 1 hour. Preheat oven to 400°; bake loaves for 35 minutes. Remove from pans and brush with oil. Makes 2 loaves.

MIXED GRAIN YEAST CORNBREAD #1

1 pkg. dry yeast	2 t. salt
2 1/2 c. cold water, divided	3 c. whole-wheat flour
1/2 c. cornmeal	3 c. flour
1/2 c. honey	Vegetable oil for loaf pans
3 T. vegetable oil	

In small bowl dissolve yeast in 1/4 cup cold water. Set aside. In a small saucepan mix cornmeal and remaining water. Bring mixture to a boil and remove from heat. Add honey, oil and salt. Pour mixture into a mixing bowl; allow to cool to lukewarm. Add yeast. Stir in whole-wheat flour; beat until well blended. Stir in enough flour to make a stiff dough. Turn out onto lightly floured board; knead until smooth and satiny. Place in an oiled bowl, turning to oil top. Cover with plastic wrap; let rise in warm place until doubled in bulk, about 1 1/2 hours. Punch down dough and divide into 2 parts. Knead until smooth. Place in 2 oiled loaf pans. Cover with a towel and let rise until doubled in bulk, about 45 minutes. Score tops with a sharp knife in 3 places. Bake at 400° for 15 minutes. Reduce heat to 375°; bake for 35 minutes longer. Makes 2 loaves.

MIXED GRAIN YEAST CORNBREAD #2

2 c. boiling water	1/2 c. warm water
1/2 c. cornmeal	1/4 c. vegetable oil
1/3 c. brown sugar, firmly packed	3/4 c. whole-wheat flour
	1/2 c. rye flour
2 t. salt	5 c. flour
2 pkgs. dry yeast	Vegetable oil for loaf pans

In a mixing bowl combine boiling water, cornmeal, brown sugar and salt. Allow to cool to lukewarm. In small bowl dissolve yeast in warm water; let stand for 5 minutes. Add yeast and oil to cornmeal mixture, stirring well. Add whole-wheat and rye flours, mixing well. Add enough flour to make a stiff dough. Turn out onto lightly floured board; knead until smooth and elastic, about 8 minutes. Place in an oiled bowl, turning to oil top. Cover with a towel, let rise in warm place until doubled in bulk, about 1 hour. Punch down dough and divide into 2 parts. Shape each part into a loaf. Place in 2 oiled loaf pans; cover with a towel. Let rise in warm place until doubled in bulk, about 40 minutes. Bake at 350° for 45 minutes until loaves sound hollow when tapped on top. Remove from pans and cool on wire rack. Makes 2 loaves.

MEXICAN-STYLE YEAST CORNBREAD

12 slices bacon, crisply fried and crumbled, drippings reserved	1 c. boiling water
	6 c. flour, divided
	2 T. sugar
2 pkgs. dry yeast	1/4 c. chopped green pepper
2 c. warm water	2 T. chopped pimientos
2 t. salt	Vegetable oil for baking dish
1 c. cornmeal, divided	

In a small bowl dissolve yeast in warm water. In a mixing bowl combine reserved bacon drippings, salt and 1/2 cup of cornmeal. Add boiling water; blend well. Allow to cool to lukewarm. Add yeast; mix well. Add 3 cups flour; beat until smooth. Mix in bacon, remaining cornmeal, remaining flour, sugar, green pepper and pimientos. Cover with a towel and let rise until doubled in bulk. Sprinkle sides and bottom of an oiled 2-quart casserole with cornmeal. Stir down dough and beat for 30 seconds. Spoon dough into casserole; sprinkle with cornmeal. Bake at 350° for 1 hour. Cool on wire rack. Makes 8 servings.

RAISIN YEAST CORNBREAD

2 pkgs. dry yeast	2 beaten eggs
1/2 c. warm water	1 1/2 c. cornmeal
1 1/3 c. scalded milk	6 c. flour
3/4 c. sugar	1 1/2 c. raisins
1 T. salt	Vegetable oil for loaf pans
1/3 c. shortening	

In a small bowl dissolve yeast in warm water. In a mixing bowl pour milk over sugar, salt and shortening. Stir until shortening has melted. Cool to lukewarm; stir in eggs and cornmeal. Add yeast and 3 cups flour. Beat until smooth. Stir in remaining flour and raisins. Beat until well blended. Cover with a towel; let rise in warm place until doubled in bulk, about 1 hour. Stir down and beat hard for 30 minutes. Divide dough into 2 parts; place in 2 oiled loaf pans. Cover with a towel; let rise in warm place until almost doubled in bulk, about 45 minutes. Bake at 375° for 50 minutes. Remove from pans and cool on wire rack. Makes 2 loaves.

RYE BREAD #1

1 c. cornmeal	2 c. rye flour
1 1/2 c. boiling water	3 T. cocoa
1/2 c. beer	2 T. salt
2 pkgs. dry yeast	2 T. vegetable oil
1 T. sugar	4 c. flour
1/2 c. warm water	

Add cornmeal to boiling water; mix well. Add beer and set aside until mixture reaches room temperature. In a small bowl dissolve yeast and sugar in warm water. Set aside until it swells. Put cornmeal mixture in mixing bowl; add rye flour, cocoa, salt, oil and yeast mixture. Combine well; turn out onto lightly floured board. Knead dough until well combined. Gradually add flour, 1/2 cup at a time, until dough is firm and evenly textured. Shape dough into a ball; place in an oiled bowl, turning to coat on all sides. Cover with a towel; let rise in warm place until doubled in bulk. Punch down dough and let rest for 2-3 minutes. Knead for 5 minutes and shape into 2 loaves. Place on baking sheet dusted with cornmeal. Cover with a towel; let rise until doubled in bulk. Bake at 425° for 10 minutes. Lower heat to 350° and bake for 40-50 minutes. Cool on wire rack. Makes 2 loaves.

RYE BREAD #2

3 pkgs. dry yeast	2 1/2 c. rye flour
1 1/2 c. warm water	2 c. sifted flour, divided
1/2 c. molasses	1/2 c. cornmeal
2 T. caraway seeds	Additional cornmeal
1 T. salt	Vegetable oil for baking dishes
2 T. softened shortening	

In a mixing bowl dissolve yeast in warm water. Add molasses, caraway seeds, salt, shortening, rye flour, 1 cup flour and cornmeal. Beat until smooth. Add enough additional flour to make a stiff dough. Turn dough out onto lightly floured board; knead until smooth and elastic, about 10 minutes. Place in an oiled bowl, turning to oil top. Cover with a towel; let rise in warm place until doubled in bulk, about 1 1/2 hours. Stir down and beat for 30 seconds. Divide dough into 2 parts; place in oiled casserole dishes sprinkled with corn-meal. Cover and let rise until doubled in bulk, about 30 minutes. Bake at 375° for 35 minutes until browned. Makes 2 loaves.

WHOLE-WHEAT YEAST CORNBREAD

1 c. milk, divided	1 T. sugar
2/3 c. water	2 T. olive oil
2 pkgs. dry yeast	2 1/2 t. salt
1 c. cornmeal	4 c. flour, divided
1 c. whole-wheat flour	Vegetable oil for bowl

In a saucepan heat 2/3 cup of milk with water until warm. In large mixing bowl dissolve yeast in milk mixture. Let sit for 15 minutes until foamy. Add cornmeal, whole-wheat flour and sugar; stir until smooth. Cover with plastic wrap and let rise in warm place for 1 hour. Add remaining 1/3 cup milk, oil, salt and 3 cups of flour. Stir mixture until it forms into a ball. Turn out onto lightly floured board; knead for 10 minutes, adding more flour to form a smooth but not sticky dough. Shape dough into a ball; place in an oiled bowl, turning to oil top. Cover with plastic wrap; let rise in warm place until dou-bled in bulk, about 1 hour. Punch down dough and turn out onto a lightly floured board. Knead for 5 minutes; divide into 2 parts. Shape each part into an oval loaf and dust with flour. Place on floured baking sheet. With a sharp knife, cut 1/4" deep cross on the top of each loaf. Loosely cover with plastic wrap; let rise in warm place for 1 hour. Put a baking pan in bottom of oven and fill with hot water. Preheat oven to 400°. Place loaves on middle rack of oven; reduce heat to 375°. Bake for 30 minutes until loaves sound hollow when tapped on bottom. Makes 2 loaves.

INDEX

CORNMEAL MUSH AND POLENTA, 120

CORNMEAL PANCAKES, 130

PIES

REGIONAL CORNBREADS, 161

CORNMEAL SIDES AND MISCELLANEOUS, 176

CORNBREAD SPECIALTIES, 203

A descendent of one of Kentucky's pioneer families, Elizabeth Ross is a graduate of Eastern Kentucky University and Smith College, Northampton, Massachusetts.

A native of Richmond, Kentucky, she now lives in a restored log house in Lawrenceburg, in the southeastern corner of Indiana. In addition to collecting Kentucky cookbooks and recipes, she draws with pen and ink and sells her prints at juried art shows.

Cornmeal Country, An American Tradition is the second cookbook published by Elizabeth Ross. Her first, *Kentucky Keepsakes, Classic Southern Recipes* won the prestigious "Best of Show" award on the QVC home shopping network when products from 20 Kentucky-based inventors, marketers and crafts people were featured nationwide. *Kentucky Keepsakes*, with over 600 down-home recipes, is a result of 30 years of collecting cookbooks and recipes as well as a contribution to preserving our culinary heritage for future generations.